I0606257

USBORNE BIG BOOK OF FACTS

Usborne Quicklinks

Scan this code for links to websites where you can find out more about some of the amazing facts in this book and test your knowledge with quizzes, or go to **usborne.com/Quicklinks** and type in the title of this book.

USBORNE BIG BOOK OF FACTS

Writers:

AMY CHIU, MEGAN CULLIS,
ALEX FRITH, MAIRI MACKINNON,
AND VICTORIA M. WILLIAMS

Illustrators:

ABIYASA ADIGUNA, LYNN BREMNER,
ROSS CRAWFORD, MAL MADE,
NICK TAYLOR AND CAROLE VERBYST

Designers:

LENKA JONES, TILLY KITCHING,
KATIE MILLER, JENNY OFFLEY, MATT PRESTON,
LAURA WOOD AND ZOE WRAY

Editors:

RUTH BROCKLEHURST,
JANE CHISHOLM AND JENNY TYLER

CONTENTS

CONTENTS

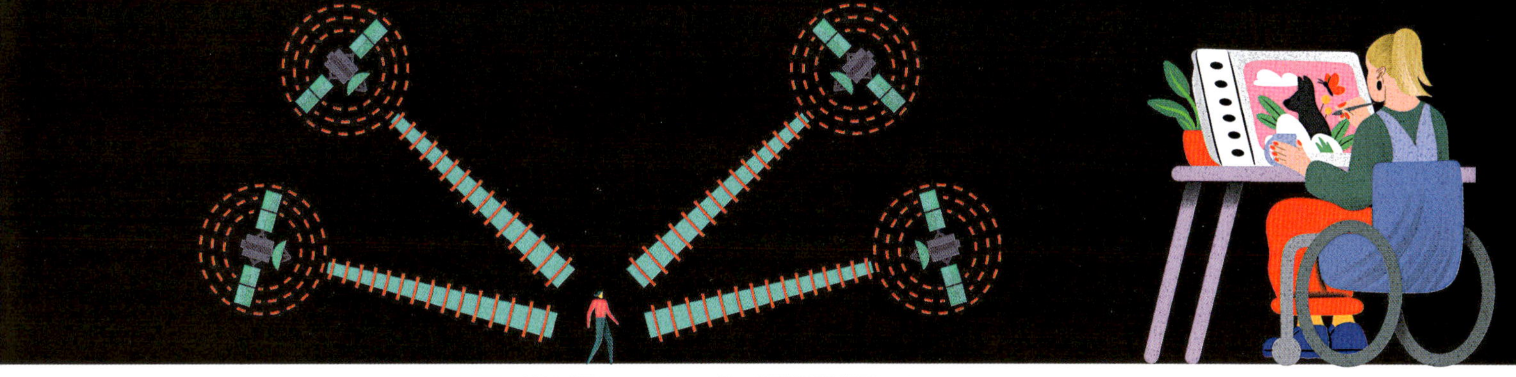

SEVEN SEVENS

In many parts of the world, 7 is considered a lucky number. Maybe because of this, people have often grouped ideas into lists of seven. Here are seven examples.

7 *Ancient wonders*

Over 2,000 years ago, Ancient Greek writers told of seven magnificent constructions that they recommended every globetrotter should see.

THE TEMPLE OF ARTEMIS AT EPHESUS
may have been paid for by Croesus, a king said to be the richest man in the world.

THE MAUSOLEUM AT HALICARNASSUS
gave its name to all future mausoleums – buildings used as tombs.

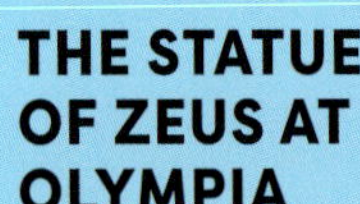

THE STATUE OF ZEUS AT OLYMPIA
held its own smaller statue, of the goddess Nike, in one hand.

THE COLOSSUS OF RHODES
was nearly as tall as the Statue of Liberty.

THE GREAT PYRAMID OF GIZA
The Great Pyramid was built over 4,600 years ago. It's the oldest wonder – and the only one still standing.

THE LIGHTHOUSE OF ALEXANDRIA
endured many earthquakes, before being destroyed 700 years ago.

THE HANGING GARDENS OF BABYLON
may be legend rather than fact. No trace of them has ever been found.

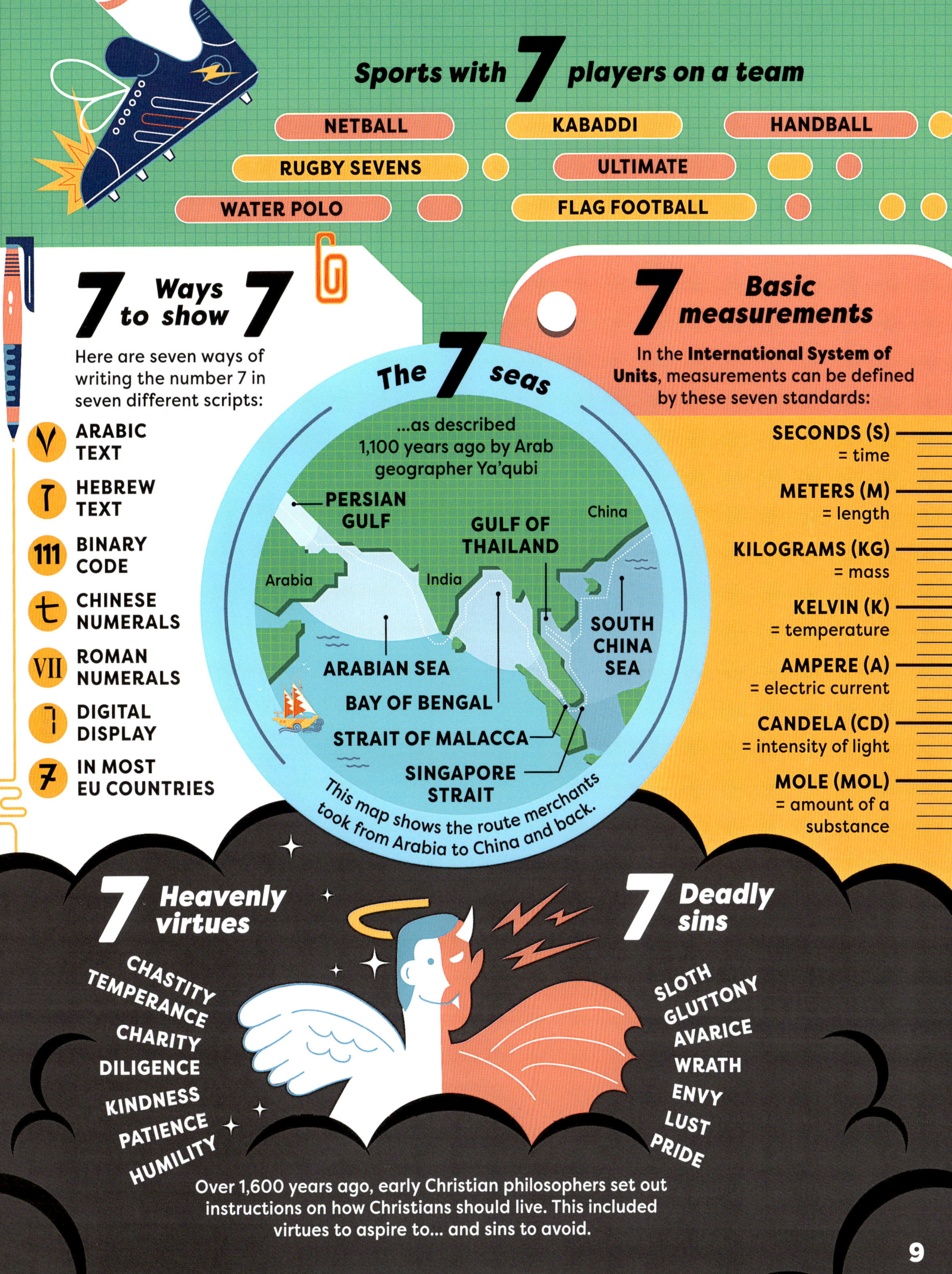
Sports with 7 players on a team
NETBALL
KABADDI
HANDBALL
RUGBY SEVENS
ULTIMATE
WATER POLO
FLAG FOOTBALL
7 Ways to show 7
Here are seven ways of writing the number 7 in seven different scripts:
٧ ARABIC TEXT
ז HEBREW TEXT
111 BINARY CODE
七 CHINESE NUMERALS
VII ROMAN NUMERALS
DIGITAL DISPLAY
IN MOST EU COUNTRIES
7 Basic measurements
In the **International System of Units**, measurements can be defined by these seven standards:
SECONDS (S) = time
METERS (M) = length
KILOGRAMS (KG) = mass
KELVIN (K) = temperature
AMPERE (A) = electric current
CANDELA (CD) = intensity of light
MOLE (MOL) = amount of a substance
The 7 seas
...as described 1,100 years ago by Arab geographer Ya'qubi
PERSIAN GULF
GULF OF THAILAND
China
Arabia
India
SOUTH CHINA SEA
ARABIAN SEA
BAY OF BENGAL
STRAIT OF MALACCA
SINGAPORE STRAIT
This map shows the route merchants took from Arabia to China and back.
7 Heavenly virtues
CHASTITY
TEMPERANCE
CHARITY
DILIGENCE
KINDNESS
PATIENCE
HUMILITY
7 Deadly sins
SLOTH
GLUTTONY
AVARICE
WRATH
ENVY
LUST
PRIDE
Over 1,600 years ago, early Christian philosophers set out instructions on how Christians should live. This included virtues to aspire to... and sins to avoid.

WORLD'S *most* DEADLY

People often fear sharks, lions and snakes – but they're *not* the biggest threat to humans. In fact, the most dangerous creature of all is the one most likely to smile at you and shake your hand.

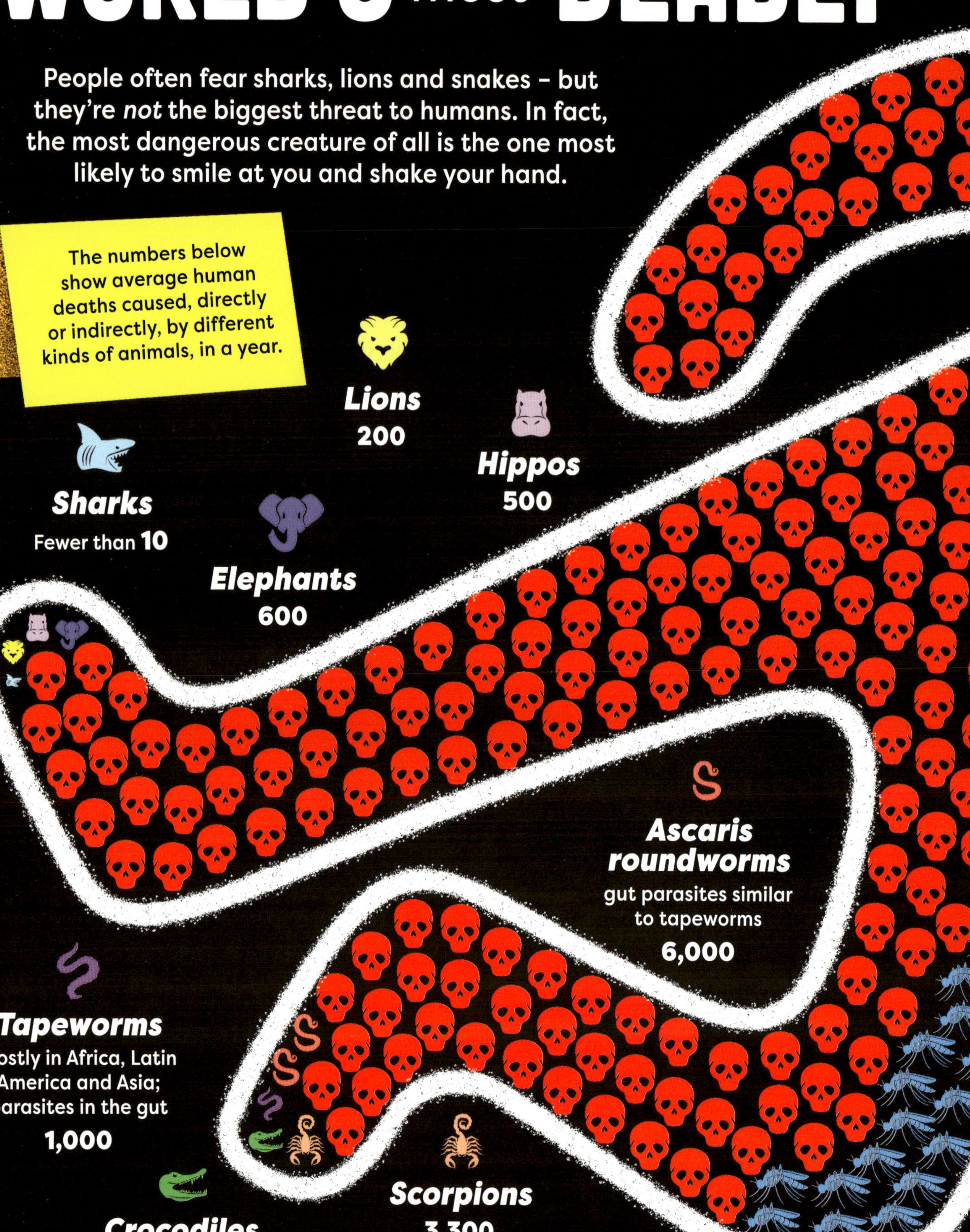

Humans

1.8 million

of which 1.35 million are caused by road traffic accidents and 0.48 million through homicide (murder or manslaughter)

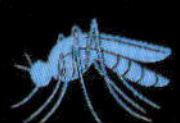

Mosquitoes

mainly in Latin America, Africa and Asia, carrying malaria and other diseases

700,000

Freshwater snails

in Africa, carrying the disease bilharzia

200,000

Snakes

110,000

Dogs

mostly in Latin America, Africa and Asia, carrying the disease rabies

60,000

Assassin bugs

mostly in Latin America, carrying Chagos disease

10,000

Most dangerous country (for humans)

AUSTRALIA has around 30 animal species that can be fatal to humans, from box jellyfish and saltwater crocodiles to funnelweb spiders and inland taipan snakes...

Least dangerous

...while NEW ZEALAND has very few animal threats: a handful of spider species and sea creatures have nasty bites and stings, but they are rare and almost always treatable.

Bigger & BIGGER

Computers store information in units called bytes. The first computers could hold just a few bytes, but today's have much bigger capacities. They can hold not just **bytes**, but **kilobytes**, **megabytes**, **gigabytes**... and more.

Quettabyte (QB) All the computerized information in the world is a little less than 1QB.

Ronnabyte (RB)

Yottabyte (YB) The total volume of information shared on the internet in 2022 was around 1YB.

Zettabyte (ZB)

Exabyte (EB)

Petabyte (PB) 1 PB is around 2,000 years-worth of digital music.

Terabyte (TB)

Gigabyte (GB) 1 GB is enough to store a 30-minute HD video.

Megabyte (MB) 1 MB is enough to store a 500-page novel.

Kilobyte (kB) 1 kilobyte = 1,000 bytes.

Byte (B)

1 byte is enough information to store a symbol, such as a letter or number.

Kilo-, Mega-, Giga-, and so on are all prefixes, used with all kinds of measurements. The names are controlled by a committee based in Paris, known as the **International Bureau of Weights and Measures**.

1 kilogram = 1,000 grams

1 megawatt = 10,000 watts

1 gigasecond = 100,000 seconds

The prefixes **quetta-** and **ronna-** were first introduced in 2022 because computer scientists needed to describe the HUGE byte capacity of new supercomputers.

SMALLER *& smaller*

Sometimes, scientists need to find ways to describe things that are **incredibly tiny**, from microbes to cells to atoms. They use a set of prefixes for length, weight and other things to measure the smallest things on Earth.

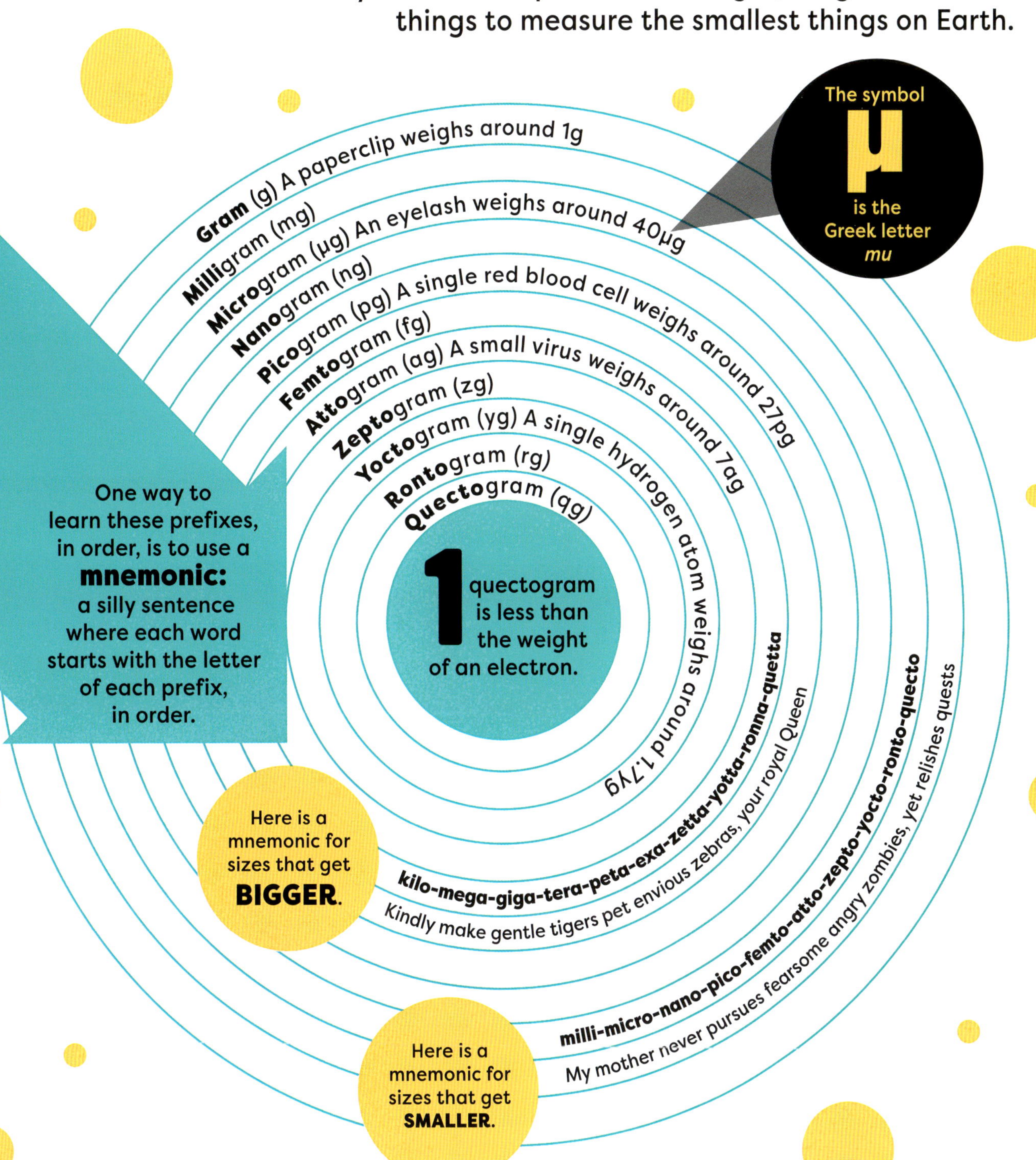

Keeping COUNT

At least 20,000 years ago, long before they learned to read and write, people learned to count. Here are some of the simplest and earliest ways.

Tally sticks

Tally marks were etched into animal bone or wood. The type and size of each mark represented different numbers.

Shepherds used tallies to count their animals. They grouped marks to make them easier to read.

Bakers kept count of the bread a customer took by filing notches on a stick and splitting it into identical halves. This way, both knew how much money the customer owed.

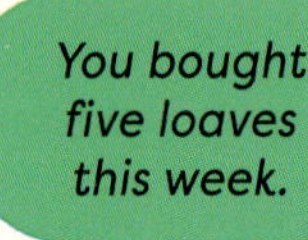

Yes, that's right – here's the money.

Knots

In Peru, the Incas recorded numbers by tying knots into lengths of string. These were called ***quipus***.

A quipu could be used to record large numbers, such as the population of a village.

Position of knot	Number of knots	Total
1,000s	1	1,000
100s	3	+ 300
10s	3	+ 30
1s	7	+ 7
		= 1,337

These were usually handled by the "keepers of the knots" – officers who worked for the king.

Fingers

Counting with our fingers obviously gave rise to a counting system based on tens, but it also led to a way of counting in multiples of 12.

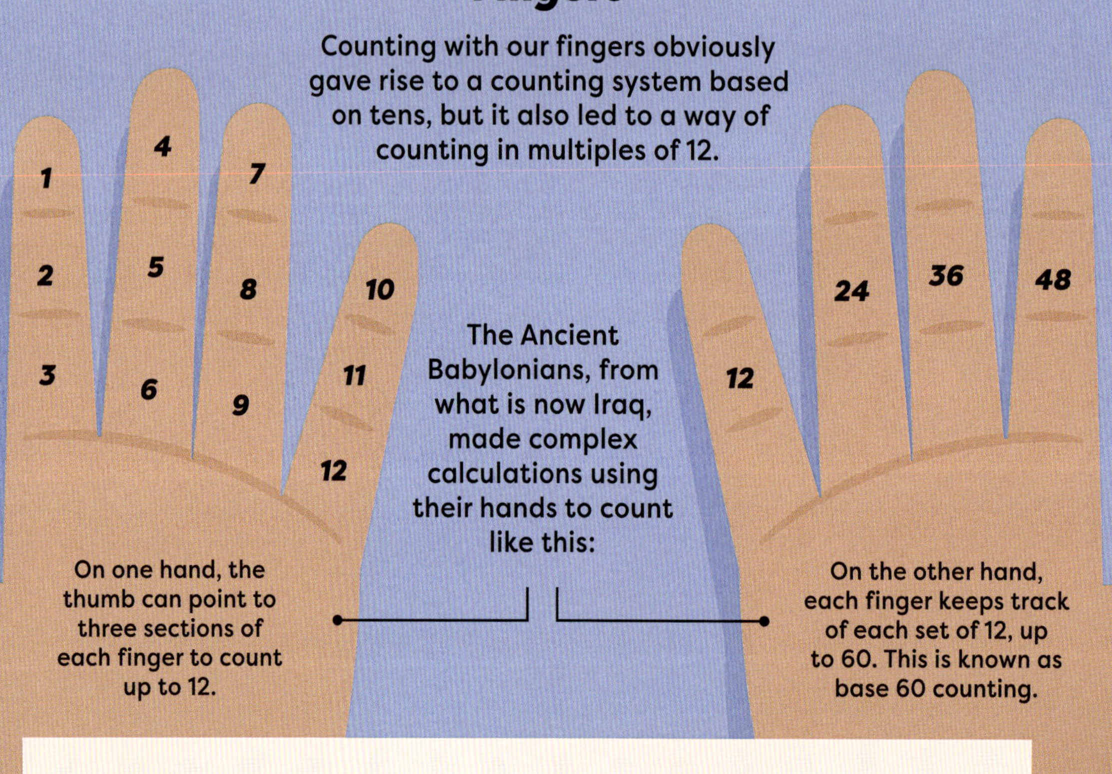

The Ancient Babylonians, from what is now Iraq, made complex calculations using their hands to count like this:

On one hand, the thumb can point to three sections of each finger to count up to 12.

On the other hand, each finger keeps track of each set of 12, up to 60. This is known as base 60 counting.

It's thanks to the Babylonians that we count... 60 seconds in a minute... 60 minutes in an hour... and 360° in a full circle.

Nothing but KNOTS

There are all kinds of knots for all kinds of uses. You can use them to tie things together, to save a life, or as decorations. Here are some examples.

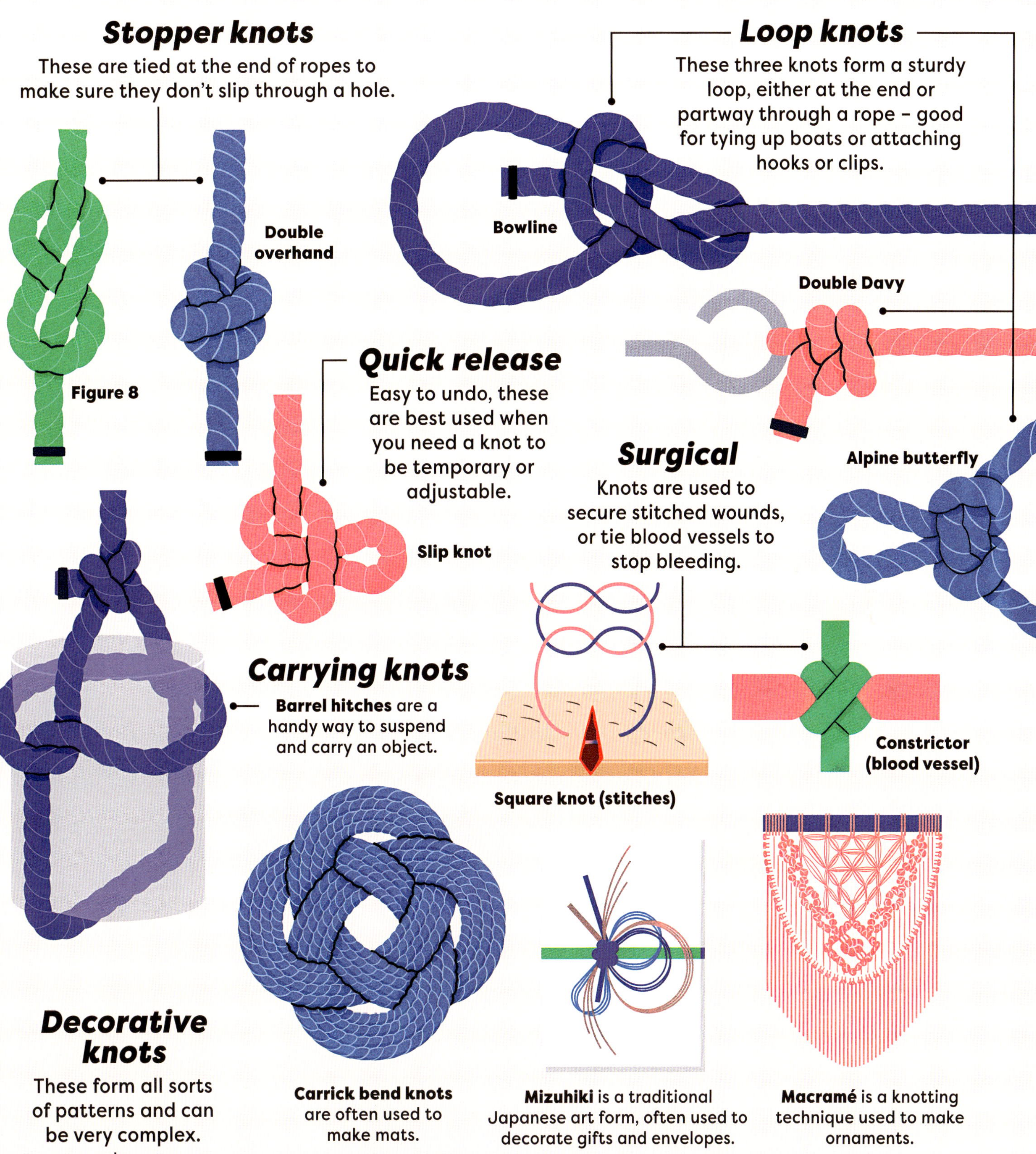

PIGMENTS *and* DYES

Pigments and dyes are traditionally created using natural materials, often from plants, animals and minerals.

KEY
- Plant
- Animal
- Mineral

REDS
- Carnelian
- Alder buckthorn bark
- Tormentil roots
- Realgar

DEEP REDS
- Beet
- Madder plant roots
- Kermes insects
- Cinnabar
- Haematite

- Walnut husk
- Goethite
- Juniper tree ashes
- Acacia tree wood

- Charcoal from burned wood
- Pyrolusite
- Black ebony leaves
- Wild walnut shell

- Titanium oxide
- Zinc oxide
- Kaolin

YELLOWS
- Saffron
- Limonite
- Orpiment
- Urine from cows fed mango leaves

GREENS
- Spinach leaves
- Alder buckthorn berries
- Malachite
- Foxglove flowers

PURPLES
- Murex sea snails
- Purple gromwell root
- Mulberries and blackberries
- Red cabbage
- Maple bark

BLUES
- Azurite
- Lapis lazuli
- Indigo flower leaves
- Dyer's wood
- Cobalt compounds

DYES dissolve in liquids.

PIGMENTS are tiny, solid particles. They stay **suspended in liquid**, floating around instead of dissolving.

SOME OF THE DEADLIEST PIGMENTS IN HISTORY...

Material	Cadmium	Arsenic	Lead	Uranium	Radium
Uses	paints	wallpaper, children's toys	paints, cosmetics	glazing bowls and plates	glowing numbers on watches
Effects	fevers, bone and kidney damage	vomiting, numbness, heart disease	nausea, organ damage, death	organ damage, cancer risk	weakens bones, cells slowly die

We still use some of these materials, but in smaller, safer amounts.

The COLORS *of* CHEMISTRY

Chemists have lots of ways to work out the properties of a substance. Some of these rely on looking at the colors produced by reactions.

THE FLAME TEST

In chemistry, there's an experiment called the **flame test**. When you burn different metal elements, they produce flames of different colors. This gives a rough idea of what elements might be in a substance.

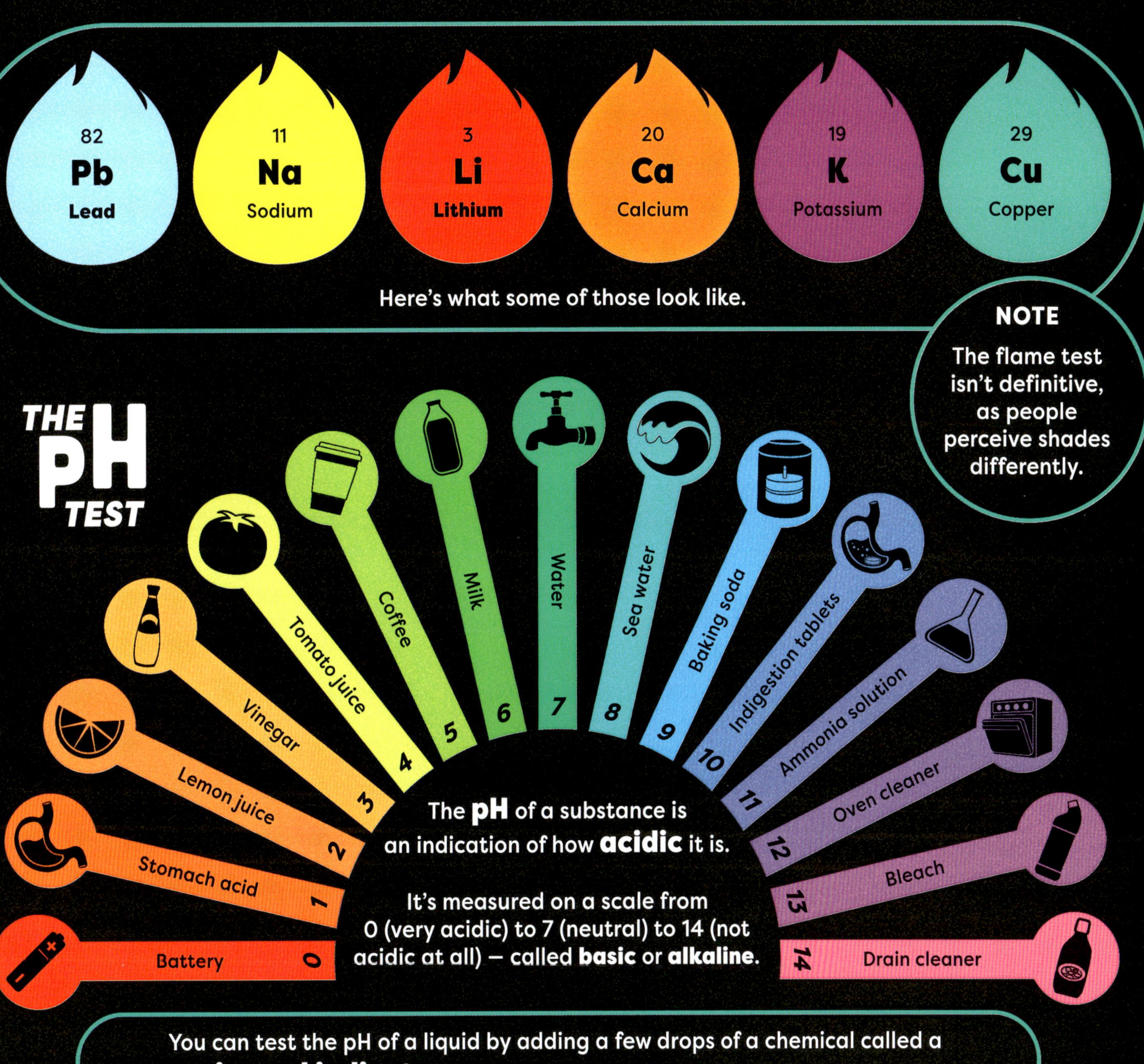

THE pH TEST

The **pH** of a substance is an indication of how **acidic** it is.

It's measured on a scale from 0 (very acidic) to 7 (neutral) to 14 (not acidic at all) – called **basic** or **alkaline**.

You can test the pH of a liquid by adding a few drops of a chemical called a **universal indicator**. The liquid changes color depending on the pH.

BONES *of the body*

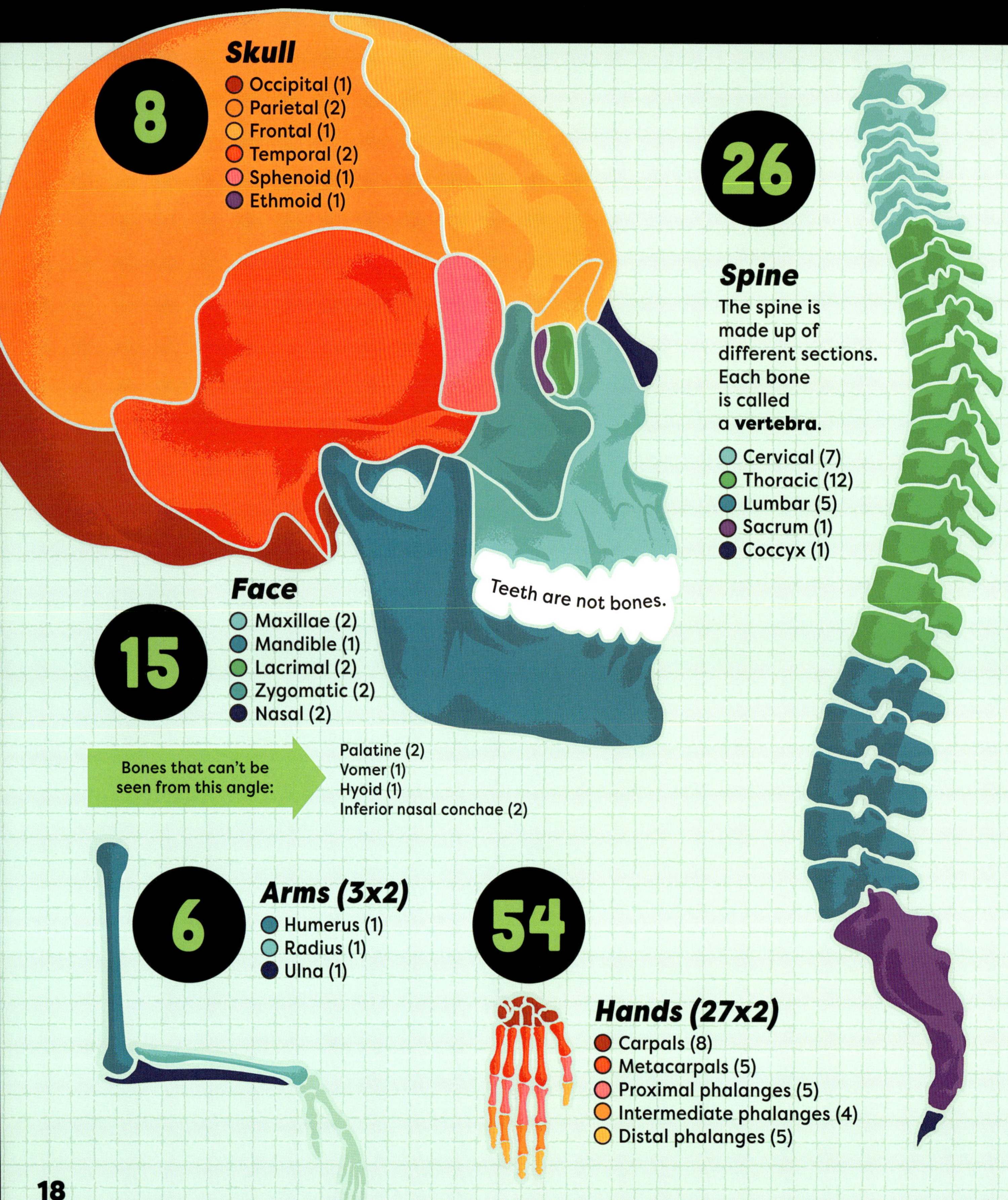

Most people are born with around 300 bones. Some of these bones fuse together to form larger bones over time, so that most adults are left with around **206 individual bones.** Here's how they add up.

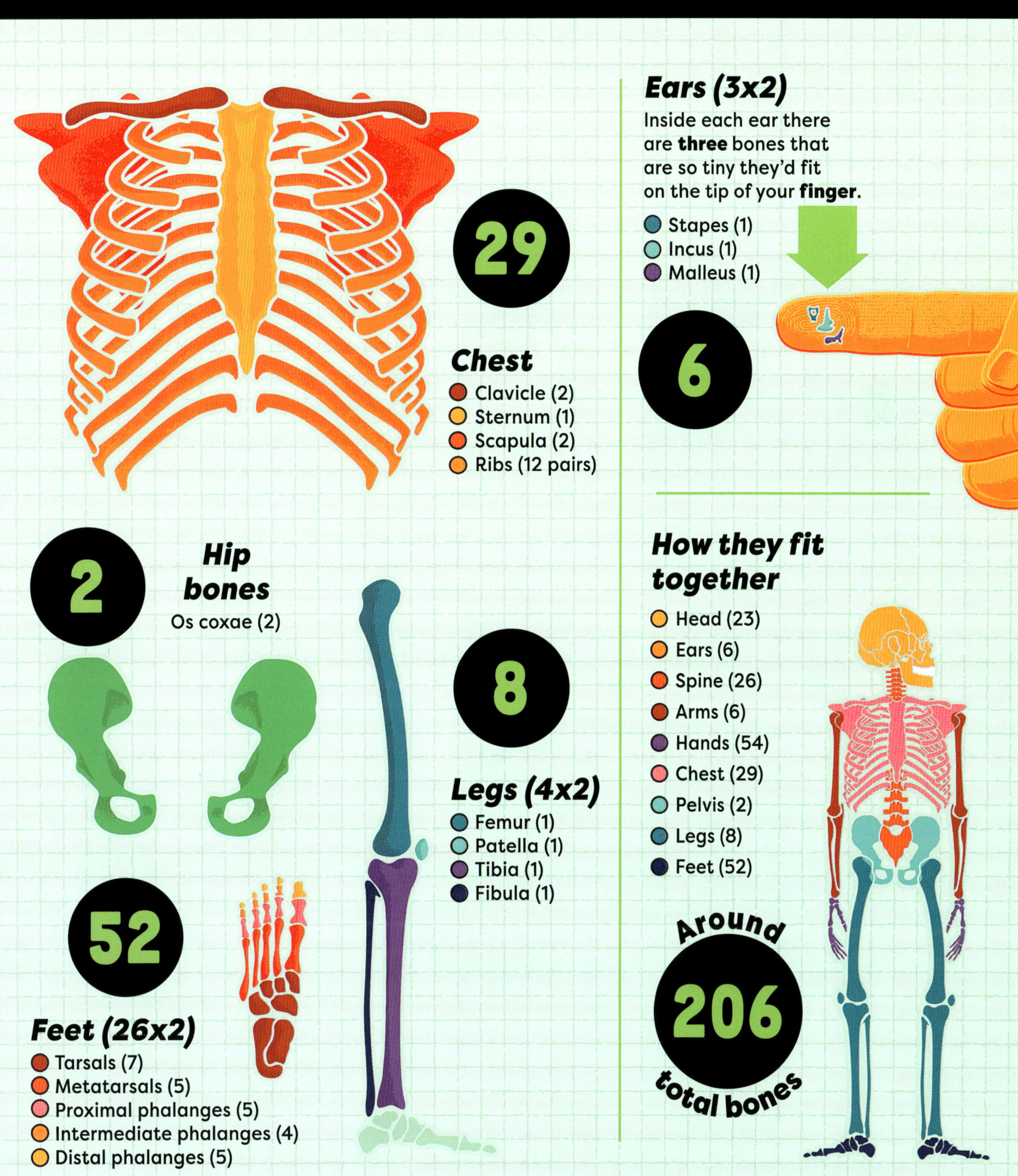

The BIRTHPLACE...

Our scientific name is *Homo sapiens*. Scientists who investigate our origins disagree on many details – but they all agree on one thing: the first humans lived, died and, gradually, evolved – in Africa.

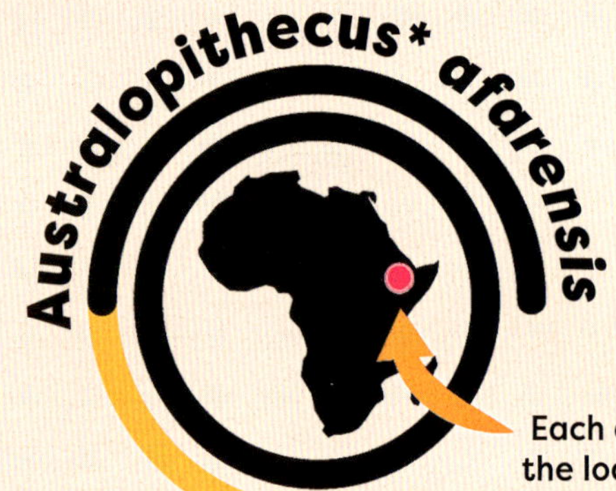

Each dot shows the location of a major find from each species.

Oldest known fossil bones date back to:

3.9 MILLION YEARS AGO

Existed from roughly:

3.3 – 2.1 MILLION YEARS AGO

Existed from roughly:

2.3 – 1.7 MILLION YEARS AGO

Skulls have a central crest

Warning!
Experts argue which of these two species, if either, was a direct ancestor to modern humans.

Walked fully upright on two legs

Made and used tools; had MUCH bigger brains than *Australopithecus*

**Australo-* doesn't mean "coming from Australia" but is from the Latin "australis" meaning "southern"... which is also why Australia was named by Europeans to mean "the southern land."*

...of HUMANKIND

After *Australopithecus*, and before the time of *sapiens*, there were several related creatures known as *Homo*. Scientists are still working to trace the story of how they all relate to each other.

Existed from roughly:
2 - 1.4 MILLION YEARS AGO

Existed from roughly:
1.7 MILLION YEARS AGO – 110 THOUSAND YEARS AGO

Oldest known fossil bones date back to:
300 THOUSAND YEARS AGO

Knew how to keep a fire going to use in other places

Warning!
Some experts believe *Homo ergaster* and *Homo erectus* are the same species, while others disagree.

Spread from Africa across Asia and Europe

Skulls are more than three times larger than *Australopithecus*

Anatomy of a HOSPITAL...

A typical general hospital has dozens of departments for different types of patients, conditions or treatments. Here are some you might find.

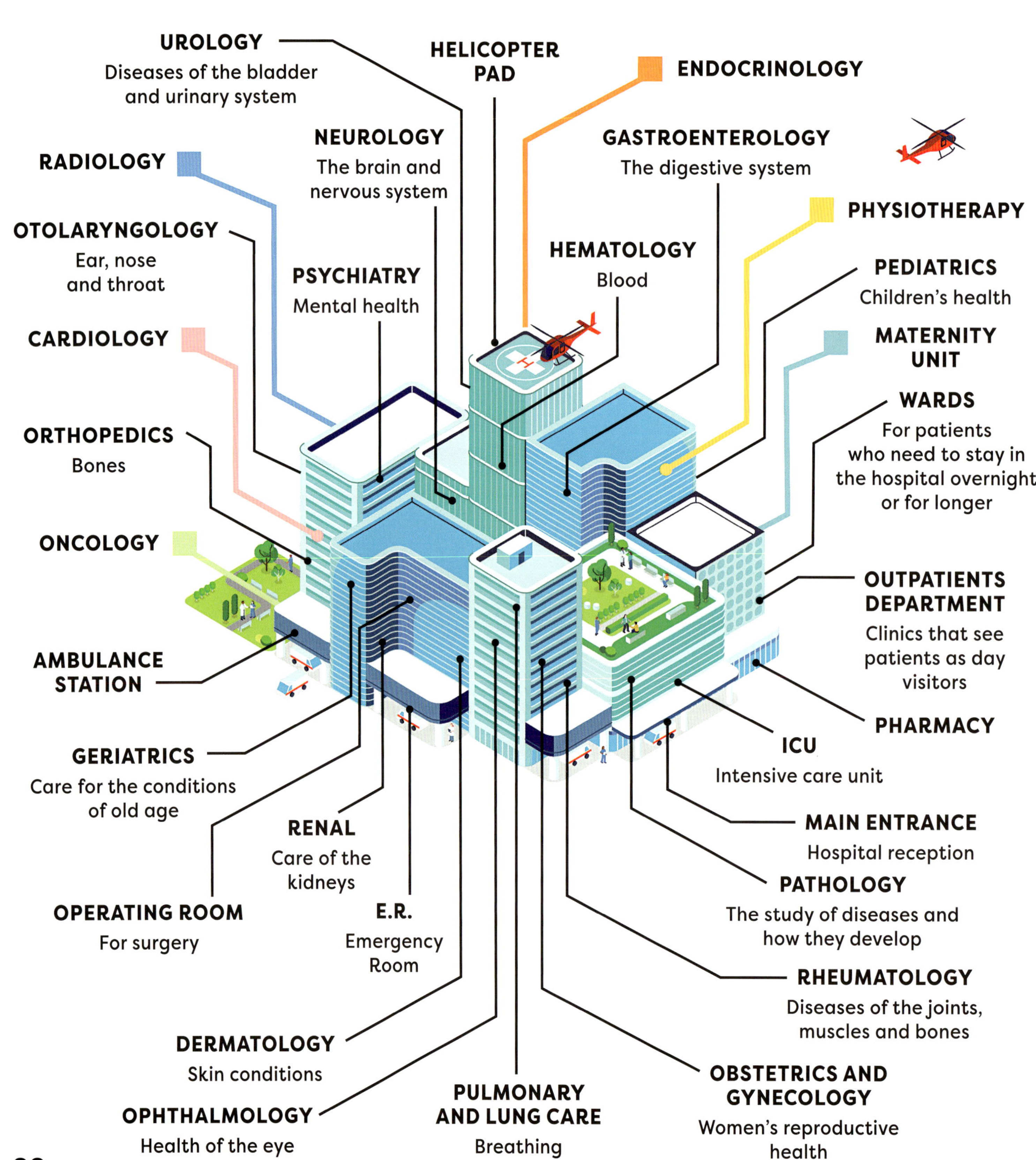

...and a little look inside

RADIOLOGY

Here you'll find X-rays, ultrasound, CT (computerized tomography) scanning and MRI (magnetic resonance imaging). These are all ways of seeing what's going on inside a patient's body.

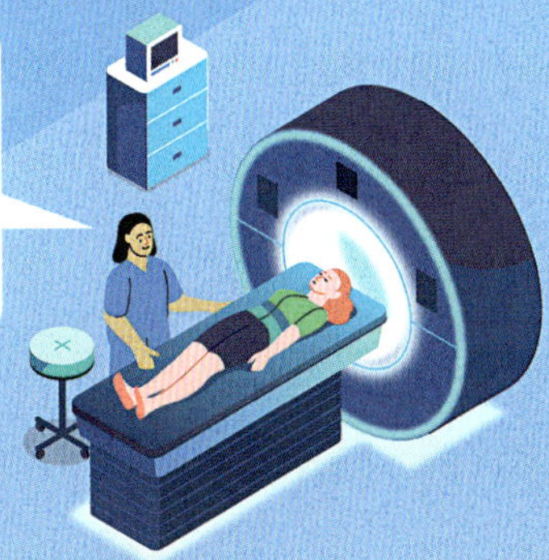

ENDOCRINOLOGY

Endocrinology deals with hormones and the organs that regulate them. Hormones help your body to function in a healthy way.

CARDIOLOGY

Care for illnesses of the heart and prevention of heart attacks

PHYSIOTHERAPY

Helping patients recover from physical injury, often by doing carefully planned exercises

ONCOLOGY

Oncology is the treatment of cancer. Cancer is always serious, but there are many treatments that can make a big difference.

MATERNITY UNIT

Maternity care (for mothers having babies) and neonatal ICU (intensive care unit for newborns)

DID YOU KNOW...

In a room of
70 people, it's
99.9%
likely that
2 of them
will share the
same birthday.

ALL LIFE
on planet Earth

It's impossible to *count* all the things that are alive on Earth... but amazingly, scientists have found a way to calculate their total *weight*.

The calculations are based on **carbon**, an element found in every living thing. Scientists estimate that the total amount of carbon is around **550 gigatons** (Gt) – that's **550 billion (550,000,000,000) tons**.

All together, the carbon in living things is more than three times the weight of Mount Everest.

This chart compares the weight of carbon of all the different groups of organisms.

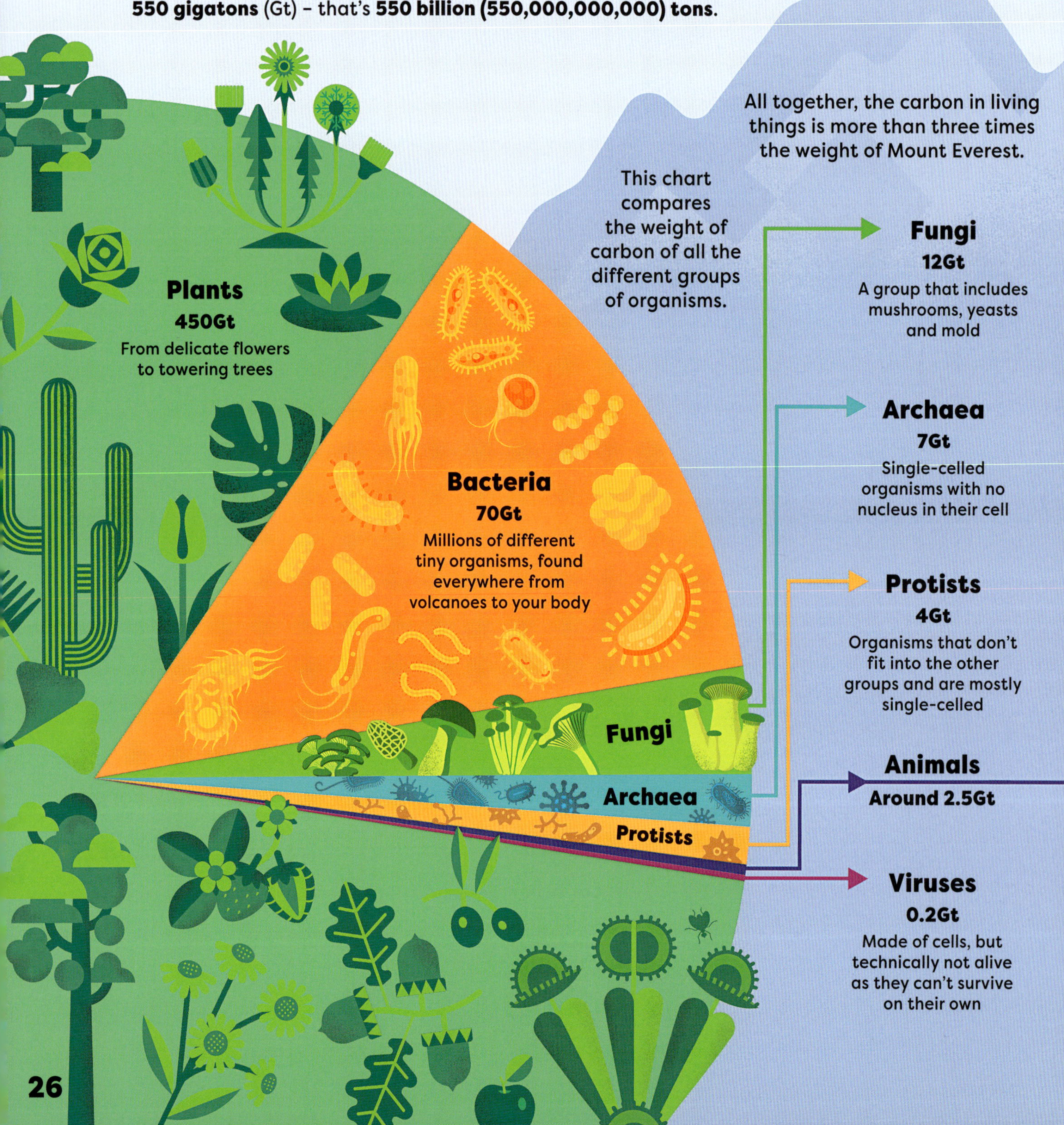

Scientists haven't studied **reptiles** or **amphibians** enough yet to estimate their total carbon weight, but they believe it wouldn't make a significant difference to the total calculation.

BIGGEST
living things

HEAVIEST → LIGHTEST

Type	Name	How BIG can it get?
TREE	GIANT SEQUOIA	Can grow nearly **100m (over 300ft)** tall, and would weigh more than **6,000 metric tons.**
FUNGUS	HONEY FUNGUS	Can spread to fill an entire forest floor – nearly **9km² (2,200 acres)**, weighing more than **400 metric tons.**
SEA ANIMAL	BLUE WHALE	Can reach over **30m (110ft)** long, and weigh close to **200 metric tons.**
MAMMAL	AFRICAN ELEPHANT	The largest ever recorded stood over **4m (13ft)** tall, and weighed close to **8 metric tons.**
BIRD	OSTRICH	Can reach up to **2.75m (9ft)** tall, and more than **155kg (345lb)** in weight.
SNAKE	PYTHON OR ANACONDA	The longest snake on record was a **10m (33ft)** reticulated python. The heaviest was a **227kg (500lb)** green anaconda.
INSECT	GOLIATH BEETLE	Goliath beetles start life as larva, which can grow to weigh over **115g (4oz)** – heavier than any adult insect.
BACTERIA	THIOMARGARITA MAGNIFICA	These are biggest known BACTERIA. Individuals can reach **20mm (0.79in)** long – about the same as an eyelash.

Smallest
LIVING THINGS

How SMALL can it get?	Name	Type
Found only on the islands of Barbados and Anguilla, these snakes are just **100mm (4in)** long.	BARBADOS THREADSNAKE	SNAKE
Male bee hummingbirds are only **55mm (2in)** long, and females are only a little bigger.	BEE HUMMINGBIRD	BIRD
Found in caves in Thailand, these bats can be as small as **29mm (1in)** in length.	BUMBLEBEE BAT	MAMMAL
Males of this predatory fish family can be just **6.2mm (0.22in)** long, many times smaller than the females.	ANGLERFISH	FISH
Often found in large groups on the surface of ponds, each individual duckweed plant can be **0.25mm (0.009in)** small.	DUCKWEED	PLANT
A type of wasp that's barely visible, just **0.14mm (0.005in)** long.	DICOPOMORPHA ECHMEPTERYGIS	INSECT
These jellyfish-like creatures are just **0.008mm (0.0003in)** long.	MYXOBOLUS SHEKEL	SEA ANIMAL
The smallest known BACTERIA is less than **0.002mm (0.00007in)** long.	PELAGIBACTER UBIQUE	BACTERIA

LONGEST → SHORTEST

Sights of the SOLAR SYSTEM

The solar system is our local corner of the universe. It includes the Sun and everything that moves around it – from space rocks to enormous planets.

The Sun makes up 99.9% of ALL the matter in the solar system.

Mercury, **Venus**, **Earth** and **Mars** are all rocky planets.

In this illustration, the relative sizes of the planets are shown to scale.

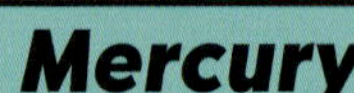

Mercury

Mercury is the smallest of the planets. It's slightly bigger than Earth's Moon.

58 million km (36 million miles) from the Sun

Venus

Temperatures can reach a scorching 482°C (900°F) on Venus.

Earth

Earth is the only planet with living things on it – as far as we know...

Mars

Mars is known as the Red Planet because its surface is covered in red iron dust.

Asteroid belt

Jupiter

Jupiter is 318 times bigger than Earth.

In a spin

As they move around the Sun, the planets each spin on an invisible line called an axis. For each planet, one full spin is a day, and one lap – or **orbit** – of the Sun is a year.

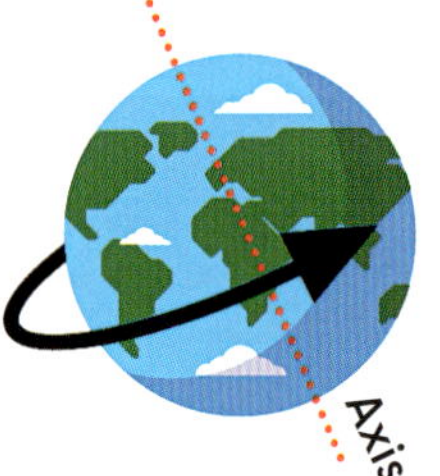

MOST of the planets spin in the same direction...

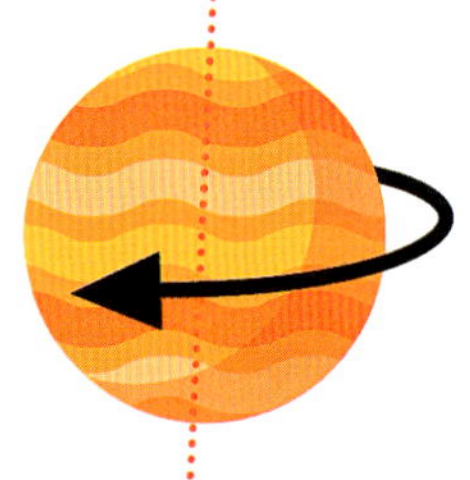

...but Venus spins very slowly in the opposite direction...

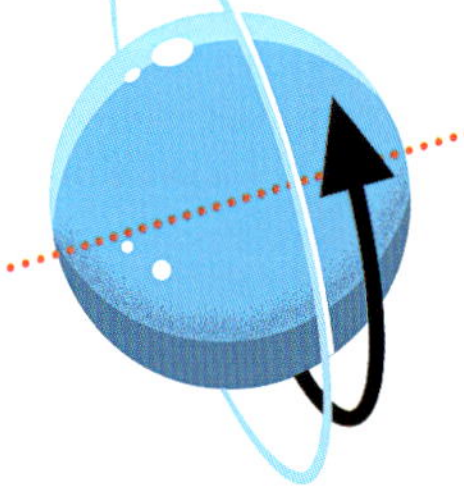

...and at some point Uranus was knocked onto its side, so it rolls like a ball.

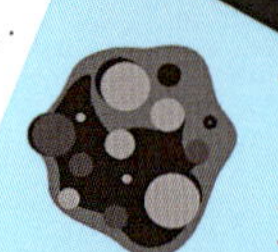

Asteroid belt

Between Mars and Jupiter, millions and millions of asteroids – lumps of rock and metal – orbit the Sun.

Naming the planets

Around the world, the planets have been named according to different traditions. Take **Mars**, for example...

In Hebrew, several planets have names that describe the way they look.

Ma'adim

"The red one"

God of war, Mars (Roman) or Ares (Greek)

In many European languages, all the planets except Earth are named after ancient gods and goddesses.

In Chinese and some other Asian languages, five planets are named after the traditional Chinese elements: water, metal, fire, wood and earth.

火星

"Fire star"

Jupiter, **Saturn**, **Uranus** and **Neptune** – known as the giant planets – are mostly made of gas or fluid.

Saturn

Saturn's rings are mostly made of ice and space dust. All of the giants have rings, but Saturn's are by far the biggest and brightest.

Neptune

Neptune is the only planet in the solar system not visible to the naked eye.

4.5 billion km (2.8 billion miles) from the Sun

Uranus

Uranus is the coldest planet, with temperatures as low as −224°C (−372°F).

Kuiper Belt

Beyond Neptune is a huge ring of icy objects – including Pluto.

Pluto

Pluto was classed as a planet until 2006, when it was downgraded to a **dwarf planet**. It's about two-thirds the size of Earth's Moon.

12:42

What's inside a **LAPTOP?**

You're probably familiar with the outside of a laptop, but do you know what's going on inside? Let's take a look...

We interact with computers using input and output devices.

Input (We give computers instructions using these.)

keyboard mouse camera microphone

Output (Computers give us results through these.)

monitor speakers printer

Monitor (screen)

White light from the back of the screen passes through many filters, which change how the light looks. Here are some examples:

Mouse

Inside the mouse, a tiny camera continuously takes photos of the surface below it. It compares each photo with the previous to calculate how far it's moved. It then tells the computer to move the screen's cursor the same amount.

Mouse button

Camera

Mirror

LED light

Hole in bottom of mouse

LET'S GO!

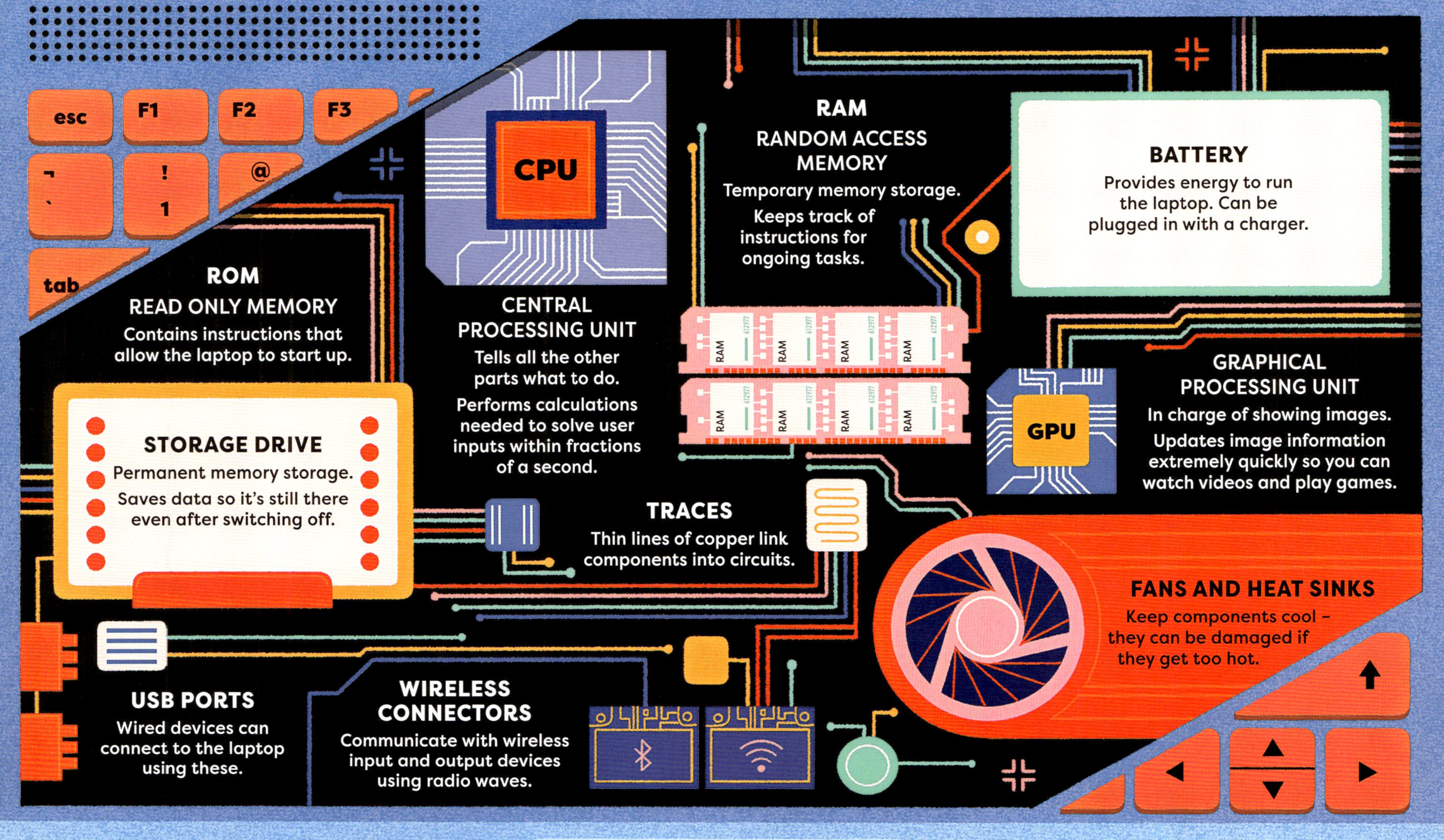

Microscopic switches called **TRANSISTORS** control electricity flow in computer circuits. A CPU alone has billions of them.

Transistors flick between on and off states. This creates electrical patterns, which carry information to other parts at lightning speed.

In the future, the average CPU might have **TRILLIONS** of transistors – that's more than the number of stars in our galaxy.

EARTHQUAKES

An earthquake is a sudden shaking of the Earth's surface. About 55 earthquakes are recorded every day around the world.

Size of earthquake – measured in magnitude (M)

Effects

Frequency

Size of earthquake	Effects	Frequency
8.0M OR GREATER	Great earthquake which can destroy entire communities	One every year or two
7.0M TO 7.9M	Major earthquake causing serious damage	About 10-15 per year
6.1M TO 6.9M	May cause a lot of damage in very populated areas	About 100 per year
5.5M TO 6.0M	Slight damage to buildings	About 350 per year
2.5M TO 5.4M	Often felt, but only causes minor damage	About 500,000 per year
2.4M OR LESS	Usually not felt	About 1,000,000 per year

9

8

7

6

5

4

3

2

Deadly earthquakes of the 21st century

INDIAN OCEAN EARTHQUAKE

Where: Indonesia, Indian Ocean

When: December 26th, 2004

Magnitude: 9.1-9.3

Fatalities: around 283,000 people

SICHUAN EARTHQUAKE

Where: Sichuan, China

When: May 12th, 2008

Magnitude: 7.9

Fatalities: 87,587 people

HAITI EARTHQUAKE

Where: Haiti (in the Caribbean Sea)

When: January 12th, 2010

Magnitude: 7.0

Fatalities: around 220,000 people

Earthquakes strike when big, rocky plates, which make up the Earth's surface, grind against each other. Some earthquakes open up huge cracks in the ground, called fissures.

VOLCANOES

Volcanoes are openings in the Earth's surface that blast out red-hot liquid rock and gases. There are more than 1,000 active volcanoes rumbling around the world today.

The power of a volcanic eruption is measured using the **Volcanic Explosivity Index**, known as the VEI.

- Volume of erupted rock
- Height of cloud
- Frequency

VEI 8

MEGA-COLOSSAL

- 240 cubic miles
- More than 31 miles
- Every 10,000 years or so

VEI 7

SUPER-COLOSSAL

- 24 cubic miles
- More than 25 miles
- Every 1,000 years or so

VEI 6

COLOSSAL (VERY LARGE OR GREAT)

- 2.4 cubic miles
- More than 18.5 miles
- Every 100 years or so

VEI 5

PAROXYSMAL (SUDDEN AND UNCONTROLLED)

- 0.24 cubic miles
- 12.5-22 miles
- Around every 10 years

VEI 4

CATACLYSMIC (LARGE SCALE AND VIOLENT)

- 0.024 cubic miles
- 6-12.5 miles
- Yearly

VEI 3

SEVERE

- 0.0024 cubic miles
- 2-9 miles
- Every few months

VEI 2

EXPLOSIVE

- 0.00024 cubic miles
- 0.5-3 miles
- Weekly

VEI 1

GENTLE

- 131,000 yards^3
- 100-1000 yards
- Daily

VEI 0

NON-EXPLOSIVE

- 13,100 yards^3
- Less than 100 yards
- Constant

Supervolcanoes

Volcanoes with VEIs of 8 are sometimes called supervolcanoes. They can cause climate change or even threaten species with extinction.

The most recent supervolcanic eruption was the Ōruanui eruption, from Taupō volcano, New Zealand. It took place 26,500 years ago.

LAB EQUIPMENT

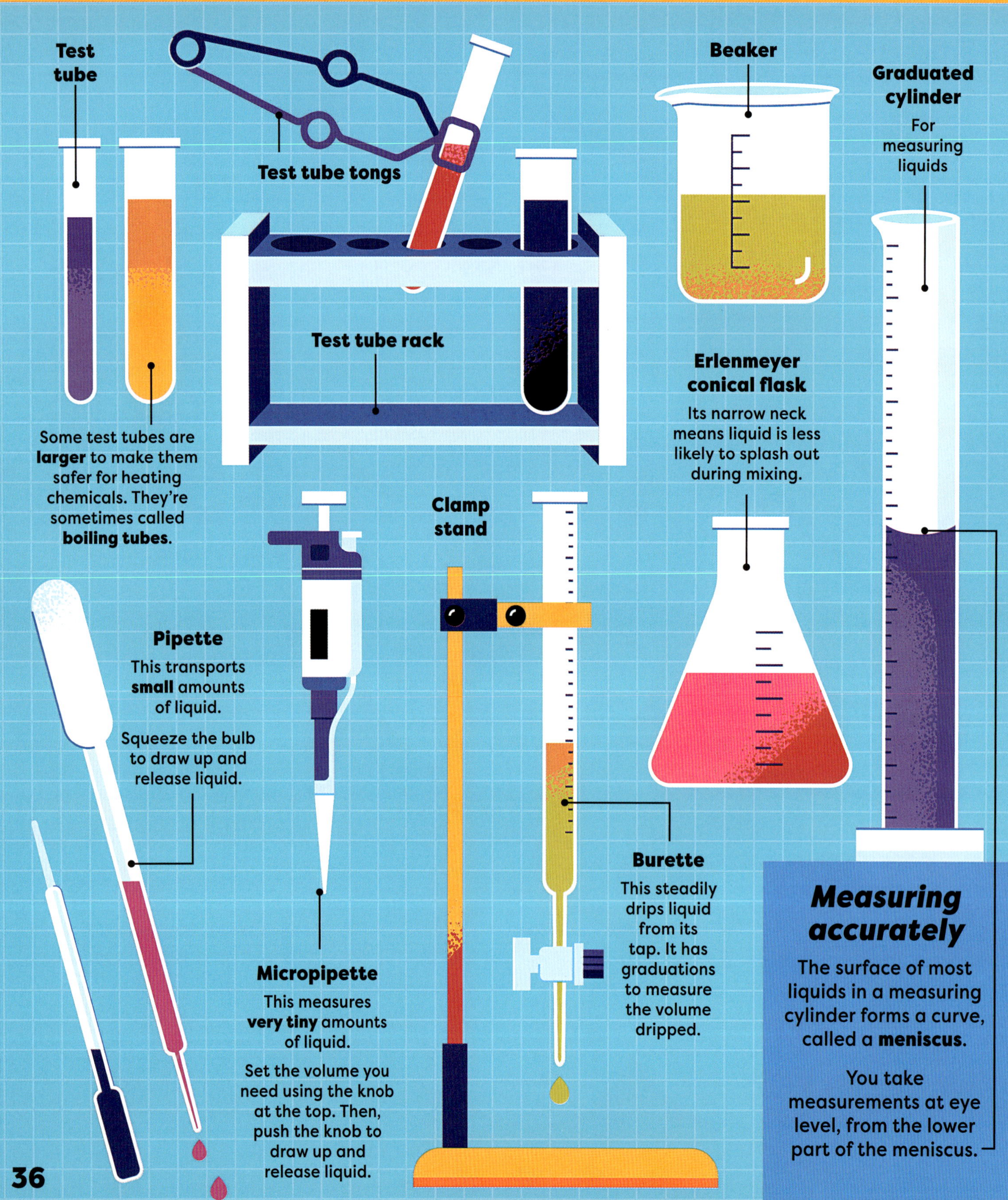

Measuring accurately

The surface of most liquids in a measuring cylinder forms a curve, called a **meniscus**.

You take measurements at eye level, from the lower part of the meniscus.

Science experiments often take place in a laboratory, where scientists can control as much as possible to get accurate results. Each lab is equipped with different tools and machines depending on what scientists are researching. Here are some common items you might find.

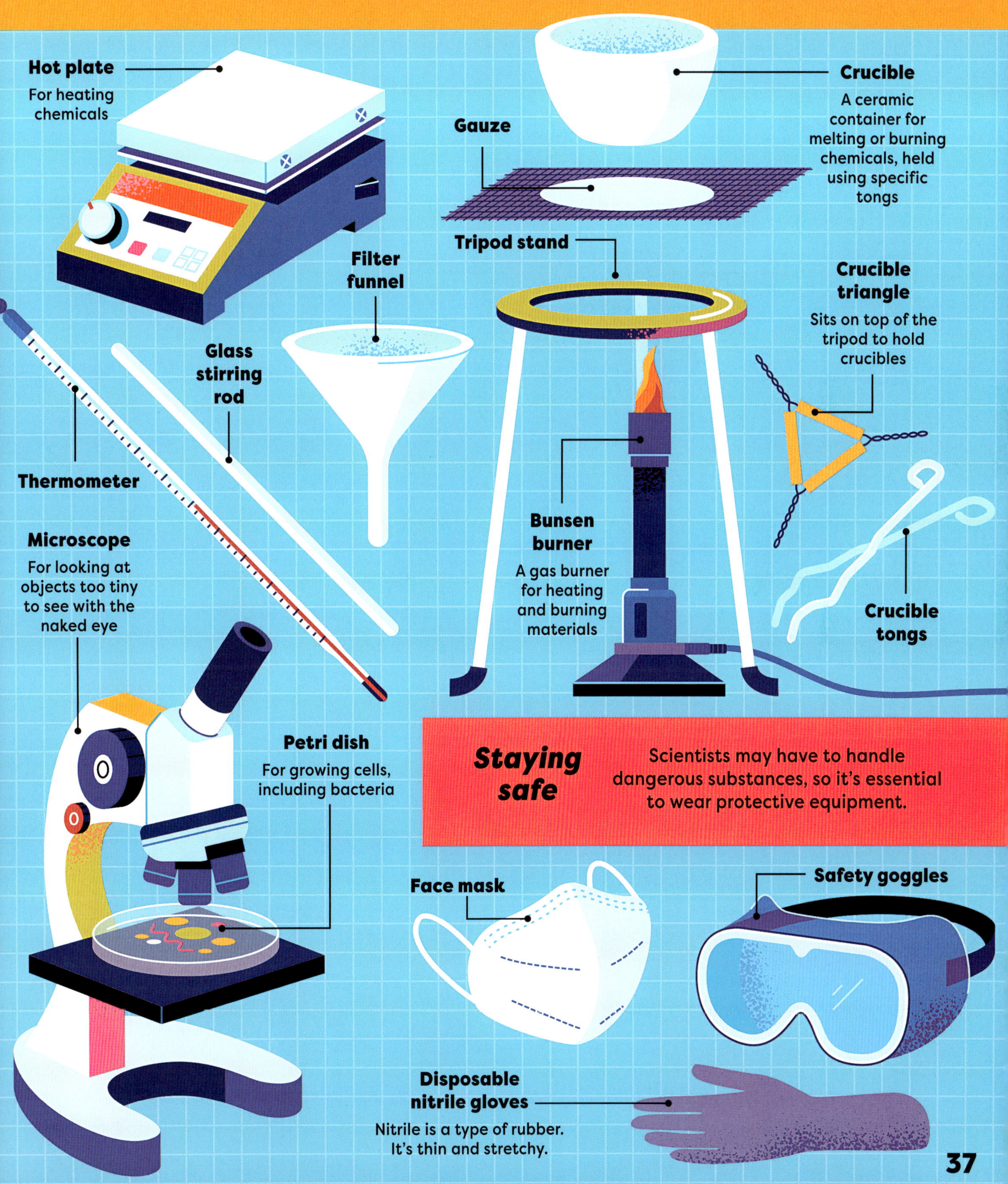

CLOUDY *with a chance of...*

Clouds form when water droplets, or ice crystals, in the air bundle together. If you know what to look for, the different clouds can tell you what weather to expect. They're shown here with their scientific names.

KEY

- Appearance
- Weather

12,000m (40,000ft) above sea level

CIRROSTRATUS

- Very thin, almost transparent, covers the sky
- Lots of moisture in the air – warm weather approaching

These lines of clouds are called **contrails**. They're left behind by aircraft engines.

CIRROCUMULUS

- Small, white patches, lined up in rows
- Fair weather, usually in the winter

CUMULONIMBUS

- Tremendous, dense and towering, with bulging areas but flat tops and dark, gloomy bottoms
- Extreme weather on the way – torrential rain, hailstorms, thunderstorms, or even tornadoes

CIRRUS

- Wispy, white streaks
- Fair weather, near warmer areas

7,000m (23,000ft) above sea level

"Cumulus" means **"heap."**

"Nimbus" means **"rain."**

Cumulonimbus is also known as **"THE KING OF CLOUDS."**

ALTOSTRATUS

- Gray, or bluish-gray, thin blankets spread over a large area
- A change of weather is coming

2,000m (6,500ft)
above sea level

Howling gales inside a cumulonimbus are powerful enough to rip a plane apart.

These storm clouds are so dangerous, pilots are trained to stay alert and **NEVER** go near them.

Have you ever walked through **FOG?** If so, you've walked through a cloud.

ALTOCUMULUS

- Gray or white small patches
- Colder weather on the way

NIMBOSTRATUS

- Thick, gray and featureless, covering the sun and sky
- Rain or snow is on the way – if it's not falling already

STRATOCUMULUS

- Gray or white large clumps
- Expect a change of weather

CUMULUS

- Round, fluffy, white tops with flatter, grayer bottoms
- Fair weather, bright, sunny days

STRATUS

- Flat and gray blanket low in the sky
- Dreary, overcast days with mist or drizzle

Natural world RECORDS

People may tell you that the tallest mountain in the world is Mount Everest, and the largest desert is the Sahara… but are they really?

On these pages, you can see record-holders in each of the world's seven continents.

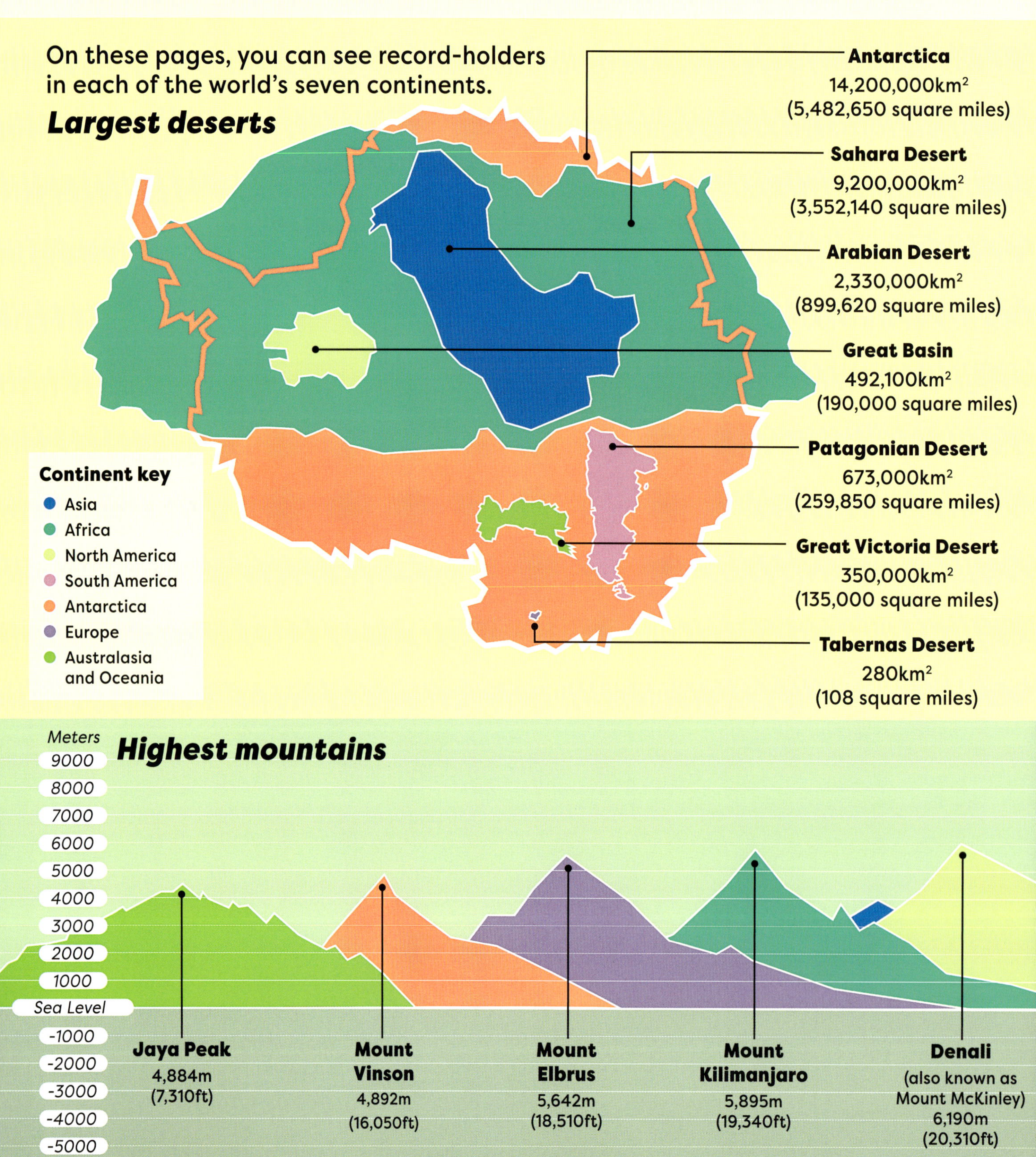

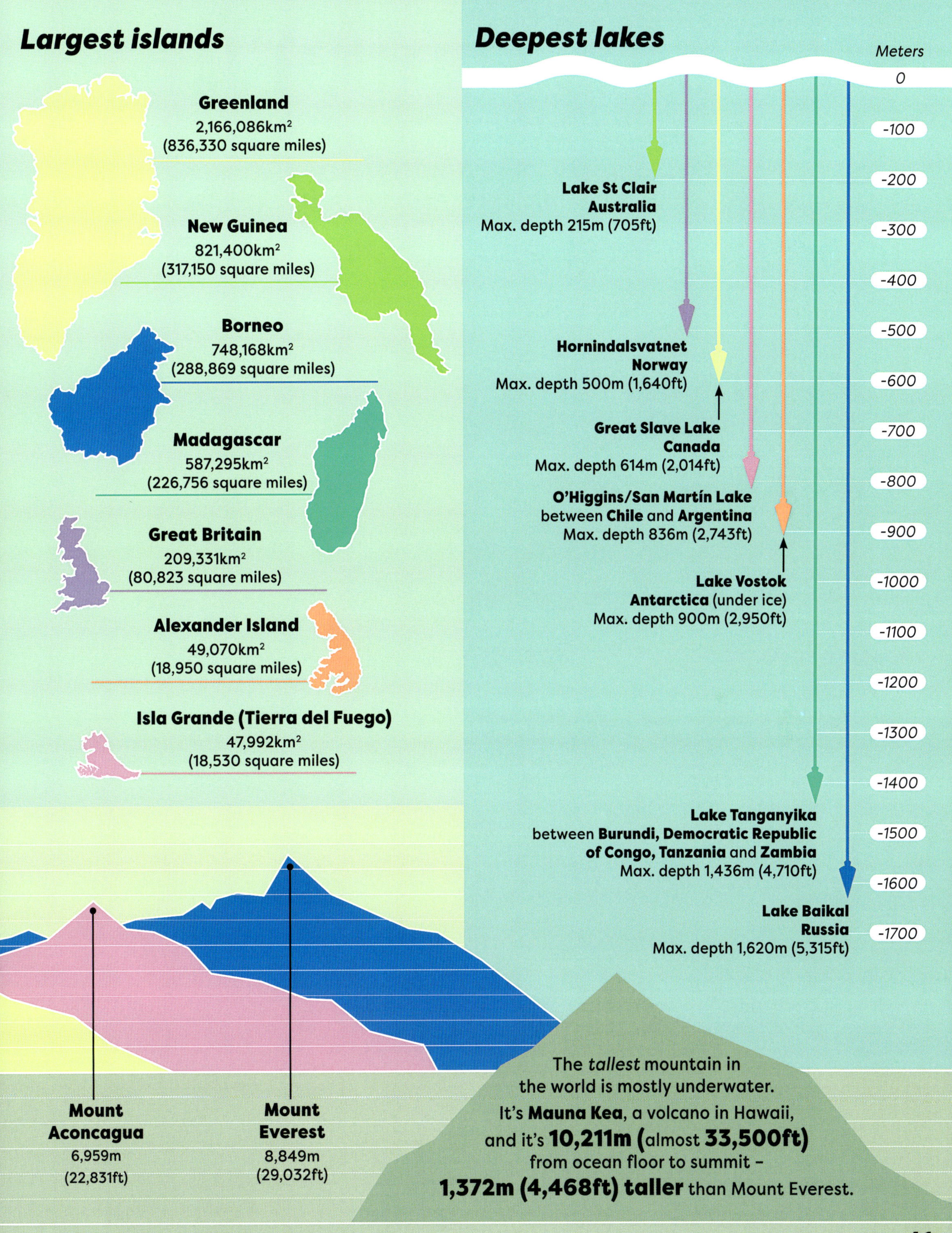
Largest islands
Greenland
2,166,086km²
(836,330 square miles)
New Guinea
821,400km²
(317,150 square miles)
Borneo
748,168km²
(288,869 square miles)
Madagascar
587,295km²
(226,756 square miles)
Great Britain
209,331km²
(80,823 square miles)
Alexander Island
49,070km²
(18,950 square miles)
Isla Grande (Tierra del Fuego)
47,992km²
(18,530 square miles)
Deepest lakes
Meters
0
-100
-200
-300
-400
-500
-600
-700
-800
-900
-1000
-1100
-1200
-1300
-1400
-1500
-1600
-1700
Lake St Clair
Australia
Max. depth 215m (705ft)
Hornindalsvatnet
Norway
Max. depth 500m (1,640ft)
Great Slave Lake
Canada
Max. depth 614m (2,014ft)
O'Higgins/San Martín Lake
between Chile and Argentina
Max. depth 836m (2,743ft)
Lake Vostok
Antarctica (under ice)
Max. depth 900m (2,950ft)
Lake Tanganyika
between Burundi, Democratic Republic of Congo, Tanzania and Zambia
Max. depth 1,436m (4,710ft)
Lake Baikal
Russia
Max. depth 1,620m (5,315ft)
Mount Aconcagua
6,959m
(22,831ft)
Mount Everest
8,849m
(29,032ft)
The tallest mountain in the world is mostly underwater.
It's Mauna Kea, a volcano in Hawaii, and it's 10,211m (almost 33,500ft) from ocean floor to summit –
1,372m (4,468ft) taller than Mount Everest.

Even in the darkest places on Earth, you'll find light. From glimmering fish at the bottom of the ocean to flashing insects hidden in underground caves – our world is full of living things that glow.

ON LAND

Some living things light up the dark themselves – a process known as **bioluminescence**.

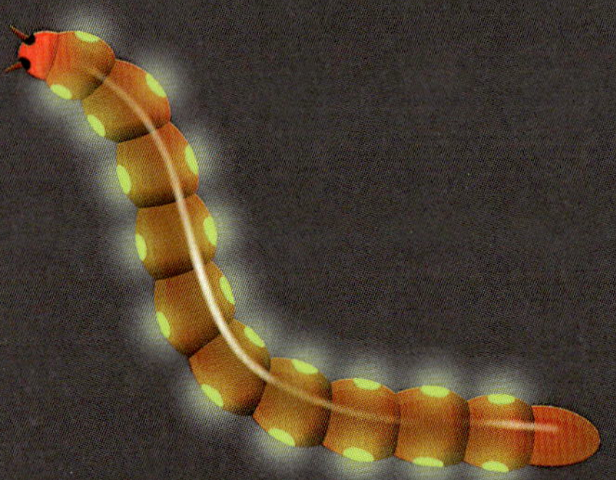

CLICK BEETLE

Click beetles glow so brightly, you could read a book by their light.

RAILROAD WORM

These little worms glimmer red and green to warn other animals away.

FIREFLY

Male fireflies flash on and off in a pattern to attract mates.

IN THE OCEAN

In the deeper parts of the ocean, where sunlight can't reach, around **76%** of creatures are bioluminescent.

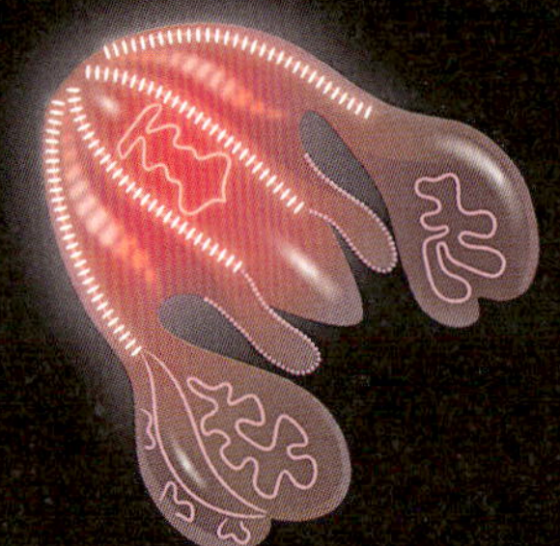

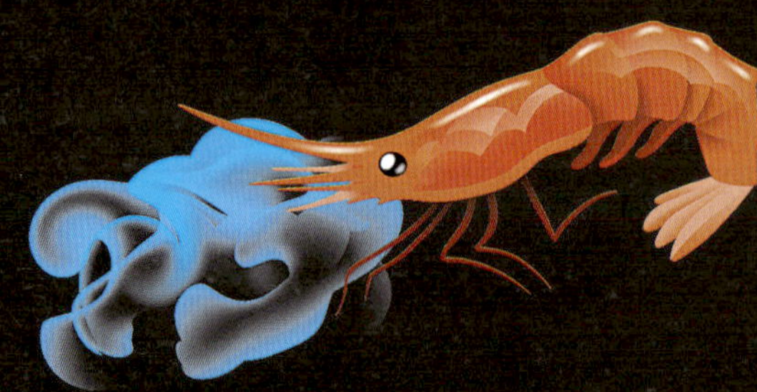

GULPER EEL

This slippery eel swishes its glowing pink tail as it searches for prey.

BLOODY-BELLY COMB JELLY

These comb jellies glow red. Most sea animals can't see red light, so the jelly is invisible.

PANDALID SHRIMP

This shrimp vomits out light to blind its predators and escape from harm. Yuck!

WHAT MAKES THINGS GLOW?

Most bioluminescent creatures have two chemicals inside them, luciferin and luciferase. When the chemicals meet and combine with oxygen, they produce light.

LUCIFERASE · LUCIFERIN · OXYGEN · PHOTON

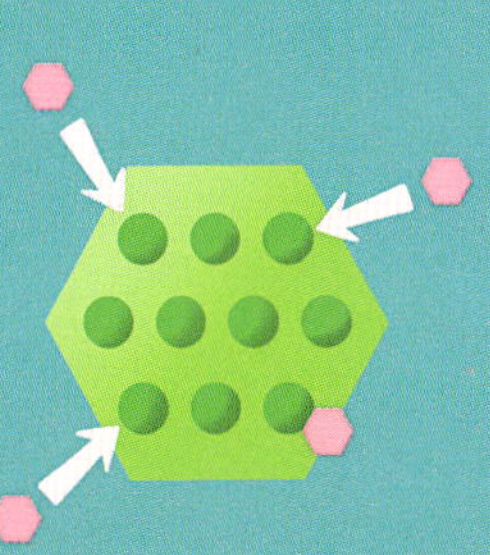

1 Luciferase meets with the luciferin.

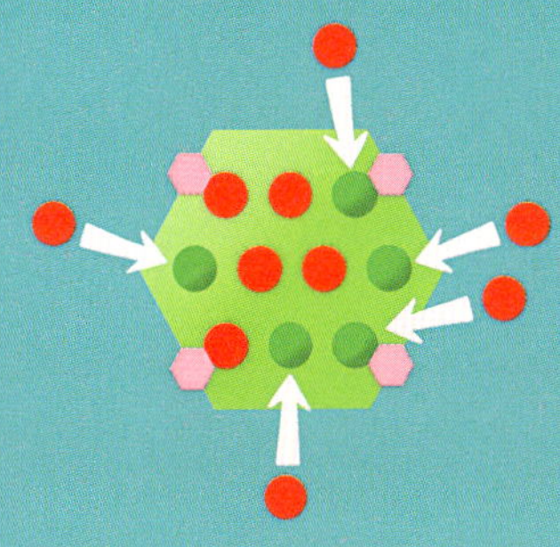

2 Together they combine with oxygen.

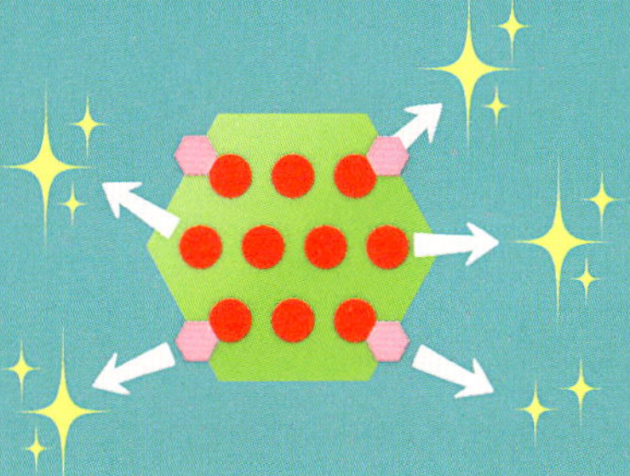

3 A **chemical reaction** takes place, which produces light particles called photons.

DIPLOCARDIA LONGA

This earthworm oozes sparkling blue slime to scare off other animals.

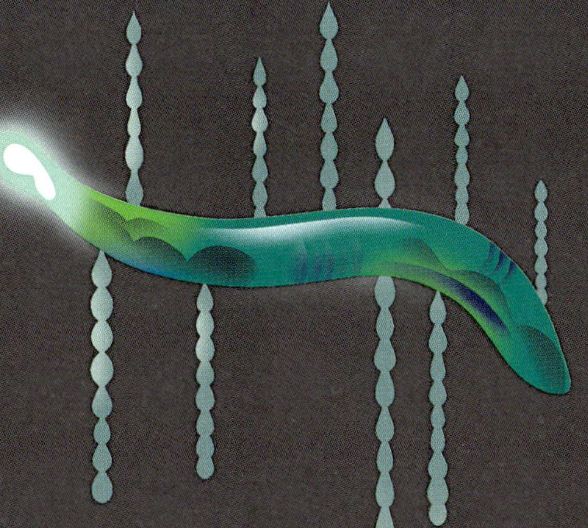

NEW ZEALAND GLOW WORM

The larvae of these glow worms use green light to lure moths into their sticky nests.

BITTER OYSTER

These frilly fungi gives off a green light as it feeds on rotting wood.

HAWAIIAN BOBTAIL SQUID

Glowing bacteria live inside this squid's body. The squid can control the brightness of the glow.

ANGLERFISH

A blue light dangles over the anglerfish's head. It uses the light to lure animals into its open jaws.

DRAGONFISH

Dragonfish use their red glow to sneak up on creatures in the dark and eat them.

DID YOU KNOW...

The Moon is...

...3,475KM

(2,159 miles) wide.

That's just smaller than the width of Australia.

TREES *of* LIFE

Oak trees grow across North America, Europe and northern Asia. One variety of oak, the English or pedunculate oak, supports **over 2,300 other species...**

...OVER 30 BIRD SPECIES,
such as goldfinch, green woodpecker, blackbird, tawny owl, blue tit and wren.

...OVER 700 SPECIES OF LICHEN.
These are complex organisms formed by fungi with seaweed-like algae, bacteria or sometimes all three.

...OVER 30 SPECIES OF MAMMALS,
such as wild boar, fallow deer, badger, rabbit, squirrel, wood mouse and 13 species of bat.

...OVER 1,200 INSECT SPECIES,
such as great oak beauty moth, purple hairstreak butterfly, oak jewel beetle and stag beetle.

...OVER 100 SPECIES OF FUNGI,
such as oak bracket fungus, penny bun mushroom, beefsteak fungus and oakbug milkcap.

...AND OVER 250 SPECIES OF PLANTS,
such as mosses, wood anemone, primrose, bluebell, wild garlic, nettle and bramble (blackberry).

OVER 1,000 SPECIES MAKE THEIR HOME IN DEAD TREES,
including ants, beetles, snails and salamanders.

EXTREME **TREES**

Trees have adapted to survive in some of the harshest environments on Earth.

DAHURIAN LARCH and TAMARACK LARCH TREES grow around the edge of the Arctic Circle. In the winter, it can be dark for up to **22 hours** a day, and for months on end temperatures can fall as low as **-65°C (-85°F)**.

BAOBAB TREES grow in regions close to the equator. They can store water in their wide trunks during the long dry seasons.

Hollow baobab trunks have been used as shelters, stables and even a prison.

DRAGON'S BLOOD TREES grow on the islands of Socotra in the Arabian Sea, where there is very little rain...

...but their close-packed leaves catch the water the trees need from clouds and sea mists.

The trees are named after the reddish resin that seeps from their trunks.

EUCALYPTUS AND BANKSIA TREES in Australia are **PYROPHYTIC PLANTS**, which means they rely on wildfires to spread their seeds.

They have seed pods encased in hard resin...

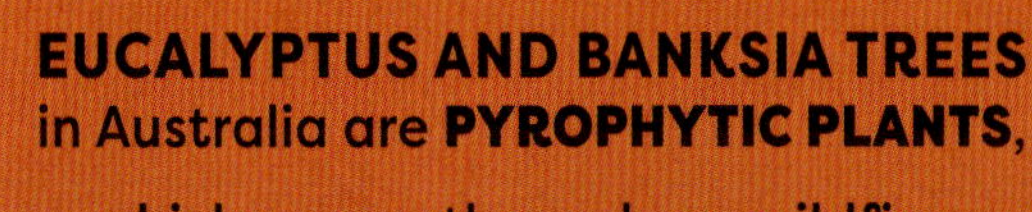

...that melts in the heat of the fire to release the seeds.

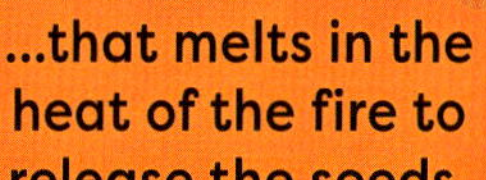

Bestselling BOOKS

From clay tablets to ebooks, people have been using books to share beliefs, stories and knowledge for over 5,000 years. Books dating back hundreds of years are still some of the most popular.

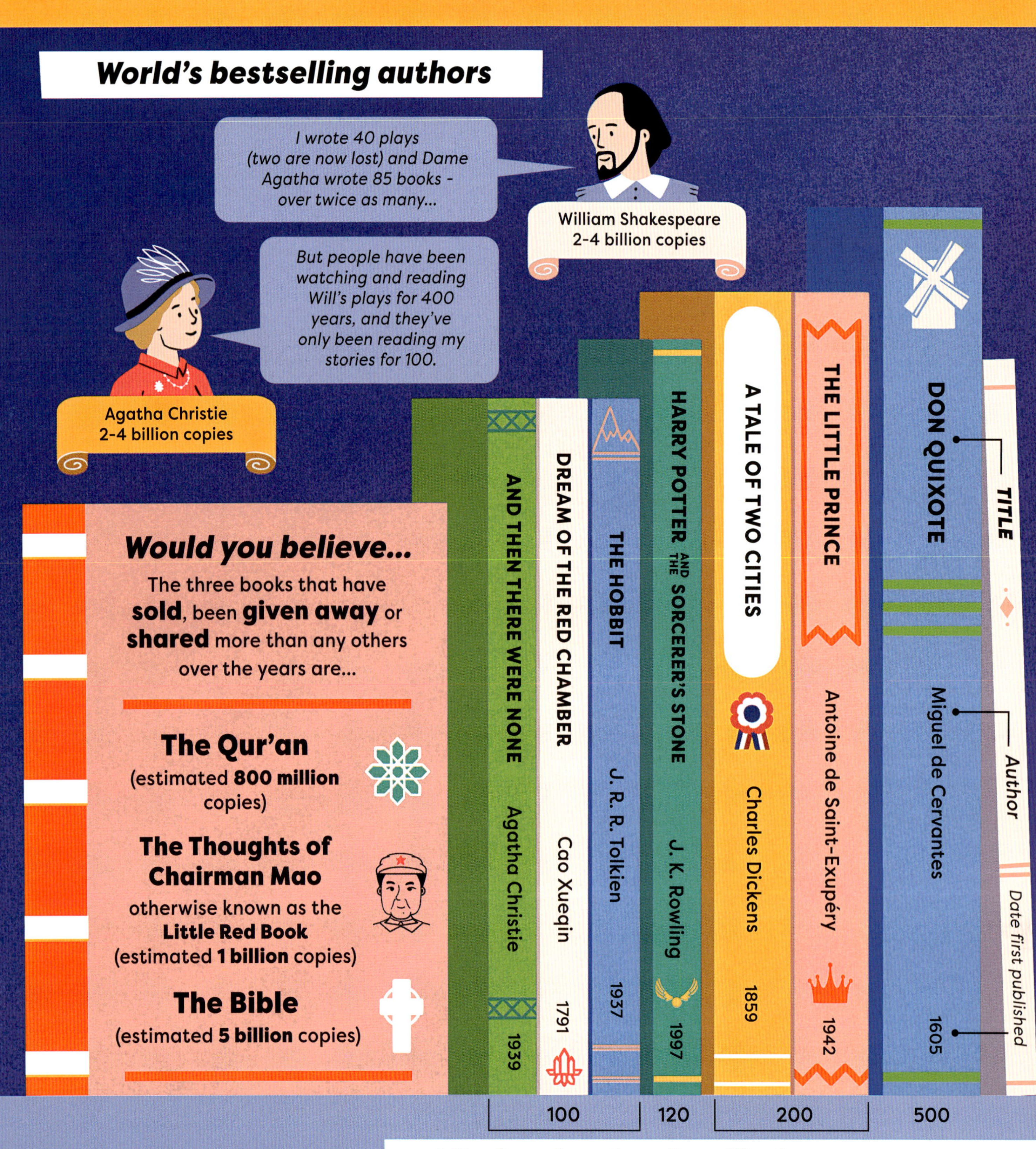

Legendary LIBRARIES

Every time a book is published in a country, copies are sent to that country's copyright or deposit libraries.

The world's largest copyright libraries are:

over **175** million items — **US LIBRARY OF CONGRESS** Washington, D.C.

over **170** million — **THE BRITISH LIBRARY** London, UK

The numbers include physical books, digital documents and sometimes sheet music, maps, photographs and drawings too.

over **54** million — **LIBRARY AND ARCHIVES CANADA** Ottawa

over **50** million — **DEUTSCHE NATIONALBIBLIOTHEK** Frankfurt, Germany

over **49** million — **NATIONAL DIET LIBRARY** Tokyo, Japan

over **43** million — **NATIONAL LIBRARY OF CHINA** Beijing

over **40** million — **BIBLIOTHÈQUE NATIONALE DE FRANCE**, Paris

over **39** million — **ROYAL DANISH LIBRARY** Aarhus and Copenhagen

Not all libraries are housed in imposing buildings. In fact, some don't have a fixed home at all.

In **Bulgaria**, you can borrow books on the beach at the **Black Sea library**.

In the **UK**, many old red **phone booths** have been repurposed as local community libraries.

In **Colombia**, **Biblioburro** donkeys bring books to children in remote rural villages.

In **Norway**, the **Epos** library ship visited villages on the west coast for 60 years. Now it's a floating bookstore and arts venue.

In **Pakistan**, the **Camel mobile library** service delivers books to the country's desert regions.

In **Italy**, the three-wheeled **Bibliomotocarro** truck visits remote villages in the south of the country.

CROCODILIANS

Imagine you can see a crocodilian in front of you.

START

To help work out which type it is, start by asking...

Where am I?

Are you in the **AMERICAS**?
YES NO

Are you in **SOUTH ASIA**?
YES NO

Are you in **SOUTH-EAST ASIA**?
YES NO

Are you in the **SOUTHERN USA**?
YES NO

Are you in **CENTRAL** or **SOUTH AMERICA**?
YES NO

Does it have a very long, thin, pointed snout, either with or without a bump on the end?
YES NO

Does it look like it's wearing spectacles?
YES NO

When its mouth is closed, can you see the top AND bottom teeth?
YES NO

Does it have a broad snout?
YES NO

Are you in the sea?
YES NO

It's a **CAIMAN**.
Caimans are closely related to alligators, but mostly live in Central and South America. There are **six** types:

Smooth-fronted caiman
Spectacled caiman
Broad-snouted caiman
Black caiman
Yacare caiman
Dwarf caiman

It's a **GHARIAL**.
Gharials are found only in Asia, and exist in **two** different types:

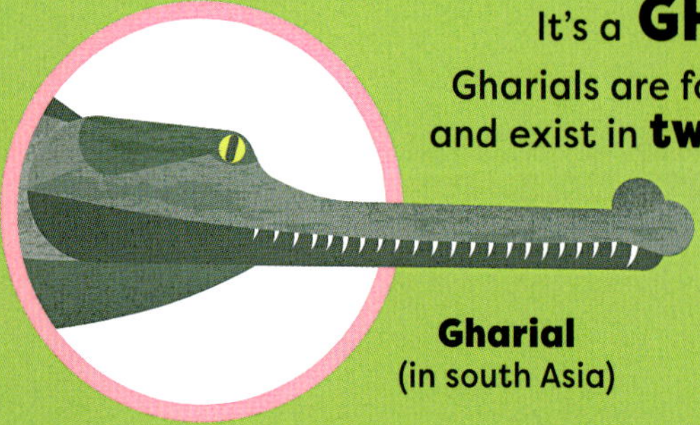

Gharial
(in south Asia)

False gharial
(in south-east Asia)

Crocodilians are a group of reptiles that can be tough to tell apart. There are **four** main types: **crocodiles, alligators, caimans** and **gharials**.

Where on earth are you? Return to the start.

Are you in **FAR EASTERN CHINA**?

YES **NO**

Are you in **AFRICA?**

YES **NO**

Are you in **OCEANIA** or **AUSTRALIA**?

YES **NO**

Are you in **EUROPE**, or **NORTHERN ASIA**?

YES **NO**

You're very lucky! It's a Chinese alligator, and they're nearly extinct.

You're probably in a zoo. There aren't any crocodilians living in the wild here.

It's a **CROCODILE**. Crocodiles live almost all over the world.

Does it have scales along the backs of its hind legs?

YES **NO**

There are at least **18** different types, including...

Cuban crocodile
Saltwater crocodile
Nile crocodile
Dwarf crocodile
Mugger crocodile
American crocodile
Freshwater crocodile
Morelet's crocodile
Orinoco crocodile

It's an **ALLIGATOR**.

There are just **two** types of alligators:

Chinese alligator
American alligator

Gods and GODDESSES

Since ancient times, people from around the world have told tales of all-powerful gods, goddesses, spirits and demons. Many of these figures are still important to people's beliefs today.

GANESHA

This elephant-headed god, from the Hindu religion, is worshipped as the god of wisdom, understanding and intellect.

ZEUS

In ancient Greek myths, this fearsome king of the gods ruled the skies and the weather. He was thought to live at the top of Mount Olympus – the tallest mountain in Greece.

FRIGG

In Norse mythology, originating in Scandinavia over 1,000 years ago, Frigg was Queen of Asgard – the home of the Norse gods and goddesses.

ZHANG GUOLAO

In Chinese mythology, Zhang Guolao is one of eight powerful gods. He had a magic mule which he could fold up and put in his pocket.

AGLOOLIK

Inuit peoples, from Arctic regions of North America and Greenland, believe that this spirit lives under the ice. Hunters pray to Agloolik hoping to be blessed with a successful catch.

AVALOKITESHVARA

Tibetan Buddhists believe that this god, with its many arms and heads, has the ability to save all living beings from suffering.

RA

In ancient Egypt, Ra was the sun god and king of all gods. Each day, he was thought to sail across the sky in a golden boat, then plunge into the darkness of the underworld.

AMATERASU

In Shinto, a religion originating from Japan, Amaterasu is the sun goddess. Her name means *that which illuminates heaven.*

BABA YAGA

More of a demonic witch than a goddess, Baba Yaga is often described in Russian folk tales as a disgusting old woman who kidnaps and eats chlldren.

MAMI WATA

With a name meaning *Mother Water*, this West African water spirit is half-human and half-fish. She can bring good fortune as well as destruction.

RANGI AND PAPA

Māori people from New Zealand believe that Rangi and Papa created the universe. They are often depicted joined in an eternal hug.

HOW ANIMALS SLEEP

Most people need 7 to 9 hours of sleep a night, although babies and children need much more. It's an important part of staying healthy. But how do our sleeping habits compare to other animals?

This chart compares the typical amount of sleep various animals need in 24 hours. The shaded sections show when each creature usually gets its rest.

Some animals get all their sleep at once. Prey animals are at risk from predators when they're asleep, so they often break their rest into short naps.

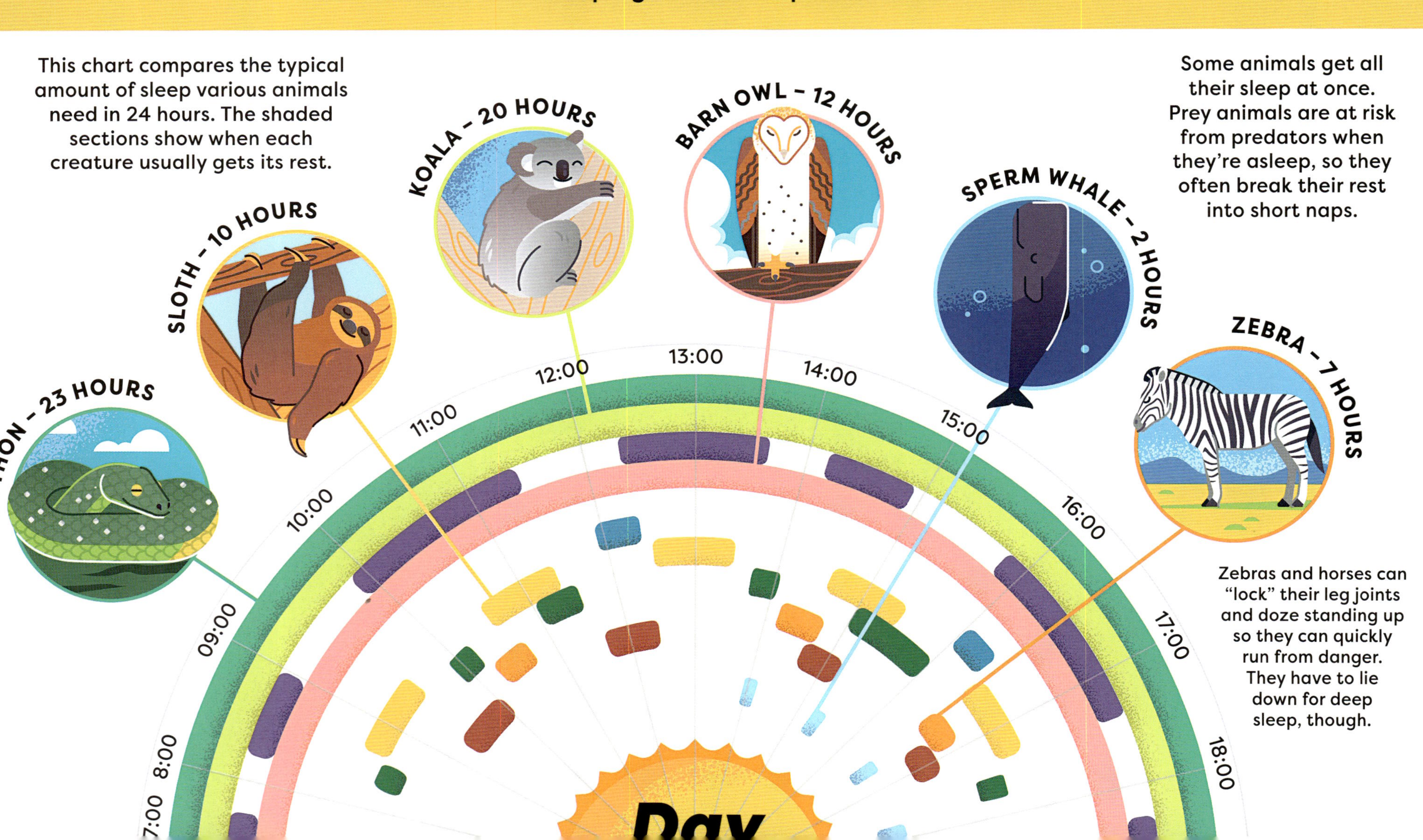

Zebras and horses can "lock" their leg joints and doze standing up so they can quickly run from danger. They have to lie down for deep sleep, though.

Night
19:00
20:00
21:00
22:00
23:00
00:00
01:00
02:00
03:00
04:00
05:00
06:00
Animals living in zoos tend to sleep longer than those in the wild.
PARROT – 12 HOURS
ELEPHANT – 2 HOURS
GORILLA – 12 HOURS
IGUANA – 8-12 HOURS
GOAT – 5 HOURS
CAT – 15 HOURS
ON THE WING
Frigatebirds fly for weeks, or even months, without landing. They catch a few seconds of sleep at a time so they don't fall from the sky.
EYES OPEN
Most species of fish don't have eyelids, so they can't close their eyes when they go to sleep.
ALL OR NOTHING
Walruses can go for days without rest, then haul themselves onto land and sleep for up to 19 hours.
TAKING TURNS
Birds and dolphins sleep with half of their brain at a time, so the other half can stay alert.
ZZZZ

The PERIODIC TABLE

The periodic table is a list of the **118 elements** – the chemicals that make up everything in the universe. It's sorted into groups according to the properties of the elements.

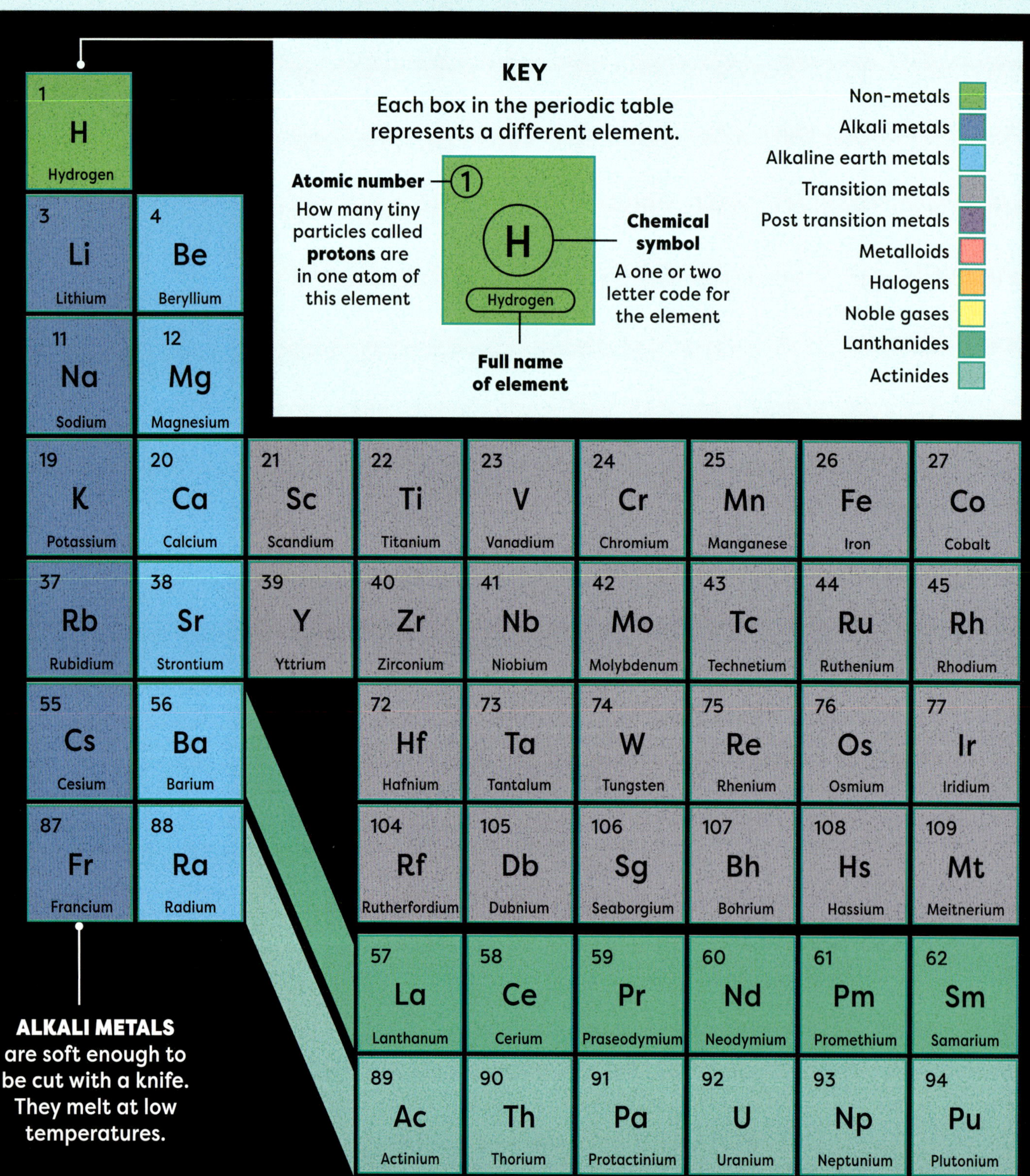

WHAT'S AN **ELEMENT** ANYWAY?

Elements are pure substances, made up of just one type of tiny particle, called an **ATOM**.

DIAGRAM OF AN ATOM

The middle of an atom is called the **NUCLEUS**. It's a clump of *even tinier* particles known as protons and neutrons.

- Proton
- Neutron

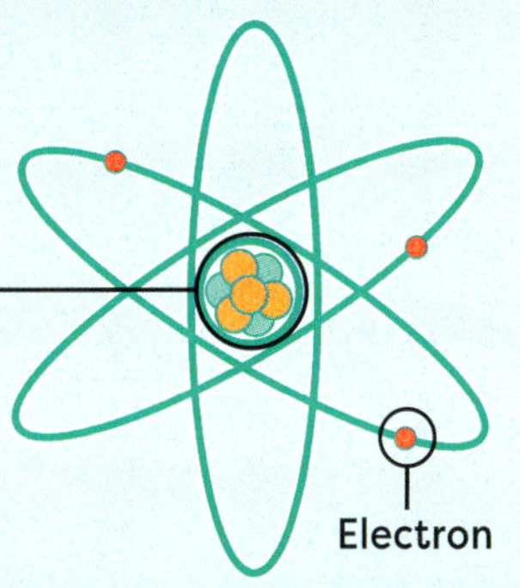

Counting the number of protons tells you which element the atom is.

This atom has three protons. It's **lithium**.

In the 1860s, a scientist named **DMITRI MENDELEEV** began arranging elements into groups in this way. He left gaps in his table for elements that were not known at the time, but which he predicted would be discovered later.

TRANSITION METALS are very useful materials. They are easily shaped and conduct electricity and heat extremely well.

								2 He Helium
			5 B Boron	6 C Carbon	7 N Nitrogen	8 O Oxygen	9 F Fluorine	10 Ne Neon
			13 Al Aluminum	14 Si Silicon	15 P Phosphorus	16 S Sulfur	17 Cl Chlorine	18 Ar Argon
28 Ni Nickel	29 Cu Copper	30 Zn Zinc	31 Ga Gallium	32 Ge Germanium	33 As Arsenic	34 Se Selenium	35 Br Bromine	36 Kr Krypton
46 Pd Palladium	47 Ag Silver	48 Cd Cadmium	49 In Indium	50 Sn Tin	51 Sb Antimony	52 Te Tellurium	53 I Iodine	54 Xe Xenon
78 Pt Platinum	79 Au Gold	80 Hg Mercury	81 Tl Thallium	82 Pb Lead	83 Bi Bismuth	84 Po Polonium	85 At Astatine	86 Rn Radon
110 Ds Darmstadtium	111 Rg Roentgenium	112 Cn Copernicium	113 Nh Nihonium	114 Fl Flerovium	115 Mc Moscovium	116 Lv Livermorium	117 Ts Tennessine	118 Og Oganesson
63 Eu Europium	64 Gd Gadolinium	65 Tb Terbium	66 Dy Dysprosium	67 Ho Holmium	68 Er Erbium	69 Tm Thulium	70 Yb Ytterbium	71 Lu Lutetium
95 Am Americium	96 Cm Curium	97 Bk Berkelium	98 Cf Californium	99 Es Einsteinium	100 Fm Fermium	101 Md Mendelevium	102 No Nobelium	103 Lr Lawrencium

NOBLE GASES are colorless, have no smell, and can't catch fire.

ACTINIDES are radioactive. They release energy as they decay.

Mendelevium is named after Mendeleev.

The ELEMENTS that make us

Chemical elements are the building blocks of absolutely **everything** there is – including us.

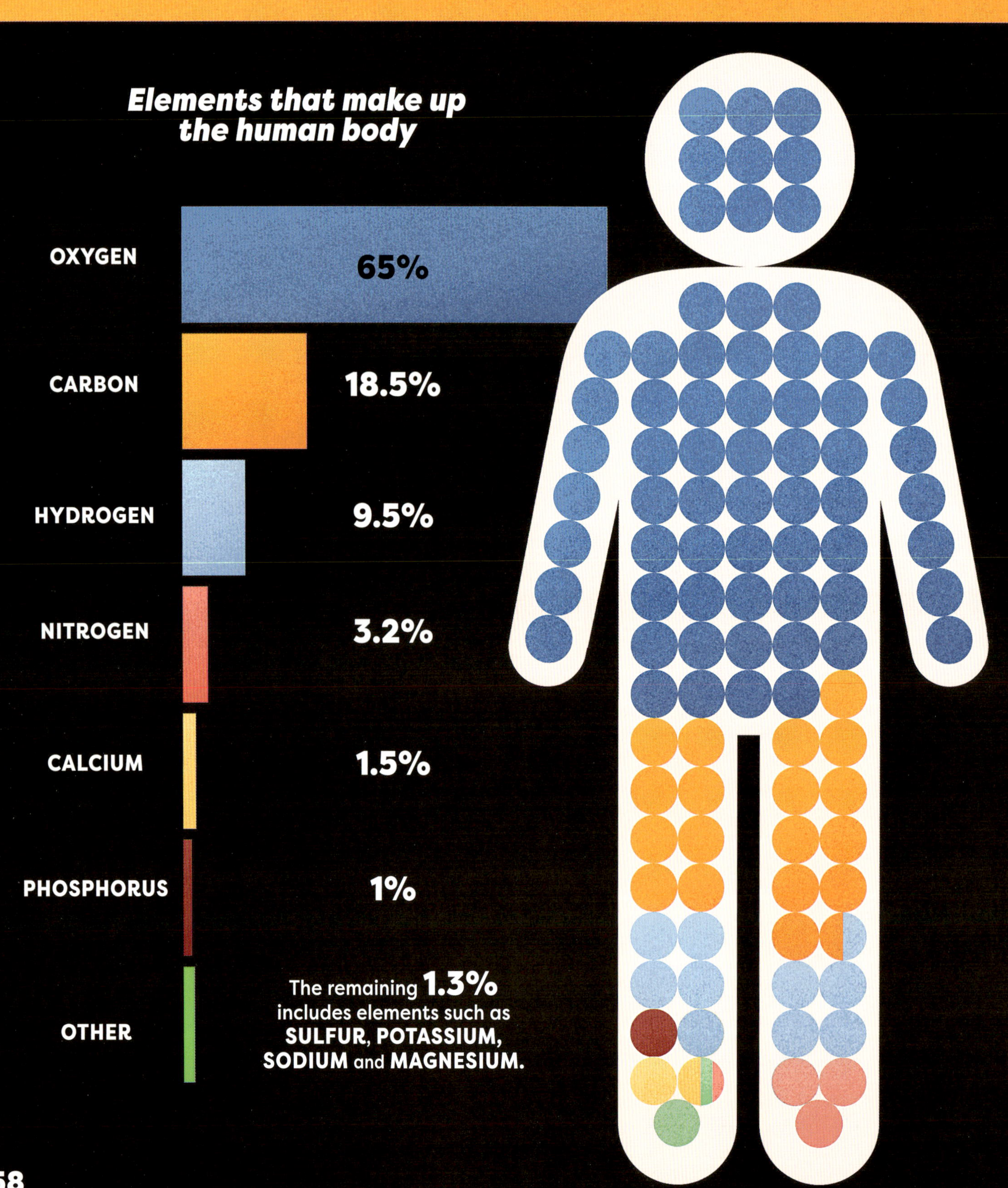

Naming the elements

Each of the **118 elements** takes its name from one of these six categories.

A MINERAL

or similar substance

CALCIUM
is from **calx** which is the word for "lime" in Latin. Calcium comes from limestone.

A SCIENTIST

CURIUM
is from Marie **Curie**, physicist and chemist.

AN ASTRONOMICAL ENTITY

NEPTUNIUM
is from **Neptune**, a planet.

A PLACE ON EARTH

NIHONIUM
is from **Nihon** which is "Japan" in Japanese.

15

9

9

29

118
ELEMENTS

48

8

A PROPERTY OF THE ELEMENT

OSMIUM
is from **osme** which means "smell" in Ancient Greek. Osmium has a very strong scent.

A CONCEPT OR CHARACTER FROM MYTHOLOGY

VANADIUM is from **Vanadis**, the Norse goddess of love and war.

Mega CITIES

In their time, each of these places could claim to be the **world's biggest city**. Visitors from near and far were amazed at their mighty buildings, bustling marketplaces and awe-inspiring inventions.

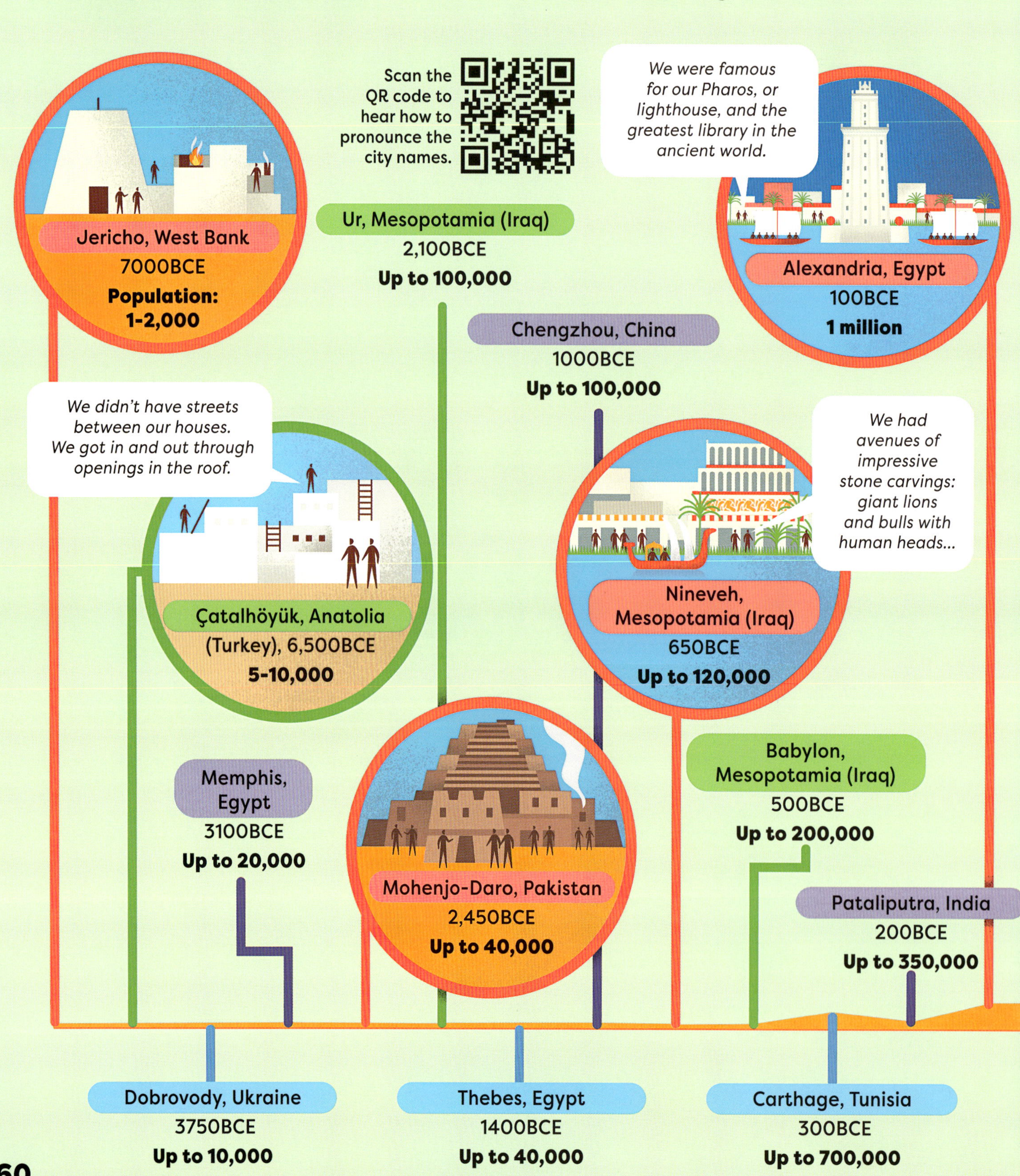

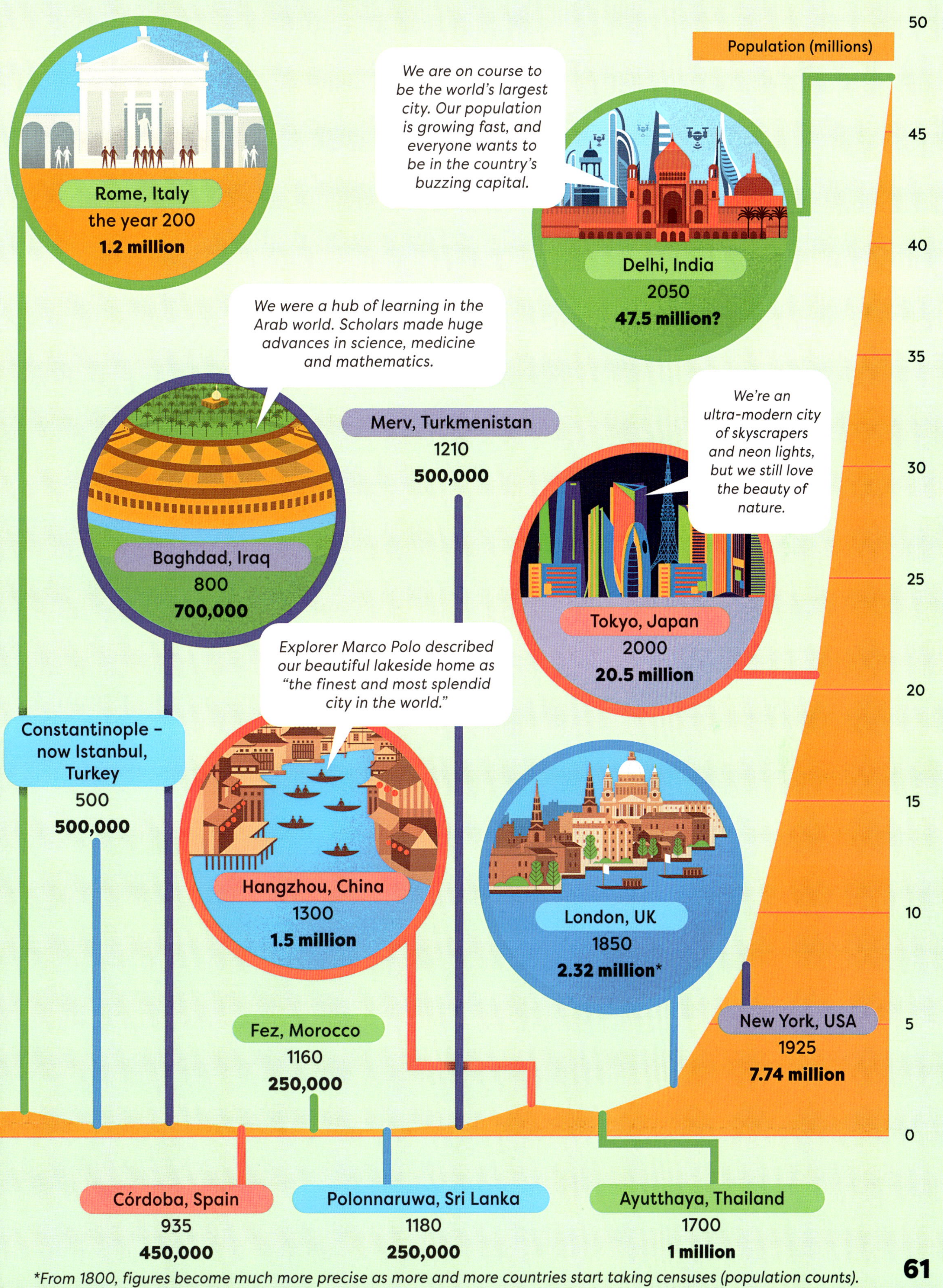

*From 1800, figures become much more precise as more and more countries start taking censuses (population counts).

DID YOU KNOW...

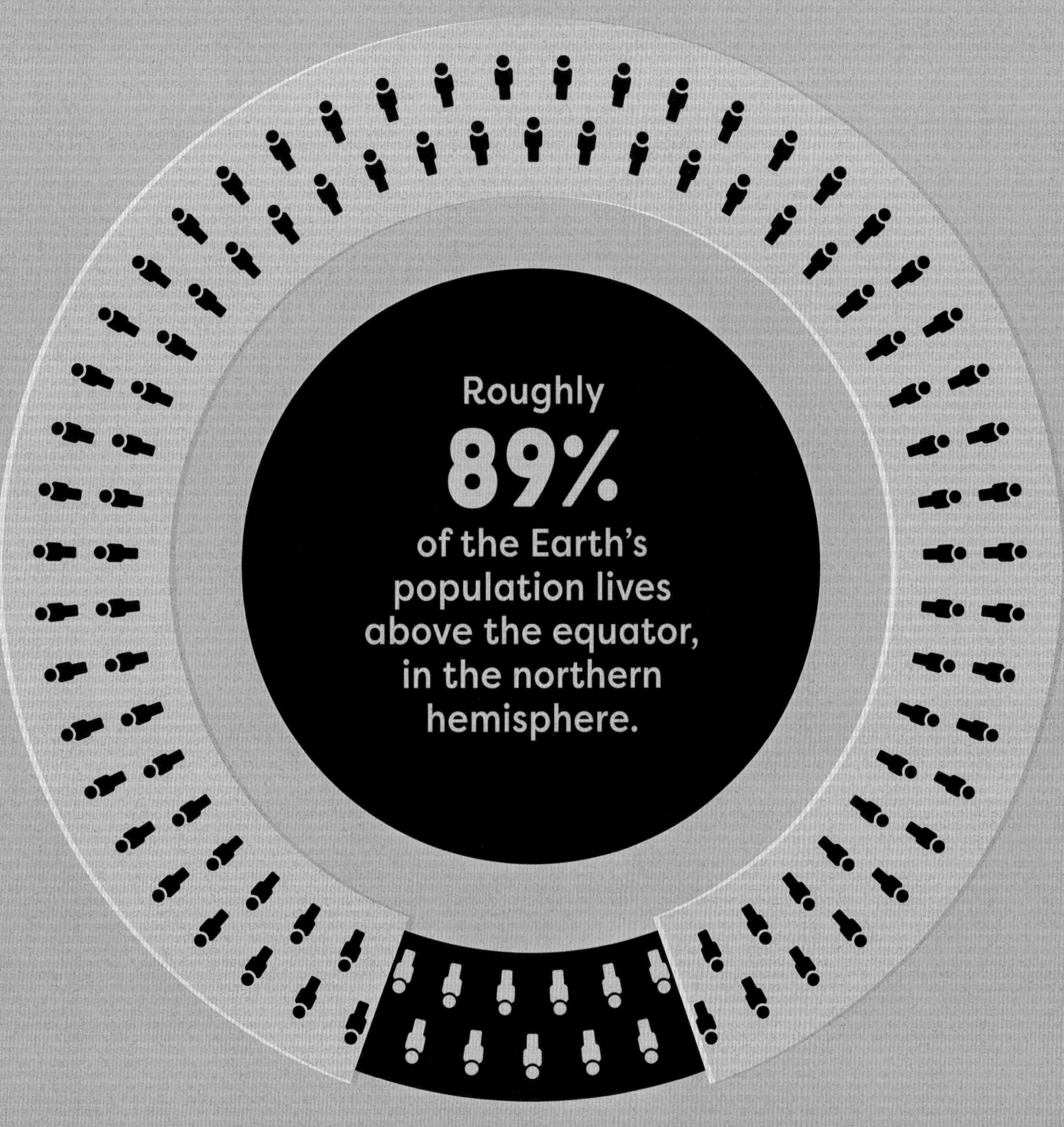
Roughly
89%
of the Earth's
population lives
above the equator,
in the northern
hemisphere.

FAMOUS *explorers*

It takes grit and determination to journey into the unknown. These fearless explorers have trekked across continents, braved the open oceans and navigated across the sky and into space.

AIR AND SPACE

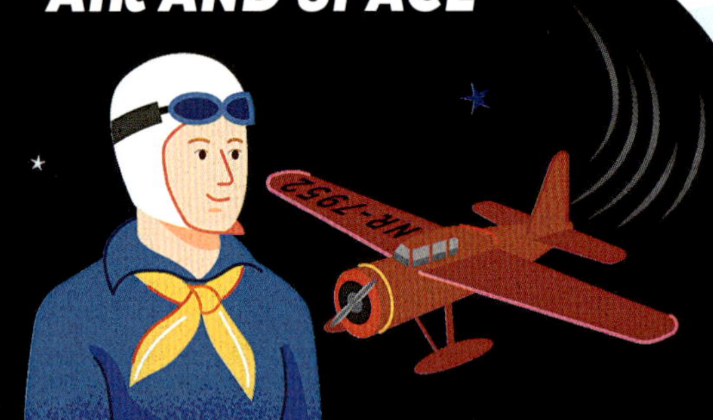

AMELIA EARHART

1897-1937

American pilot Amelia Earhart broke many aviation world records, including being the first woman to fly solo across the Atlantic Ocean. Sadly, her attempt to become the first woman to fly around the world ended in her disappearance.

NEIL ARMSTRONG

1930-2012

On July 20, 1969, American astronaut Neil Armstrong became the first person to walk on the Moon. Part of the Apollo 11 mission, he spent over 21 hours exploring the surface of the Moon.

POLAR EXTREMES

MATTHEW HENSON

1866-1955

African American explorer Matthew Henson may have been the first person to stand on the North Pole. In 1909, he reached the pole with the help of fellow explorer Robert Peary, forty dogs and four local hunters.

ROALD AMUNDSEN

1872-1928

This Norwegian explorer became the first person to sail through the Northwest Passage – a dangerous route between the Antarctic and Pacific Ocean. On December 14th, 1911, he became the first person to reach the South Pole.

OPEN OCEANS

ZHENG HE

1371-1433

Chinese admiral Zheng He commanded a fleet of ships on seven voyages around Asia and East Africa. He took with him gifts of gold, silver and silk, and returned with zebras, giraffes and spices.

I discovered a great many islands, inhabited by numberless [many] people.

CHRISTOPHER COLUMBUS

1451-1506

Italian explorer Christopher Columbus made four voyages across the Atlantic. He found land that was previously unknown to Europeans, although it was home to over two million people. This land was America.

JEANNE BARET

1740-1807

In 1766, French scientist and explorer Jeanne Baret snuck onto a French naval ship dressed as a boy and set sail across the Pacific Ocean. During her travels, she collected exotic plants to bring home and study.

ACROSS CONTINENTS

MARCO POLO

1254-1324

This Italian merchant journeyed into Asia and visited China, where he stayed for 17 years. His adventures were documented in the famous book, *The Travels of Marco Polo.*

IBN BATTUTA

1304-1368

Moroccan scholar Ibn Battuta's adventures took him through India, China, southeast Asia and Africa. He wrote about his experiences in his book *Rihla,* meaning *The Travels.*

I said I could and I would. And I did.

NELLIE BLY

1864-1922

Inspired by Jules Verne's novel, *Around the World in Eighty Days,* American journalist Nellie Bly took a trip around the world in 72 days. She wrote a column about her travels in the *New York World.*

The rise of POP MUSIC

Pop is a genre of music that began in the 1950s in the United States – it is usually catchy, memorable and appeals to lots of different people. Pop is influenced by all kinds of sounds and styles of music.

Pop from the US spread across the world with the help of television. It brought *rock and roll* – a genre inspired by African-American music – into the spotlight and made some artists superstars.

Popular artists*:
Elvis Presley
Frank Sinatra
Fats Domino
Brenda Lee
Chuck Berry

Popular artists:
The Beatles
Elvis Presley
The Beach Boys
The Rolling Stones
Simon & Garfunkel

Portable radios became the latest accessory because they gave listeners more choice. British rock bands, made up of groups of artists writing and performing their own songs, invaded the US charts.

New sound systems allowed musicians to play to huge live audiences. **Hard rock** ruled the stage with heavy, electric sounds, while **disco** – a type of dance music – brought energy to dancefloors.

Popular artists:
Pink Floyd
Eagles
Led Zeppelin
Queen
Elton John

Popular artists:
Michael Jackson
Madonna
Phil Collins
U2
Queen

Music could now be recorded digitally and processed by computers. More and more artists began to use new electronic instruments, such as synthesizers and electronic drums.

*The names listed above are the best-selling artists of each decade based on global sales.

Best-selling albums

Each one of these represents a million copies sold worldwide.

Michael Jackson – ***Thriller***, 1982
70 million copies

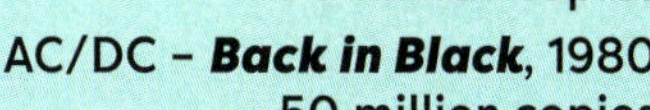

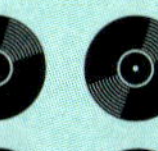

AC/DC – ***Back in Black***, 1980
50 million copies

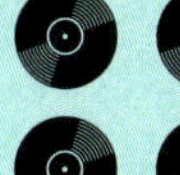

Whitney Houston/Various – ***The Bodyguard***, 1992
45 million copies

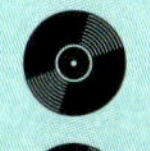
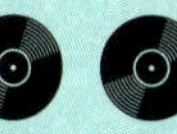
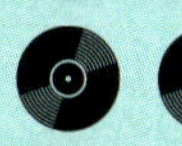

Pink Floyd – ***Dark Side of the Moon***, 1973
45 million copies

Eagles – ***Their Greatest Hits*** *(1971-1975)*, 1976
44 million copies

Boy bands and girl groups, aimed specifically at teenagers, exploded into the US charts. Electronic music continued to grow and the pulsing sounds of **rave** and **techno** filled dancefloors.

Popular artists:
Mariah Carey
Céline Dion
Garth Brooks
Whitney Houston
Nirvana

Popular artists:
Eminem
Linkin Park
Coldplay
Britney Spears
Beyoncé

In the early 2000s, pop acts ruled the US charts with upbeat, bubbly tunes. By the end of the decade, **hip hop** and **rap** – which had emerged in the 70s and 80s – had become mainstream.

Music could now be streamed online, giving listeners even more choice. Pop tunes became shorter and more repetitive. Many artists sang in a whisper – perfect for people listening on headphones.

Popular artists:
Taylor Swift
Drake
Ed Sheeran
Adele
BTS

Popular artists:
Bad Bunny
Taylor Swift
BTS
Drake
The Weeknd

Music from lots of different decades is coming back into popularity. Teenage artists are writing and producing their own songs – some from laptops in their bedrooms. Many artists gather loyal fans through social media.

Our place in the UNIVERSE

We are here

The Sun

Planet Earth is part of the **solar system...**

(FInd out more about the solar system on page 30.)

...which is in the **Milky Way** galaxy...

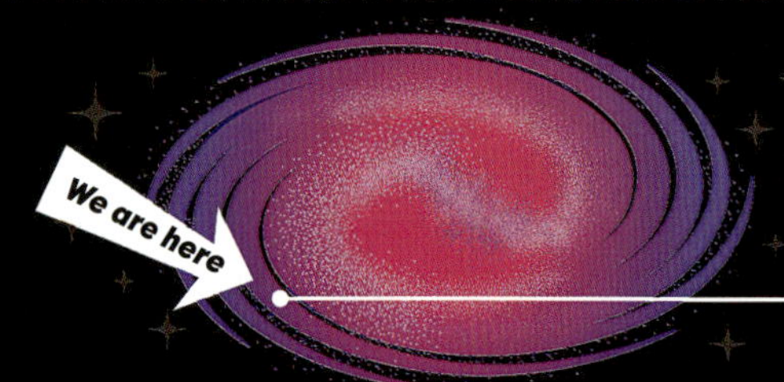

Earth is in one of the outer spiral arms

...which is part of the **Local Group** of galaxies...

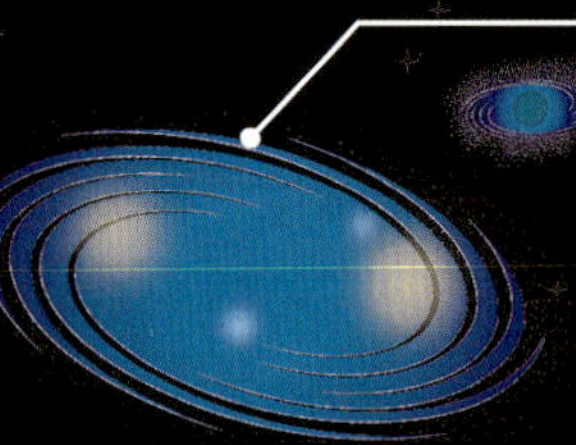

Andromeda, our nearest galaxy

Milky Way

...which is part of the **Virgo supercluster** of galaxies...

Virgo is the name for the largest of 100 galactic groups in this patch

...which is part of the even larger **Laniakea Supercluster,** one of around 10 million superclusters in the known universe.

We are here

Virgo Supercluster

Is anyone else OUT THERE?

How science fiction authors have imagined aliens

Warlike aliens from Mars invade Earth. At first they easily destroy any and all human opposition, but ultimately the invaders catch a virus, and all die.

Human explorers discover an ocean planet. The ocean seems to communicate telepathically – but it is SO alien that experts argue, endlessly, whether or not it is a living thing.

Aliens known only as Overlords come to Earth. They are SO superior to humans that they easily take over the world – without any fighting – and bring peace.

Human colonists find planet Pax, where certain local plants can think and communicate. Humans and plants unite to defeat a new enemy.

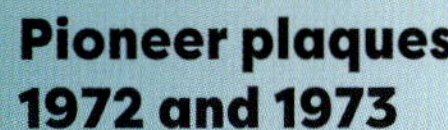

Things a planet needs to sustain life

 Ice or water

 An atmosphere of gases

 A magnetic field

 A rocky crust made up of plates

 Not too far from, or too close to, a star

Attempts by scientists to contact aliens

Pioneer plaques 1972 and 1973  Pictures on a disc were attached to two probes sent to Jupiter, Saturn and beyond.

Arecibo message 1974  A radio message was beamed out to a cluster called Messier 13.

Golden Disc on Voyager I and II 1977  Playable discs were attached to probes sent beyond the solar system.

Cosmic Calls 1 and 2 1999 and 2003 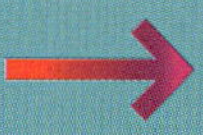 Radio messages were broadcast to various nearby stars.

METI International 2017  Radio messages were broadcast to Luyten's Star, which hosts several earth-like planets.

SPEAKING *your* LANGUAGE

There are over **8 billion** (8,000 million) people in the world today, speaking over **7,000 languages**. Some have just a handful of speakers; English and Chinese have over a billion. On the right are the ten most widely-spoken languages in the world.

 NUMBER OF SPEAKERS WORLDWIDE

 OFFICIAL LANGUAGE IN THESE COUNTRIES (used by governments to make laws, and in official documents)

Scan this QR code to hear these ten hellos. If you can learn these, you'll be able to say hello to people all over the world.

English

Mandarin Chinese

Hindi

 India

Standard Arabic

OVER 275 MILLION

 Over 20 countries from north-west Africa across the Middle East to Iraq

OLÁ!

Portuguese

OVER 260 MILLION

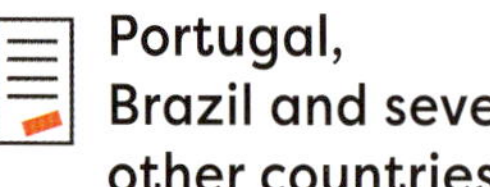

ELLO!

OVER 1,450 MILLION

USA, Canada, UK, Australia, New Zealand and over 50 other countries

Ni hao!

OVER 1,140 MILLION

China, Singapore

Namaste!

¡HOLA!

Spanish

OVER 550 MILLION

Spain, Mexico, Argentina, Peru, Chile and 16 other countries

BONJOUR!

French

OVER 300 MILLION

France, Belgium, Switzerland, Canada and over 20 others, including many African countries

আসসালামু আলাইকুম

Assalamu alaikum!

Bengali

OVER 270 MILLION

Bangladesh; also an officially recognized language in India

ЗДРАВСТВУЙТЕ!

Sdrasdvuitye!

Russian

OVER 250 MILLION

Russia, Belarus, Kazakhstan and Kyrgyzstan

السلام علیکم

Assalam-a-alaikum!

Urdu

OVER 230 MILLION

Pakistan; also an officially recognized language in India

Human RIGHTS

Everyone is born with basic human rights. Most countries in the world recognize these core human rights below, based on the **UNIVERSAL DECLARATION OF HUMAN RIGHTS.**

YOUR FUNDAMENTAL HUMAN RIGHTS

THE RIGHT TO LIFE

Nobody, including the government, can try to end your life.

FREEDOM FROM TORTURE (MENTAL AND PHYSICAL) AND INHUMAN TREATMENT

THE RIGHT TO A FAIR TRIAL AND NO PUNISHMENT WITHOUT LAW

You are innocent until proven guilty.

FREE SPEECH AND PEACEFUL PROTEST

You have a right to speak freely and express your views aloud.

FREEDOM OF THOUGHT, RELIGION AND BELIEF

THE RIGHT TO AN EDUCATION

No child can be denied an education.

RESPECT FOR YOUR PRIVATE LIFE, FAMILY LIFE AND YOUR HOME

PROTECTION FROM DISCRIMINATION

Everyone's rights are equal. You should not be treated unfairly because of your gender, race, disability, sexuality, religion or age.

FREEDOM FROM SLAVERY AND FORCED LABOR

THE RIGHT TO LIBERTY AND FREEDOM

You must not be sent to prison without good reason.

The Universal Declaration of Human Rights was written by the United Nations in 1948, and has since been translated into **over 500 languages**.

Human DEVELOPMENT

Experts use a measurement called the **HUMAN DEVELOPMENT INDEX (HDI)** to compare the quality of life in different countries.

HDI is measured between 0 and 1. A country with a high HDI scores well in each of the following categories:

STANDARD OF LIVING

How wealthy are the businesses and people living in this country?

LIFE EXPECTANCY

How healthy are people in this country, and how long do they live?

KNOWLEDGE

How educated are people living in this country?

The countries with the highest HDI in the world score above 0.9. These include:

AUSTRALIA
DENMARK
ICELAND
NORWAY
SWEDEN
SWITZERLAND

Human NEEDS

American psychologist Abraham Maslow suggested that people have five different levels of need. He called this **MASLOW'S HIERARCHY OF NEEDS.**

5 **SELF-ACTUALIZATION**
Being creative, content and achieving your full potential in life

4 **ESTEEM NEEDS**
Having self-respect and feeling good about yourself

3 **BELONGING AND LOVE NEEDS**
Feeling accepted, loved and included by friends and family

2 **SAFETY NEEDS**
Feeling and being safe from harm

1 **PHYSIOLOGICAL NEEDS**
Access to food, water, shelter and air

According to Maslow, each level of need must be met before the next level can be reached. A person's physiological needs must be met first and the rest can be built up from there.

Behind the scenes on a MOVIE SET

Films only last a couple of hours, but making one can take years. Hundreds of people are involved, many just as important as the actors you see on screen. Here are some of the stars who work behind the scenes.

SCREENWRITER
Writes the **screenplay** – the script for what the characters will say and do, as well as instructions for camera and editing crews

SET DESIGNER
Creates and arranges indoor spaces, from choosing furniture to their layout

GAFFER
Figures out which lights to use and where to fix them

BOOM OPERATOR
Holds the boom microphone, which is used to record speech and sounds

CAMERA CREW
Work the many different cameras to record the scenes

Here, the cast is being filmed in an almost empty stage known as a **green screen**.

My camera is on a track so it moves smoothly.

CAST
Act as the characters in the film

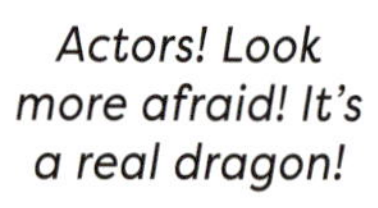

Actors! Look more afraid! It's a real dragon!

DIRECTOR
Instructs crew members on all creative aspects of the film

PRODUCER
Organizes the time, money, materials and people needed to make the film

STUNT DOUBLE
Takes the place of cast members when they perform dangerous scenes, such as fights and explosions

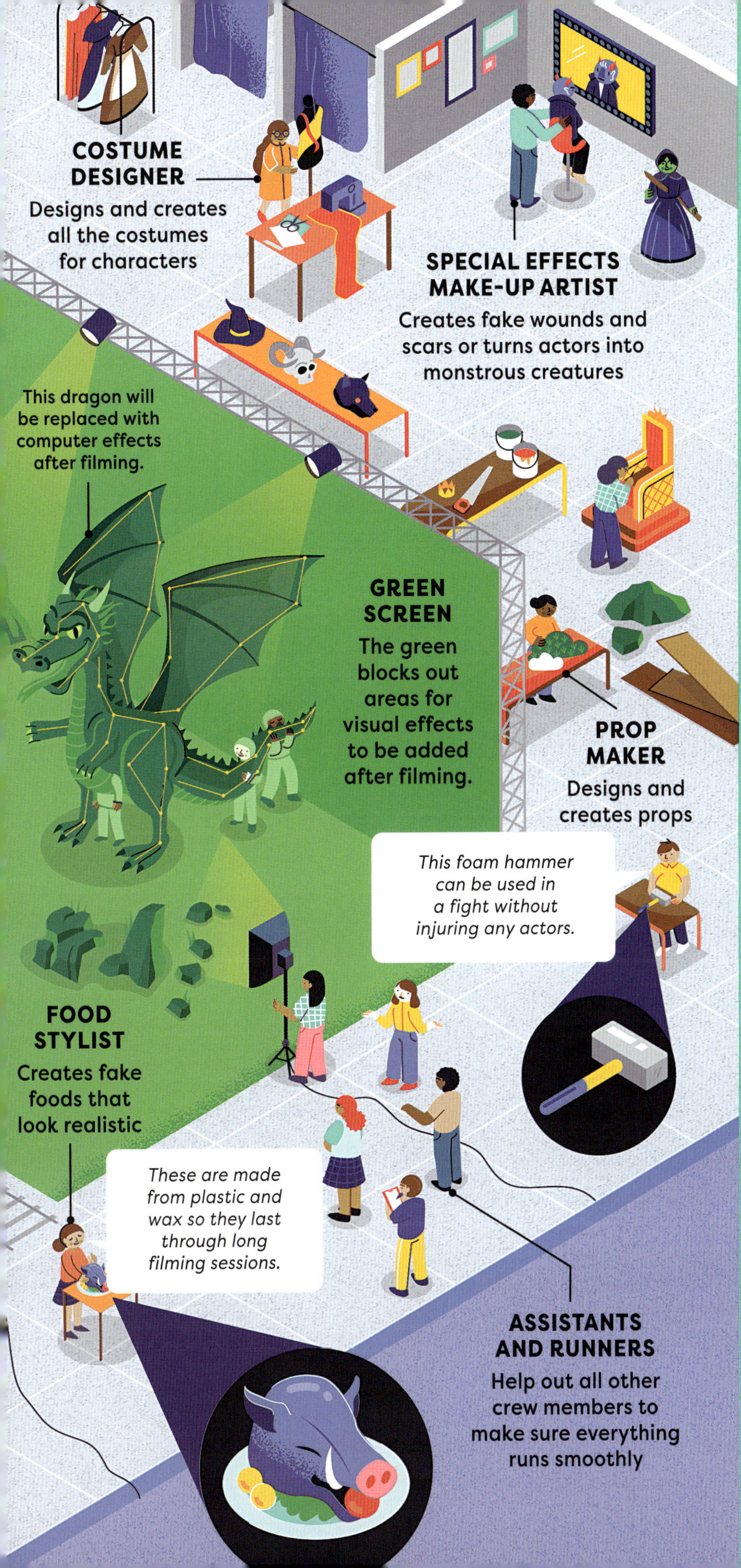

COSTUME DESIGNER
Designs and creates all the costumes for characters
SPECIAL EFFECTS MAKE-UP ARTIST
Creates fake wounds and scars or turns actors into monstrous creatures
This dragon will be replaced with computer effects after filming.
GREEN SCREEN
The green blocks out areas for visual effects to be added after filming.
PROP MAKER
Designs and creates props
This foam hammer can be used in a fight without injuring any actors.
FOOD STYLIST
Creates fake foods that look realistic
These are made from plastic and wax so they last through long filming sessions.
ASSISTANTS AND RUNNERS
Help out all other crew members to make sure everything runs smoothly

After filming...

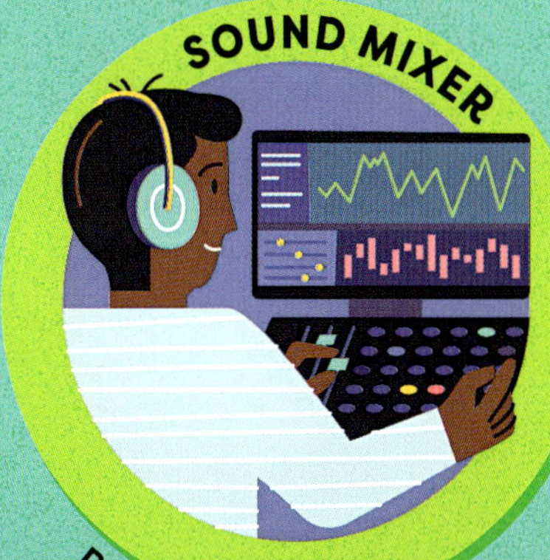

SOUND MIXER
Puts all sound and music together at the right volumes

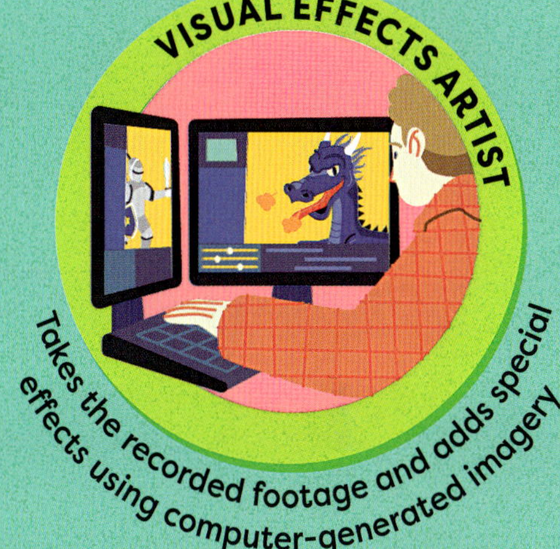

VISUAL EFFECTS ARTIST
Takes the recorded footage and adds special effects using computer-generated imagery

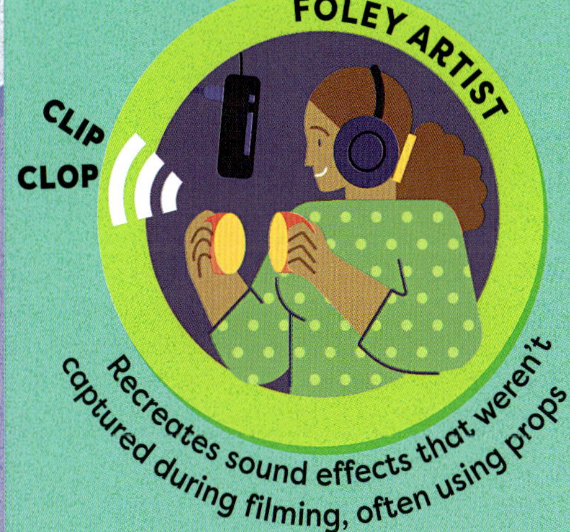

FOLEY ARTIST
CLIP
CLOP
Recreates sound effects that weren't captured during filming, often using props

...it's a wrap!

GOING, GOING, GONE

When over **75%** of the Earth's species die out at nearly the same time, scientists refer to this as a **MASS EXTINCTION**.

So far in the Earth's history, there have been **five** mass extinctions – and many scientists believe that we're going through a **sixth** one right now.

1

Ordovician-Silurian extinction

450-440 million years ago

Death rate: **86%** **of all species**

Possible causes: global cooling, oxygen depletion, heightened volcanic activity

Effects: sea levels dropped and water temperatures cooled, which disrupted habitats.

2

Late Devonian extinction

375-360 million years ago

Death rate: **75%** **of all species**

Possible causes: global cooling or volcanic activity under the sea

Effects: the world's oceans were deprived of oxygen and they became toxic to sea life.

3

Permian-Triassic extinction – "The Great Dying"

252 million years ago

Death rate: **96%** **of all species**

Possible causes: volcanic activity in Siberia

Effects: toxic gases were released into the atmosphere and the Earth became uninhabitable to most animals.

WHAT BECAME EXTINCT?

Here are just some of the many species that died out.

PLAESIOMYIDAE

Also known as lamp shells, these creatures lived on the sea floor

GRAPTOLITES

Tiny floating sea animals that lived together in groups, or colonies

STROMATOPOROIDS

Sea sponges that lived in groups and built rocky, underwater reefs

CYSTOIDS

Sea creatures that attached themselves to the sea floor with a stalk

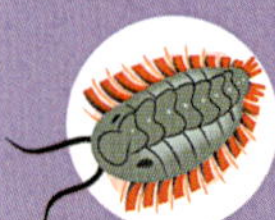

TRILOBITES

Sea creatures with hard outer casings that could swim, scuttle or float

GORGONOPSIANS

Powerful land animals that had sharp teeth to stab and tear prey

Living fossils

More than **99%** of plant and animal species that have EVER lived on Earth are extinct. However, some species that are alive today have been around for hundreds of millions of years. These species are known as LIVING FOSSILS. Here are just three examples.

GLYPHEOID LOBSTERS

GINKGO TREE

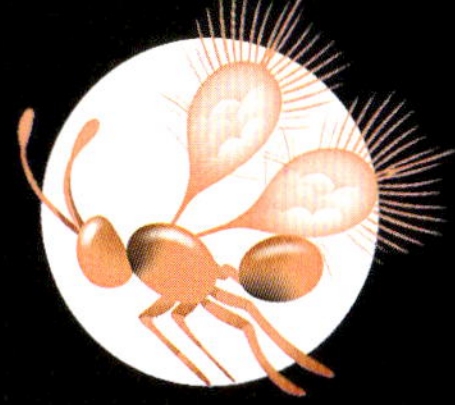

FALSE FAIRY WASPS

250 MYA | 150 MYA | 50 MYA | NOW

4

Triassic-Jurassic extinction

201 million years ago

Death rate:
80%
of all species

Possible causes: volcanic activity, asteroid impact, gradual climate change

Effects: dinosaurs, pterosaurs, crocodiles and small mammals were left to roam the Earth.

PHYTOSAURS
Crocodile-like scaly reptiles that lived in water and on land

CONODONTS
Long, soft-bodied sea animals with fins and teeth

5

Cretaceous extinction

66 million years ago

Death rate:
60-76%
of all species
including dinosaurs

Possible causes: a massive asteroid hitting the Earth

Effects: fires and earthquakes were probably triggered across the globe, and global temperatures dropped.

PTEROSAURS
Flying reptiles with beaks and head crests, which ate other animals

MOSASAURS
Reptiles with long, muscular tails that lived in shallow waters

6

Holocene extinction

11,700 years ago to now

Death rate:
Not yet known

Possible causes: overhunting, overfishing, climate change and the spread of diseases

Effects: habitats are being destroyed and extinction rates are estimated to be **100-1,000** times the natural rate.

MAMMOTHS
Enormous animals from the elephant family with long, curved tusks

RAPHINAE
Flightless birds, including the dodo, from the islands of Mauritius

Taking FLIGHT

325 million years ago (MYA)

INSECTS EVOLVED WINGS AND BEGAN FLYING

228 MYA

PTEROSAURS EMERGED

17 December, 1903

THE WRIGHT FLYER

First engine-powered aircraft to fly a human

Built by the Wright brothers, its longest flight lasted 59 seconds.

8 – 29 August, 1929

THE GRAF ZEPPELIN

First airship to fly around the world

It took 21 days, 5 hours and 31 minutes. Passenger Grace Hay Drummond-Hay became the first woman to fly around the world.

20 – 21 May, 1932

AMELIA EARHART

First woman to fly solo across the Atlantic Ocean

Her journey lasted 14 hours and 56 minutes.

14 October, 1947

BELL X-1

First aircraft to fly faster than the speed of sound

This was such an achievement, it was kept top secret by the US military for months.

12 April, 1961

VOSTOK 1

First capsule to launch a person into outer space

On board was Yuri Gagarin. He orbited the Earth once – a journey which took 108 minutes.

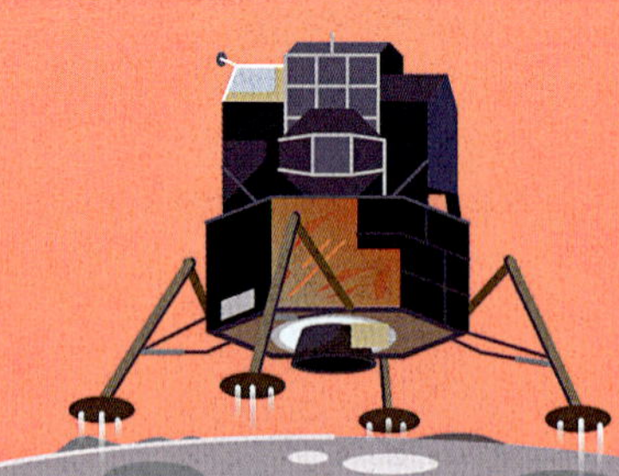

20 July, 1969

LUNAR MODULE EAGLE

First spacecraft to land humans on the Moon

As part of the Apollo 11 mission, astronauts Neil Armstrong and Buzz Aldrin spent 21 hours and 36 minutes on the Moon's surface.

Human evolution period

150 MYA
BIRDS EVOLVED FROM DINOSAURS

52 MYA
FIRST BATS

The only flying mammal

540s
FIRST PAPER KITES FLOWN IN CHINA

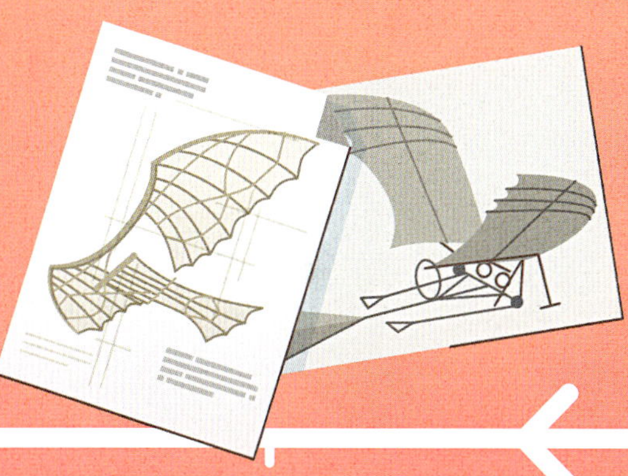

1480s
LEONARDO DA VINCI

First known designs for flying machines, gliders and parachutes

Leonardo was an Italian artist and scientist. He didn't build his designs, but even if he had, they wouldn't have worked.

1783
MONTGOLFIER BALLOON

First hot air balloon to fly with human passengers

Made by the Montgolfier brothers. Their earlier balloon carried a sheep, a duck and a rooster.

1804
CAYLEY GLIDER

First glider to carry humans

Made by George Cayley. He spent his life working on gliders and studying the science behind flight – we still use his knowledge today.

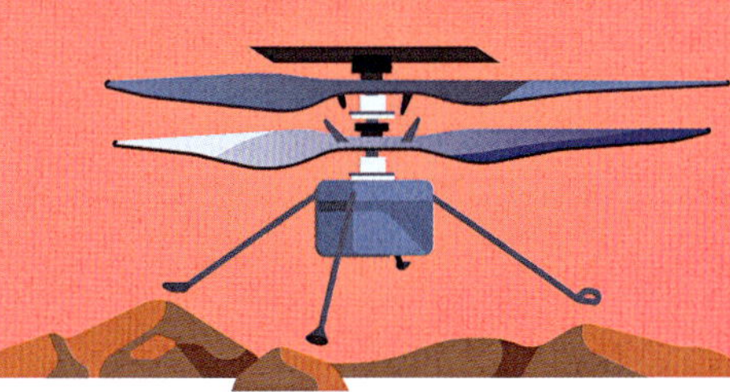

20 November, 1998
THE ZARYA MODULE

First component of the International Space Station (ISS) to launch into space

The first crew members of the ISS arrived in 2000, and it has never been empty since.

19 April, 2021
INGENUITY MARS HELICOPTER

First remote-controlled, powered unit to fly on another planet

It took off for a test flight and hovered for about 3m (10ft) before landing again.

Future achievements in flight might include planes powered by renewable energy.

DID YOU KNOW...

Dinosaurs first walked the Earth over **230 MILLION YEARS AGO.**

But sharks were swimming in the oceans more than **200 MILLION YEARS** *before* that.

So they've been around for over

450 MILLION YEARS.

INDEPENDENCE DAYS

Many countries have been ruled by another country in the past. For most, the day they won their freedom is marked each year by a celebration known, in a local language, as *Independence Day*.

This calendar shows the dates of independence days of over **130 countries** around the world. The year they gained independence is shown in brackets.

January

Date	**Country** (year)
1	**Haiti** (1804)
1	**Sudan** (1956)
4	**Myanmar** (1948)
31	**Nauru** (1968)

February

Date	Country (year)
4	**Sri Lanka** (1948)
7	**Grenada** (1974)
15	**Serbia** (1804/1835)
18	**Gambia** (1965)
22	**St Lucia** (1979)
23	**Brunei** (1984)
25	**Kuwait** (1961)
27	**Dominican Republic** (1844)

March

Date	Country (year)
1	**Bosnia and Herzegovina** (1992)
6	**Ghana** (1957)
12	**Mauritius** (1968)
20	**Tunisia** (1956)
21	**Namibia** (1990)
25	**Greece** (1821)
26	**Bangladesh** (1971)

April

Date	Country (year)
4	**Senegal** (1960)
17	**Syria** (1946)
18	**Zimbabwe** (1980)
27	**Togo** (1960)
27	**Sierra Leone** (1961)

May

Date	Country (year)
14/15	**Paraguay** (1811)
21	**Montenegro** (2006)
24	**Eritrea** (1991)
25	**Jordan** (1946)
26	**Georgia** (1918)
26	**Guyana** (1966)
28	**Azerbaijan** (1918)

June

Date	Country (year)
1	**Samoa** (1962)
12	**Philippines** (1898)
25	**Mozambique** (1975
25	**Slovenia** (1991)
26	**Madagascar** (1960
27	**Djibouti** (1977)
29	**Seychelles** (1976)

BRR
BRR
BRRRR

Celebrations are often marked by fireworks, parades, food, drinks, music, dancing, flag-waving, and kite-flying.

Scan this QR code to find out more about different countries' independence days and how they're celebrated.

July

- 1 **Somalia** (1960)
- 1 **Burundi** (1962)
- 1 **Rwanda** (1962)
- 3 **Belarus** (1944 and 1991)
- 4 **USA** (1776)
- 5 **Venezuela** (1811)
- 5 **Algeria** (1962)
- 5 **Cape Verde** (1975)
- 6 **Malawi** (1964)
- 7 **Solomon Islands** (1978)
- 9 **Argentina** (1816)
- 9 **South Sudan** (2011)
- 10 **Bahamas** (1973)
- 12 **São Tomé and Príncipe** (1975)
- 12 **Kiribati** (1979)
- 17 **Slovakia** (1992)
- 20 **Colombia** (1810)
- 23 **Egypt** (1952)
- 26 **Liberia** (1847)
- 6/27 **Maldives** (1965)
- 8/29 **Peru** (1821)
- 30 **Vanuatu** (1980)

August

- 3 **Niger** (1960)
- 5 **Burkina Faso** (1960)
- 6 **Bolivia** (1825)
- 6 **Jamaica** (1962)
- 7 **Ivory Coast** (1960)
- 10 **Ecuador** (1822)
- 11 **Chad** (1960)
- 13 **Central African Republic** (1960)
- 14 **Pakistan** (1947)
- 15 **Korea** (1945)
- 15 **India** (1947)
- 16/17 **Gabon** (1960)
- 17 **Indonesia** (1945)
- 19 **Afghanistan** (1919)
- 24 **Ukraine** (1991)
- 25 **Uruguay** (1825)
- 27 **Moldova** (1991)
- 31 **Malaysia** (1957)
- 31 **Trinidad and Tobago** (1962)
- 31 **Kyrgyzstan** (1991)

September

- 1 **Uzbekistan** (1991)
- 6 **Eswatini** (1968)
- 7 **Brazil** (1822)
- 8 **North Macedonia** (1991)
- 9 **Tajikistan** (1991)
- 15 **Costa Rica** (1821)
- 15 **El Salvador** (1821)
- 15 **Guatemala** (1821)
- 15 **Honduras** (1821)
- 15 **Nicaragua** (1821)
- 15/16 **Mexico** (1810)
- 16 **Papua New Guinea** (1975)
- 18 **Chile** (1810)
- 19 **St Kitts and Nevis** (1983)
- 21 **Belize** (1981)
- 21 **Armenia** (1991)
- 22 **Mali** (1960)
- 24 **Guinea-Bissau** (1973)
- 27 **Turkmenistan** (1991)
- 30 **Botswana** (1966)

October

- 1 **Cyprus** (1960)
- 1 **Nigeria** (1960)
- 1 **Tuvalu** (1978)
- 1 **Palau** (1994)
- 2 **Guinea** (1958)
- 4 **Lesotho** (1966)
- 9 **Uganda** (1962)
- 10 **Fiji** (1970)
- 12 **Equatorial Guinea** (1968)
- 24 **Zambia** (1964)
- 27 **St Vincent and the Grenadines** (1979)

November

- 1 **Antigua and Barbuda** (1981)
- 3 **Dominica** (1978)
- 3 **Micronesia** (1986)
- 9 **Cambodia** (1953)
- 11 **Poland** (1918)
- 11 **Angola** (1975)
- 18 **Latvia** (1918)
- 18 **Morocco** (1956)
- 22 **Lebanon** (1943)
- 25 **Suriname** (1975)
- 28 **Albania** (1912)
- 28 **Mauritania** (1960)
- 28 **East Timor** (1975)
- 30 **Barbados** (1966)

December

- 1 **Portugal** (1640)
- 6 **Finland** (1917)
- 9 **Tanzania** (1961)
- 12 **Kenya** (1963)
- 16 **Kazakhstan** (1991)
- 24 **Libya** (1951)
- 29 **Mongolia** (1911)

BOOM!

2-D shapes

A 2-D (two-dimensional) shape is the outline of a flat object with two dimensions: length and width. Do you know your hexagons from your heptagons? Here are some examples of ***POLYGONS*** – flat shapes with multiple corners and straight sides.

EQUILATERAL TRIANGLE
(3 sides, all of equal length)

SCALENE TRIANGLE
(3 sides, all of different length)

ISOSCELES TRIANGLE
(3 sides, with two of equal length)

SQUARE
(4 sides of equal length)

A square is a type of rectangle, but a rectangle isn't a square.

RECTANGLE
(4 sides)

KITE
(4 sides)

Four-sided polygons are also called quadrilaterals.

TRAPEZOID
(4 sides)

PARALLELOGRAM
(4 sides)

PENTAGON
(5 sides)

HEXAGON
(6 sides)

HEPTAGON
(7 sides)

OCTAGON
(8 sides)

NONAGON
(9 sides)

DECAGON
(10 sides)

Polygons with hundreds or thousands of sides may look like circles – but they aren't.

CHILIAGON
(1,000 sides)

HEXAGONS IN NATURE

Hexagons are strong shapes, even at small sizes, and found throughout nature. Compared to other shapes of the same size, they can be built using less material too.

HONEYCOMB

Bees turn honey into wax for honeycomb. They use honeycomb to store their eggs, honey and pollen.

SNOWFLAKES

Water molecules are bent at the same angle as two sides of a hexagon. As they freeze, they form hexagonal shapes.

VOLCANIC ROCK COLUMNS

As molten lava cools, it shrinks and cracks into stable columns. These are usually hexagonal, but can have anything from three to eight sides.

3-D *shapes*

A 3-D (three-dimensional) shape has three dimensions: length, width and height.

Anatomy of a 3-D shape

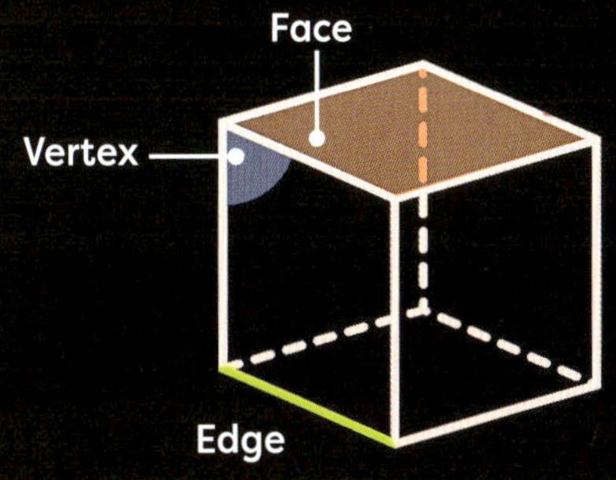

The amount of space a 3-D shape takes up is called its **VOLUME**.

A **NET** is what a 3-D shape would look like if it were opened up. 3-D shapes can have more than one net – a cube can be made from these 11 different nets.

Polyhedrons Shapes with flat faces and straight edges

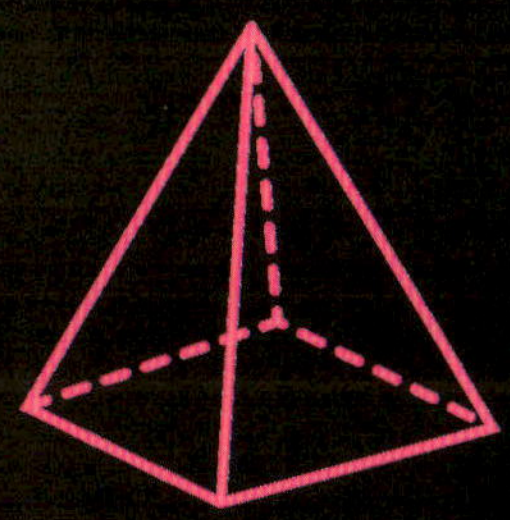

SQUARE PYRAMID
(5 faces)

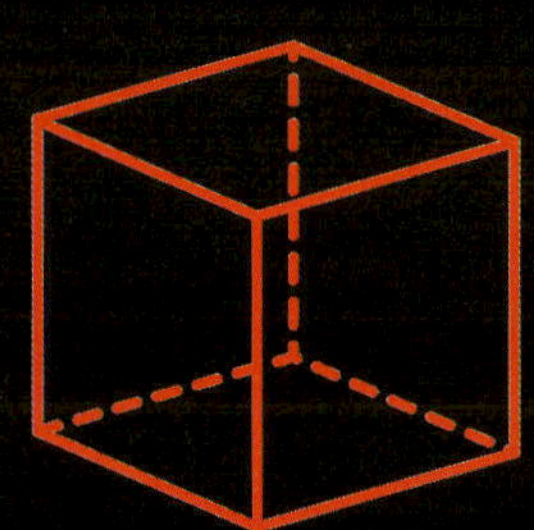

CUBE
(6 faces)

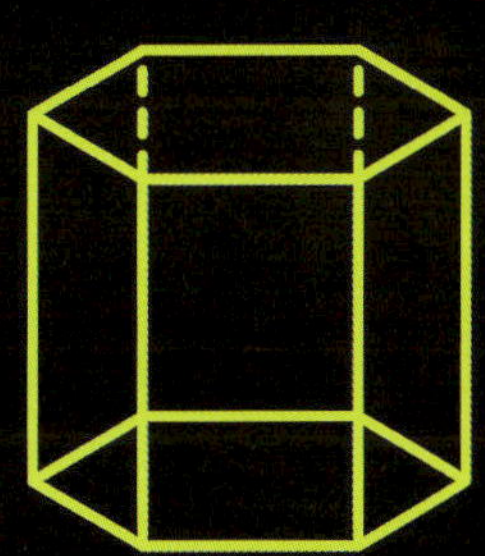

HEXAGONAL PRISM
(8 faces)

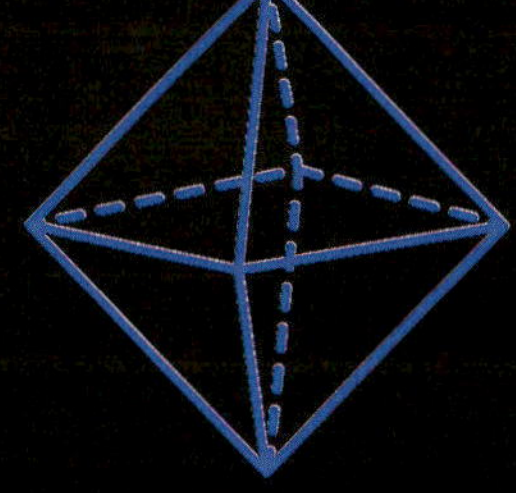

OCTAHEDRON
(8 faces)

ICOSAHEDRON
(20 faces)

Non-polyhedrons Shapes with at least one curved face

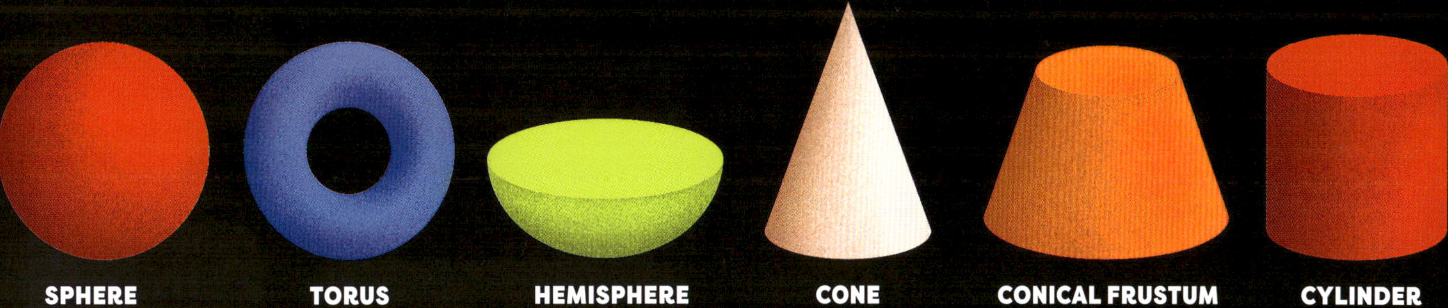

SPHERE (1 face) **TORUS** (1 face) **HEMISPHERE** (2 faces) **CONE** (2 faces) **CONICAL FRUSTUM** (3 faces) **CYLINDER** (3 faces)

Wild WINDS

The wind can blow a gentle breeze or a violent storm. One way of measuring its **force**, or how strong it is, is by using the **Beaufort scale** – a scale based on observations of the sea.

(Beaufort scale)

FORCE	*WIND DESCRIPTION*	WIND SPEED	*Sea conditions*
0	*Calm*	0-1km/h (0-1mph)	*Sea like a mirror*
1	*Light air*	1-5km/h (1-3mph)	*Ripples*
2	*Light breeze*	6-11km/h (4-7mph)	*Small wavelets*
3	*Gentle breeze*	12-19km/h (8-12mph)	*Large wavelets*
4	*Moderate breeze*	20-28km/h (13-18mph)	
5	*Fresh breeze*	29-38km/h (19-24mph)	
6	*Strong breeze*		
7	*Near gale*		
8	*Gale, fresh gale*		
9			
10			

Destructive winds

At high speeds, winds can tear down homes, rip up roads and destroy whole towns and cities. Here are some of the most destructive types.

TORNADO

A rapidly rotating column of air that connects a thunderstorm to the ground.

Speed: up to **483km/h** (300mph)

DERECHO

A group of thunderstorms moving together.

Speed: over **93km/h** (58mph)

Size: over **640km** (400 miles)

TROPICAL CYCLONE

A giant, circular storm of swirling winds that forms over warm, tropical oceans.

Size: up to **2,000km** (1,243 miles) wide

Local winds

Winds that blow in specific areas of the world are called local winds. They are given **special names** by the locals.

BERG
Mountain
South Africa, Namibia

CHINOOK
Snow-eater
Rocky Mountains, Canada and the USA

FOEHN EFFECT
Spring breezes
European Alps

HABOOB
Blasting
Sudan

HARMATTAN
Wind from a distant place
West Africa

MISTRAL
Master wind
Southern France

Windy cities of the world

Gusts of wind in these cities can regularly reach force ten or over on the Beaufort scale.

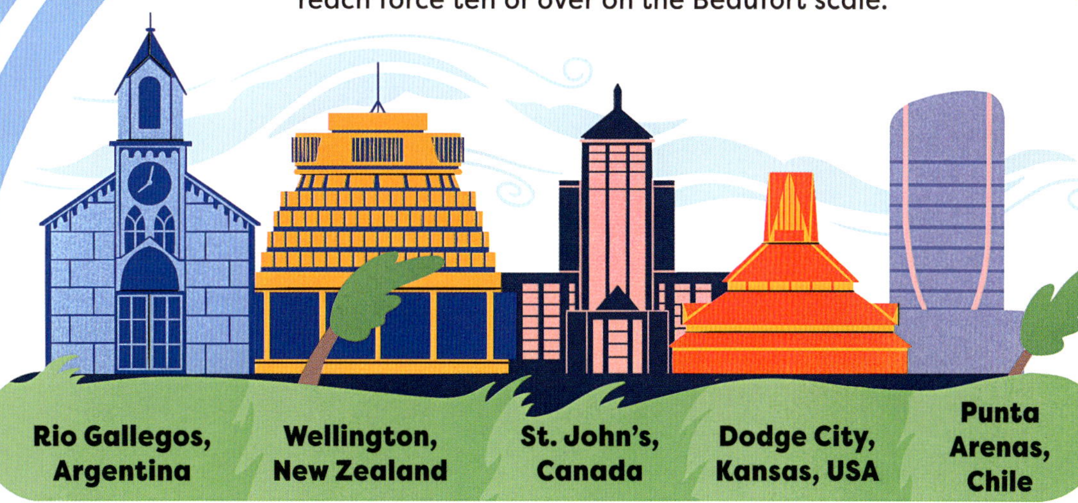

Chicago, USA, is nicknamed the **Windy City**. But it's probably less to do with the weather and more to do with the city's 19th century politicians, who were thought to be boastful and full of bluster.

Small waves

Moderate waves

39-49km/h (25-31mph) Large waves

50-61km/h (32-38mph) Sea heaps up

62-74km/h (39-46mph) Moderately high waves

Severe gale 75-88km/h (47-54mph) High waves

Storm 89-102km/h (55-63mph) Very high waves

11 Violent storm 103-117km/h (64-72mph) Exceptionally high waves

12 Hurricane 118-133km/h (73-83mph) Huge waves, sea is completely white

In Taiwan and mainland China, storms are *so* powerful weather scientists have extended the Beaufort scale to **17** – a ***tropical typhoon.***

Wind gods

Since ancient times, wind has been seen as something to be both feared and respected. Many early civilizations associated the wind with gods and goddesses.

Greek god of the cold north wind

Hindu god of the winds

Chinese goddess of the wind

All SYSTEMS *go*

Your body is made up of different groups of organs and other body parts that work together to do specific jobs. These groups are called body systems, and there are 11 of them.

1. INTEGUMENTARY
2. MUSCULAR
3. SKELETAL
4. CIRCULATORY (Cardiovascular)
5. LYMPHATIC
6. NERVOUS
7. REPRODUCTIVE
8. DIGESTIVE
9. URINARY
10. RESPIRATORY
11. ENDOCRINE

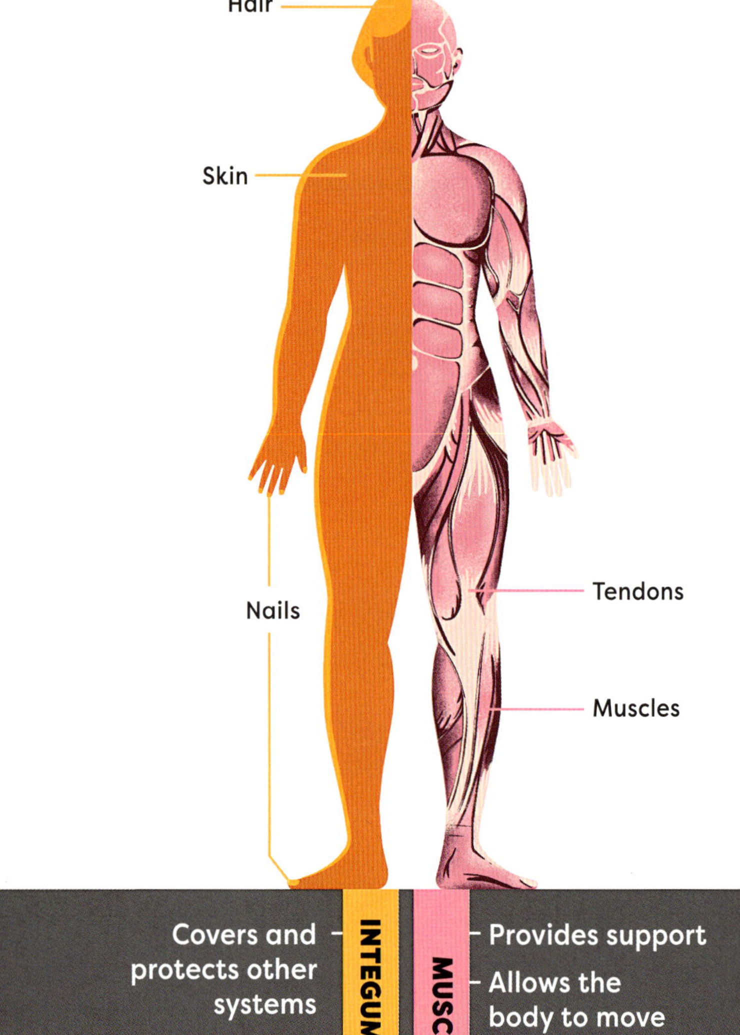

INTEGUMENTARY

- Covers and protects other systems
- Contains sensory receptors

MUSCULAR

- Provides support
- Allows the body to move
- Helps regulate temperature

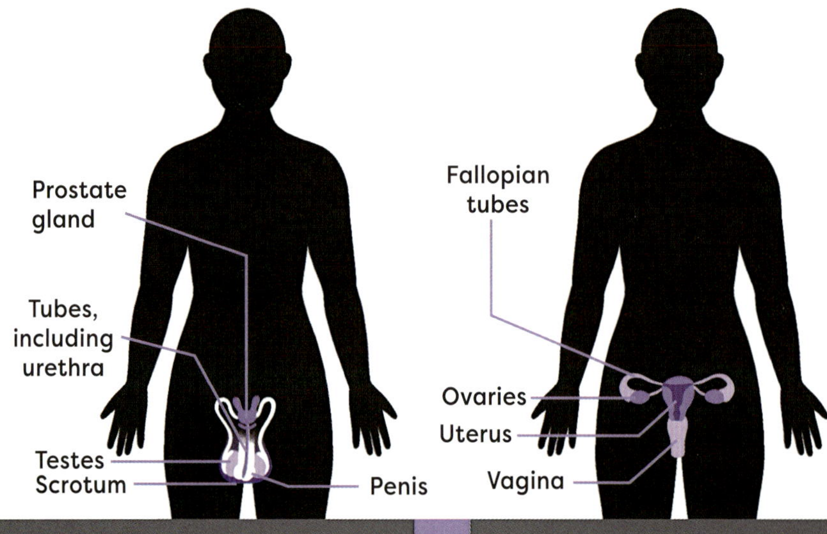

REPRODUCTIVE

- Makes the hormones and cells needed for sexual development and reproduction
- Makes the hormones and cells needed for sexual development and reproduction
- Can protect, nurture and give birth to babies

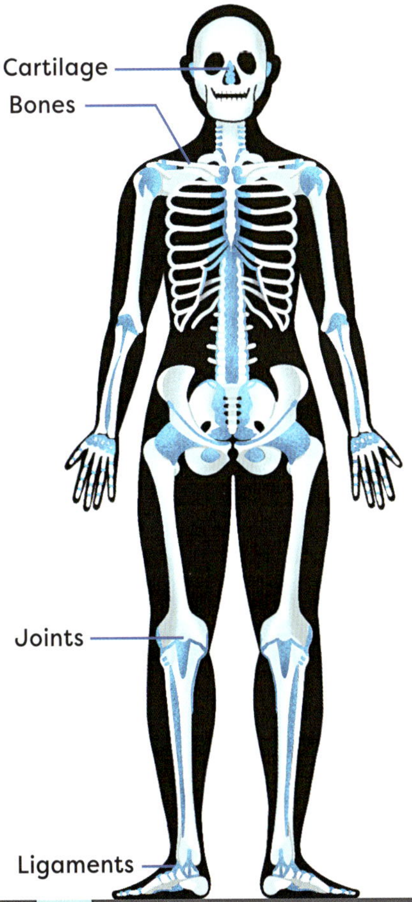

Cartilage
Bones
Joints
Ligaments

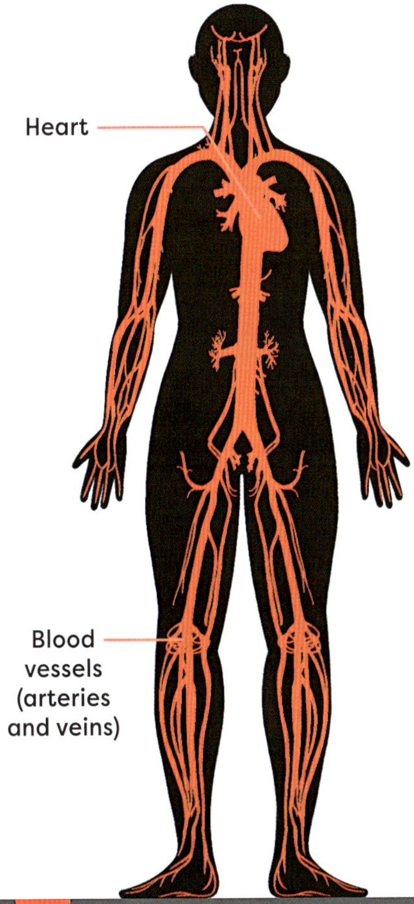

Heart
Blood vessels (arteries and veins)

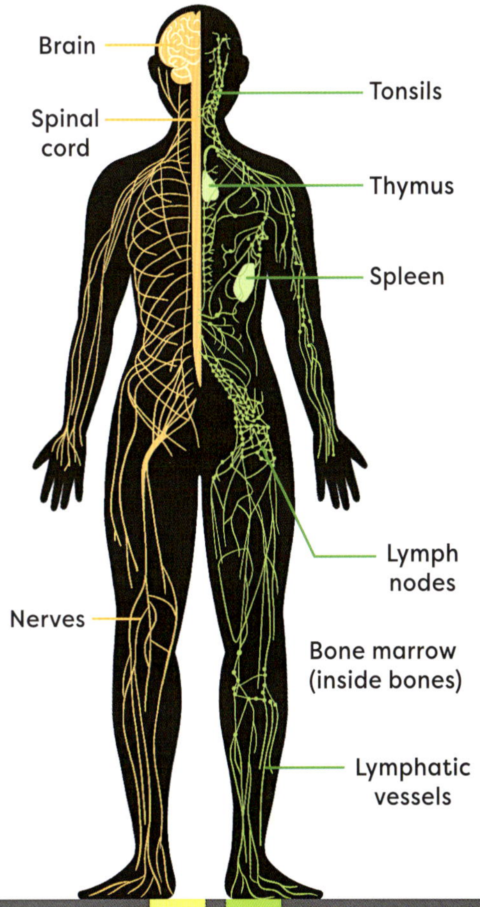

Brain
Spinal cord
Nerves
Tonsils
Thymus
Spleen
Lymph nodes
Bone marrow (inside bones)
Lymphatic vessels

SKELETAL
- Provides structure and helps with movement
- Protects internal organs

CIRCULATORY
- Circulates blood
- Transports oxygen, nutrients and waste products
- Helps regulate temperature

NERVOUS
- Processes information from the senses
- Sends signals around the body
- Activates other systems

LYMPHATIC
- Defends the body against infections and diseases
- Balances fluid levels

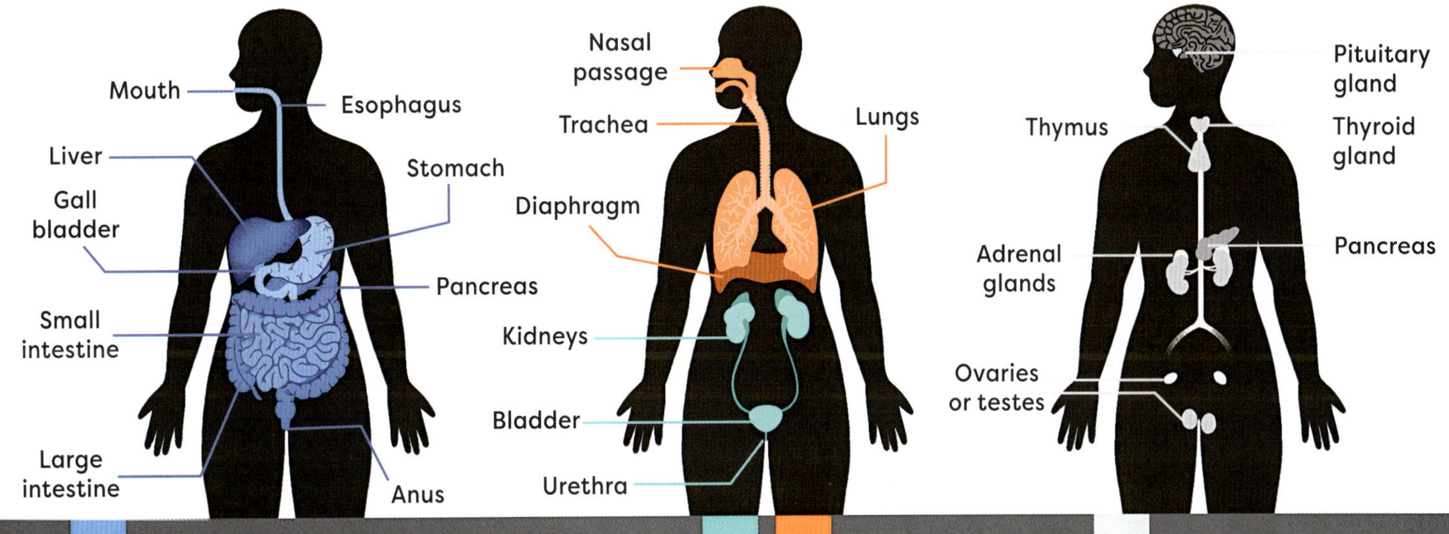

DIGESTIVE
- Breaks down food
- Absorbs nutrients
- Processes waste

URINARY
- Makes and passes urine to remove waste filtered from the blood

RESPIRATORY
- Brings air into and out of the lungs
- Absorbs oxygen, removes carbon dioxide

ENDOCRINE
- Makes hormones
- Regulates bodily processes

WHEN *did it* HAPPEN?

This long and winding line shows how many years ago certain major events happened in the history of the universe.

The Big Bang
13.8 billion years ago (YA)

Birth of earliest known star
13.7 billion YA

Formation of earliest known galaxy
13.6 billion YA

Formation of the Milky Way galaxy
13.5 billion YA

Formation of the Sun and planets in the solar system
4.57 billion YA

Origin of the Moon
4.53 billion YA

Earliest known life on Earth
3.9 billion YA

Earth gains an oxygen-rich atmosphere
2.5 billion YA

Wide variety of life forms spread all over Earth
540 million YA

Extreme cold kills off over 80% of living things
445 million YA

The time of the dinosaurs, ended by a meteorite strike
230-65 million YA

Earliest known human-like life
2.2 million YA

The dates on this timeline are based on the latest evidence found by historians, archeologists, paleontologists and astronomers.

As experts uncover new evidence, some of the dates will change.

From Africa, humans migrate to all continents 30,000 - 60,000 YA
Oldest known musical instruments 42,000 YA
Earliest known works of art 500,000 YA
Earliest known stitched clothes 40,000 YA
Oldest known wheeled vehicle 5,500 YA
Oldest known writing 5,500 YA
Oldest known farming of crops 12,000 YA
First powered flight over 120 YA
Oldest known farming of sheep and goats 10,000 YA
Oldest known wars around 12,000 YA
First rocket in space over 75 YA
First human-made object to leave the solar system 2012
First person on the Moon 1969

Parts of a FLOWER

A flower is the part of a plant that usually makes the seeds. Seeds are living things, which grow – or **REPRODUCE** – into new plants.

Most flowers have a **FEMALE** and a **MALE** part.

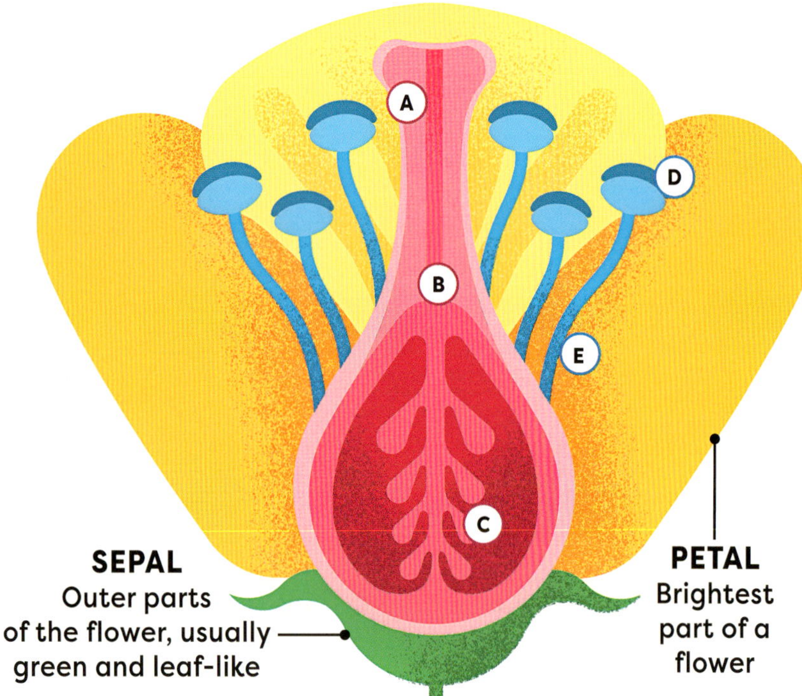

SEPAL
Outer parts of the flower, usually green and leaf-like

PETAL
Brightest part of a flower

Pistil

The FEMALE part of the flower is made up of 3 sections:

STIGMA (A)
A sticky lump that traps and holds the pollen

STYLE (B)
A stalk that connects the stigma to the ovary

OVARY (C)
The bottom part of pistil that contains the ovules (egg cells)

Stamen

The MALE part of the flower is made up 2 sections:

(D) **ANTHER**
Where tiny grains, called pollen, are produced

(E) **FILAMENT**
A stalk that holds up the anther

Making a seed

Most flowering plants produce seeds that will grow into new plants. There are three steps in this process:

1 **POLLINATION**

A pollen grain is released from the anther and sticks to the stigma. It grows a pollen tube, which reaches down through the style into the ovary.

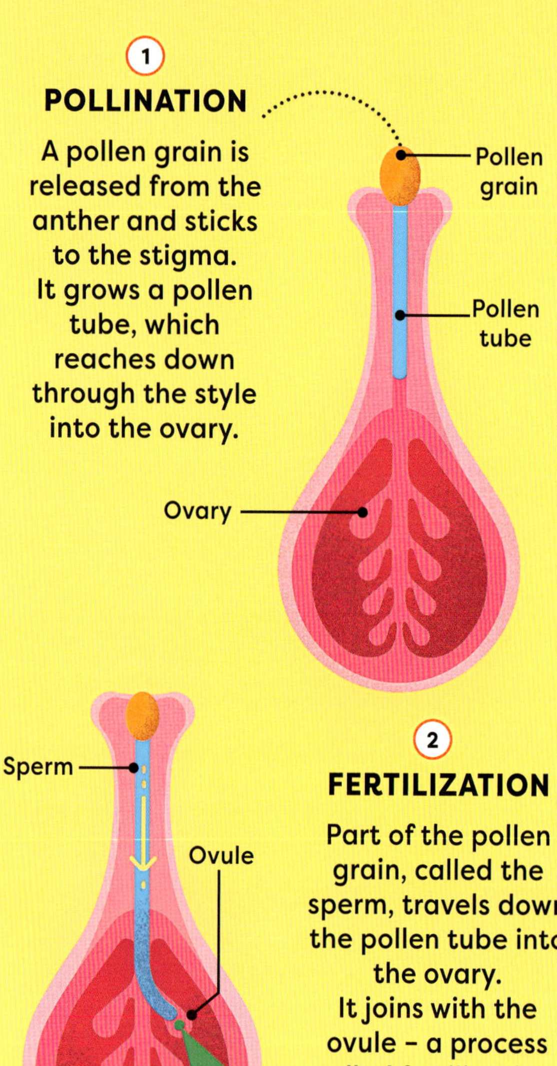

2 **FERTILIZATION**

Part of the pollen grain, called the sperm, travels down the pollen tube into the ovary. It joins with the ovule – a process called fertilization.

3 **SEED FORMATION**

The fertilized ovule grows into a tiny version of the plant, called an embryo. A hard protective shell forms around it to make a seed.

Parts of a LEAF

APEX
Tip of the leaf

LAMINA
The leaf's flat surface, containing chlorophyll

VEINS
Tiny tubes that carry water and nutrients from the rest of the plant to the leaf

MIDRIB
Keeps the leaf strong and sturdy in the wind

MARGIN
The edge of the leaf

PETIOLE
The stalk of the leaf, that attaches to the stem of the plant

Producing food

A leaf uses sunlight to produce food. This process is called **PHOTOSYNTHESIS.**

Chlorophyll, a green chemical in the leaf, absorbs energy from the sunlight. This changes carbon dioxide and water into food, called glucose, and oxygen.

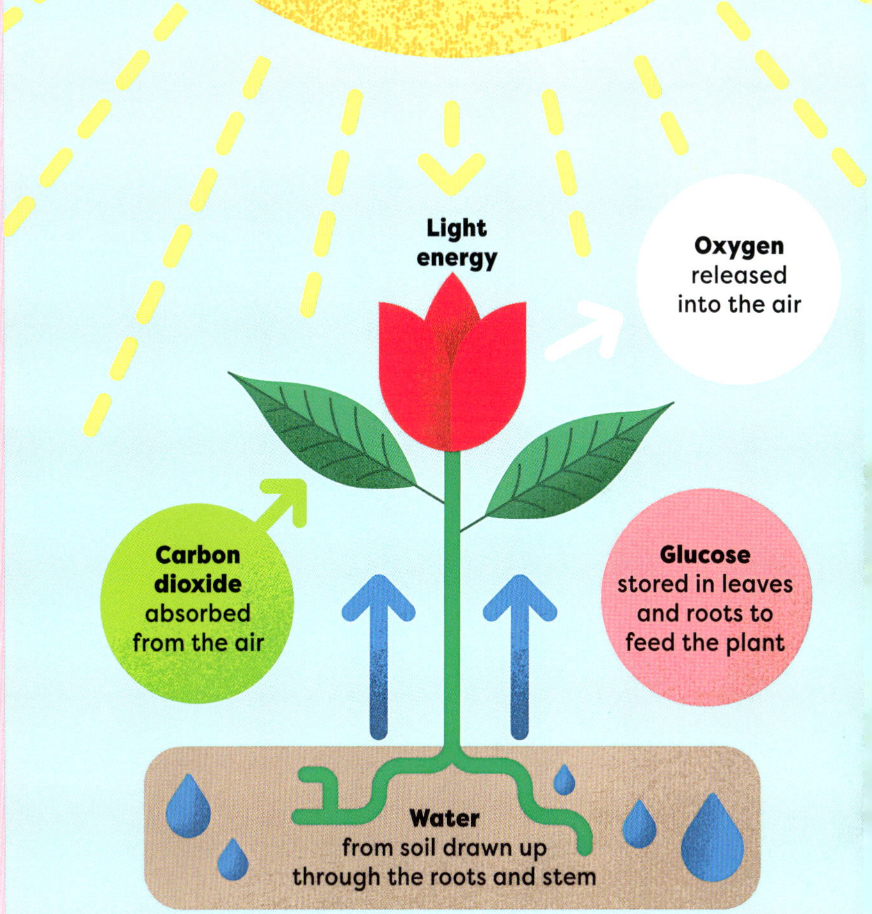

Light energy

Oxygen released into the air

Carbon dioxide absorbed from the air

Glucose stored in leaves and roots to feed the plant

Water from soil drawn up through the roots and stem

Leaves grow in many shapes and sizes, and there are names for all of them. Here are some.

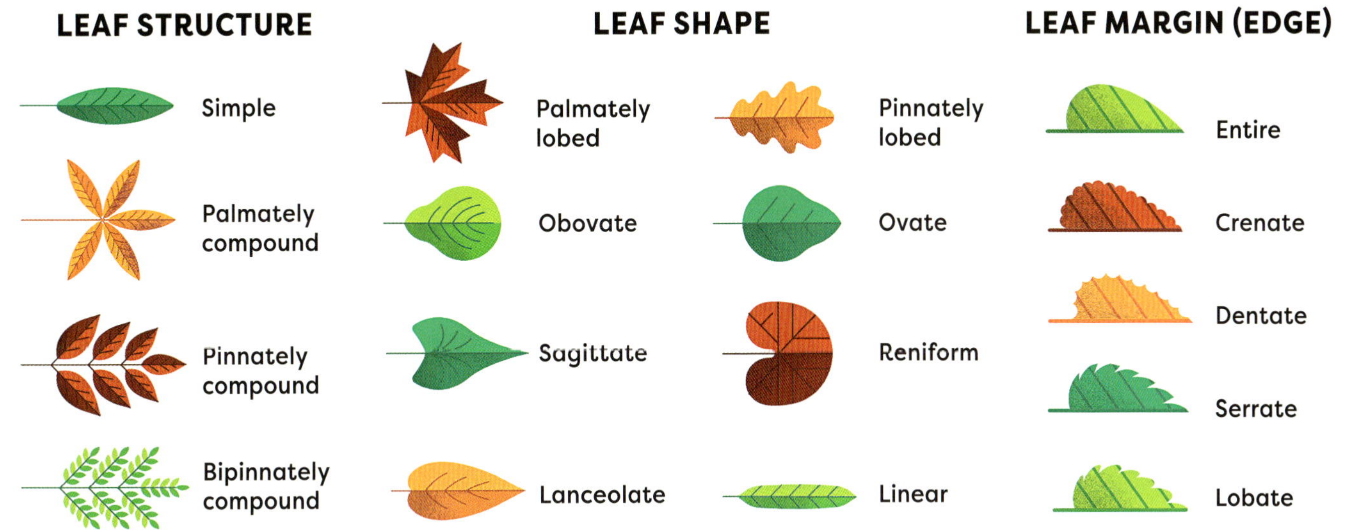

The tallest TOWERS

At the time they were completed, each of these constructions could claim to be the tallest EVER.

These are all **freestanding structures**. That means they're not supported by any wires or other external forms of support.

1
Maximum known height **146.6m (481ft)**

2
Maximum known height **160m (525ft)**

3
169m (555ft)

4
312m (1,024ft)

5
319m (1,046ft)

6
381m (1,250ft)

7
540m (1,762ft)

8
553.33m (1,815.39ft)

10
828m (2,716.5ft)

1 **GREAT PYRAMID**
Giza, Egypt
Originally constructed over **4,500** years ago.

2 **LINCOLN CATHEDRAL**
Lincoln, England
Completed **1311**

3 **WASHINGTON MONUMENT**
Washington, D.C., USA
Completed **1884**

4 **EIFFEL TOWER**
Paris, France
Completed **1889**

5 **CHRYSLER BUILDING**
New York City, USA
Completed **1930**

6 **EMPIRE STATE BUILDING**
New York City, USA
Completed **1931**

7 **OSTANKINO TOWER**
Moscow, Russia
Completed **1967**

8 **CN TOWER**
Toronto, Canada
Completed **1975**

9 **BURJ KHALIFA**
Dubai, UAE
Completed **2009**

Tallest twin building

PETRONAS TOWERS
Kuala Lumpur, Malaysia
Completed **1996**
Height **452m (1,483ft)**

Tallest mast

KVLY-TV MAST
Blanchard, North Dakota, USA
Constructed **1963**
Height **629m (2,063ft)**

Tallest electricity tower

YANGTZE RIVER CROSSING POWERLINE LINK
Jiangsu, China
Constructed **2022**
Height **385m (1,263ft)**

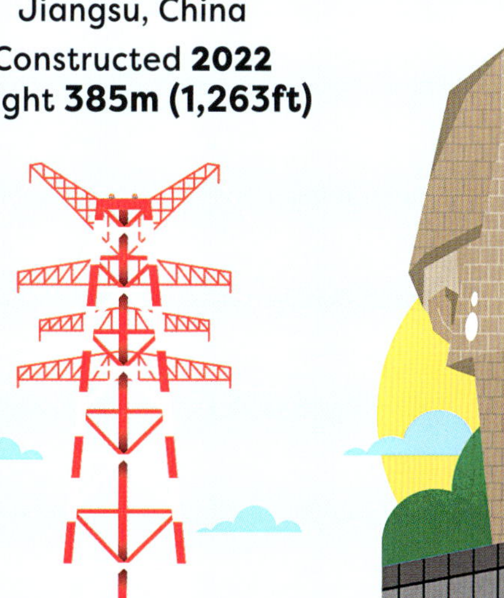

Tallest statue

STATUE OF UNITY
Kevadia, Gujarat, India
Completed **2018**
Height **182m (597ft)**
(not including base pedestal)

Tallest bridge

MILLAU VIADUCT
Millau, France
Constructed **2004**
Height **343m (1,125ft)**

Tallest tower to come?

As building materials and engineering techniques develop, it will be possible to build far taller buildings than these. But so far, no one has managed. The Jeddah Tower in Saudi Arabia is designed to be more than 1km (3,280ft) tall. Construction began in 2013 but the project has suffered several delays.

Pick a CARD...

Playing cards originated in China 1,200 years ago and spread to Europe 500 years later. Sets of cards are usually sorted into groups, known as **suits**, each with its own symbol. Many countries have their own traditional cards with different suits.

Chinese suits

The most popular version of traditional Chinese playing cards has three suits.

Coins

These are a type of old coin called **qian**.

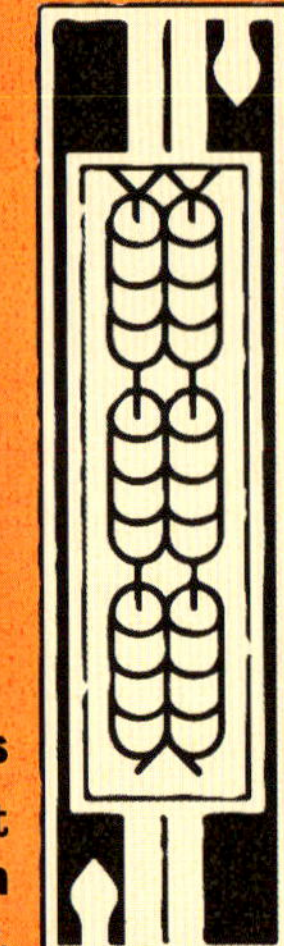

Strings

These represent **stacks of qian** strung together.

Myriads

These are characters from a novel from over 500 years ago, called *Outlaws of the Marsh*.

European suits

Most European sets are sorted into four suits. The most commonly used around the world today are based on the French cards, which consist of the suits **Spades**, **Diamonds**, **Clubs** and **Hearts**.

FRENCH: Spades, Diamonds, Clubs, Hearts

ITALIAN: Batons, Coins, Cups, Swords

SPANISH: Clubs, Coins, Cups, Swords

GERMAN: Bells, Hearts, Leaves, Acorns

SWISS: Acorns, Roses, Shields, Bells

CARDS AROUND THE WORLD

Here are more examples of different types of playing cards from around the world:

Italian
TAROT

A tarot set is based on the traditional Italian deck **plus 22 illustrated cards.**

Around the 18th century, people claimed these playing cards had mystical powers and began using them for fortune-telling.

Japanese
HANAFUDA

Hanafuda sets are sorted into twelve suits – one for each month, represented by a flower or tree.

Also known in Korea as **hwatu**.

Persian and Indian
GANJIFA

Ganjifa are traditional cards originally from Persia (now Iran) dating back to the 16th century. They're usually circular and **hand-painted**, made from wood or stiffened cloth. Historically, Ganjifa were symbols of status. They were made from ivory, tortoiseshell and precious gems.

DID YOU KNOW...

At its largest, around the year 211, the Roman army would have worn out
1,350,000
pairs of marching sandals in a single year.

HELLO? HELP!

What do you do if you can't rely on a phone or an internet connection, but you need to send a message or call for help? Here are a few options that might help in a sticky situation.

DISTRESS SIGNALS

When someone's life is in danger...

Burn a red flare
Most flares burn brightly for at least a minute.

Wave arms
Move arms slowly up and down.

Mayday
Call out "MAYDAY" three times over radio.

MAYDAY, MAYDAY, MAYDAY!

SOS
This is often sent using Morse code as three short, three long and three short signals.

Morse code can be sent using either sound or light. Each letter is encoded as a series of short "dit" and long "dah" signals.

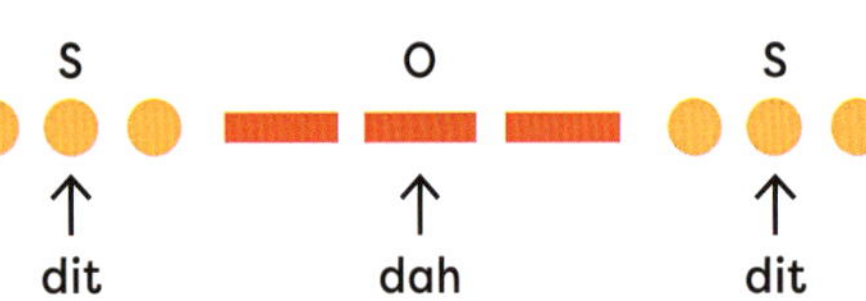

URGENCY SIGNALS

When help is needed...

I need assistance
Make a symbol on the ground to catch an aircraft's attention.

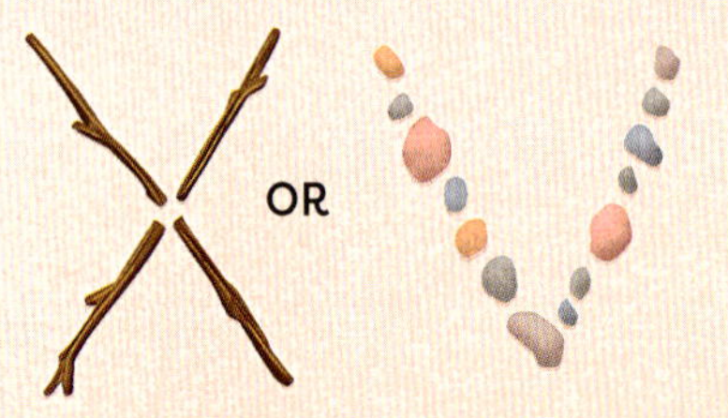

Pan-pan
Declare "PAN-PAN" three times over radio.

PAN-PAN, PAN-PAN, PAN-PAN!

FLAG SEMAPHORE

This is a system used by sailors to represent letters A–Z and numbers 0–9.

The person sending signals holds flags or rods to be seen more easily.

The signals shown here are used internationally, but the Japanese have an extra set.

INTERNATIONAL SPELLING ALPHABET

The International Radiotelephony Spelling Alphabet is a set of unique code words for the letters A-Z. It's used to spell out information over phones or radios, when sound isn't always clear.

For example, pilots communicate over fuzzy radios. They must know this alphabet to understand instructions.

These code words were chosen as they're easily pronounced by most people, no matter what language they speak.

To help with pronunciation, Alfa and Juliett are spelled "wrong" on purpose.
Alfa should be ***Alpha***
Juliett should be ***Juliette.***

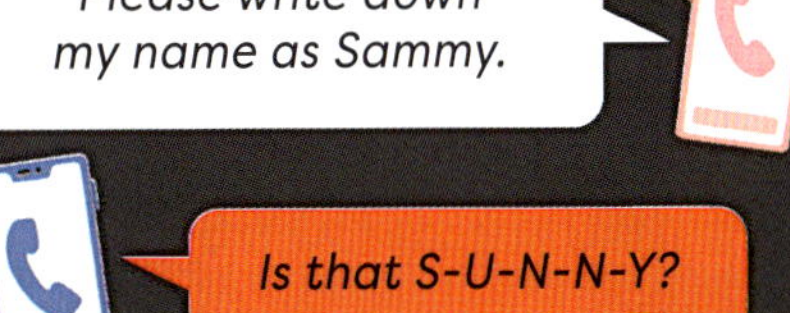

Please write down my name as Sammy.

Is that S-U-N-N-Y?

No, it's Sierra-Alfa-Mike-Mike-Yankee.

LETTER	CODE WORD	PRONUNCIATION
A	ALFA	AL-fah
B	BRAVO	BRAH-voh
C	CHARLIE	CHAR-lee SHAR-lee
D	DELTA	DELL-tah
E	ECHO	ECK-oh
F	FOXTROT	FOKS-trot
G	GOLF	golf
H	HOTEL	ho-TELL
I	INDIA	IN-dee-ah
J	JULIETT	JEW-lee-ETT
K	KILO	KEY-loh
L	LIMA	LEE-mah
M	MIKE	mike
N	NOVEMBER	no-VEM-ber
O	OSCAR	OSS-cah
P	PAPA	pah-PAH
Q	QUEBEC	keh-BECK
R	ROMEO	ROW-me-oh
S	SIERRA	see-AIR-rah
T	TANGO	TANG-go
U	UNIFORM	YOU-nee-form OO-nee-form
V	VICTOR	VIK-tah
W	WHISKEY	WISS-key
X	X-RAY	ECKS-ray
Y	YANKEE	YANG-key
Z	ZULU	ZOO-loo

F OR 6

G OR 7

H OR 8

I OR 9

J

K OR 0

L

M

S

T

U

V

W

X

Y

Z

ANIMALS *and us*

We've been sharing our lives with other species for thousands of years. Some animals keep us company, while we farm others for meat. But when did it all happen?

KEY

The rings around the animals on this timeline show the main reasons they became domesticated.

- FOOD (yellow)
- PEST CONTROL (red)
- CLOTHING (purple)
- PROTECTION (green)
- TRANSPORTATION (blue)
- COMPANIONSHIP (pink)
- MANURE (orange)

DOGS

At least 20,000 years ago, Asia

Modern pet dogs are descended from wolves. Wolves and early dogs helped with hunting and kept predators away from where humans lived.

It's hard to be sure when and where humans first started to keep each type of animal, but these dates and places are based on the best evidence archeologists have found so far.

ZEBU (HUMPED COWS)

8,000 years ago, South Asia

GEESE

7,000 years ago, Southeast Asia

LLAMAS

7,000 years ago, Peru

GUINEA PIGS

6-7,000 years ago, South America

BACTRIAN CAMELS

6,000 years ago, Central Asia

Camels are strong and tough, which made them ideal for riding or for carrying heavy loads over long distances and tricky terrain.

HORSES

5,500 years ago, Central Asia

Horses were first kept for their meat and milk. Eventually, people worked out how to use their power and speed for pulling carts or for riding.

Tame or domesticated?

A **TAME** animal is not dangerous or scared of humans.

A truly **DOMESTICATED** animal is one kept as a pet or on a farm. It depends on humans for its food, and usually looks and behaves differently to its wild ancestors.

SHEEP AND GOATS

10-11,000 years ago, Middle East

Grazing animals were the easiest to domesticate, because they're easiest to feed; all they need is an area of grass or other plants.

CATS

10-12,000 years ago, Middle East

Cats were first attracted by the mice and rats that lived in people's grain stores.

Some scientists say cats are only partly domesticated, because they can still find their own food.

PIGS

9,000 years ago, Middle East

Wild boar, the ancestor species of pigs, have coarse fur, and the males grow much longer tusks.

COWS

10,500 years ago, Middle East

Cows have been farmed for thousands of years for milk, meat and leather, and for manure to help crops grow. They're also used pull and carry things.

CHICKENS

3,500 years ago, Southeast Asia and Oceania

The chickens farmed now are much bigger than their wild ancestors, and lay more eggs.

DUCKS

2,500 years ago, China

TURKEYS

2,000 years ago, North and Central America

Several Indigenous American groups domesticated turkeys, but the Maya were probably the first.

ABOVE the Earth

The Earth is surrounded by a mixture of gases called the **atmosphere**. It's divided into **five** main layers.

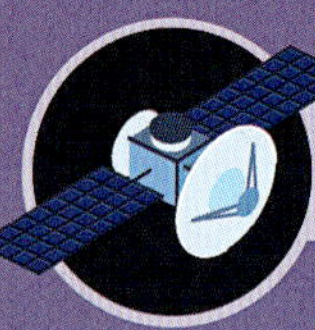

5 EXOSPHERE

Lots of satellites orbit in the exosphere and thermosphere below.

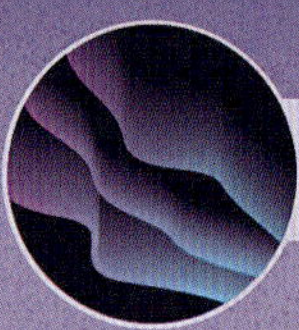

4 THERMOSPHERE

The auroras – the spectacular natural light shows we know as the Northern and Southern Lights – are created in this layer.

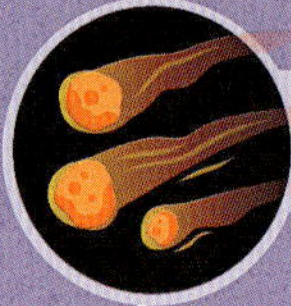

3 MESOSPHERE

Meteoroids (space debris usually created by asteroids colliding) burn up in the gases of this layer, turning into shooting stars.

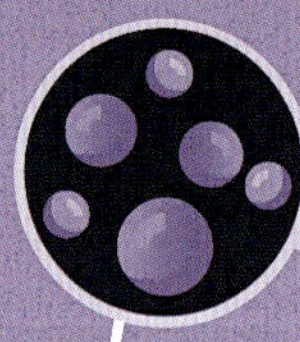

2 STRATOSPHERE

This layer contains almost **20%** of all the gas in the atmosphere.

1 TROPOSPHERE

About **75%** of the gas and **99%** of water in the atmosphere is in the troposphere.

10,000km (6,200 miles)

700km (435 miles)

80km (50 miles)

50km (31 miles)

Up to **12km (7.5 miles)** above Earth's surface

EARTH

INSIDE the Earth

Our planet has several **layers**, each hotter than the one above it.

Parts of the mantle are warm and soft enough to move. They push the rock above, erupting as volcanoes and causing earthquakes.

CRUST 8-40km (5-25 miles) thick. This is Earth's rocky outer shell.

MANTLE 2,900km (1,800 miles) thick

OUTER CORE 2,250km (1,400 miles) thick. This is a layer of hot liquid metal.

INNER CORE 1,300km (800 miles) thick

Scientists think temperatures reach **6,000°C (10,800°F)** in parts of the inner core, but it's under so much pressure that it stays solid and can't melt.

and into the DEPTHS

The world's oceans are divided into **zones,** based on distance from the surface.

DEPTH

EPIPELAGIC ZONE
The Sunlight Zone

Well-known ocean creatures such as sharks, sea turtles, dolphins and whales are mostly found in this zone. It's close enough to the surface for sunlight to reach.

0m/ft

200m (656ft)

MESOPELAGIC ZONE
The Twilight Zone

It's cold and dim in the Twilight Zone. Some of the animals that live here can make their own light.

1km (0.6 miles)

BATHYPELAGIC ZONE
The Midnight Zone

Below 1,000m (0.6 miles) it's permanently dark. Oxygen levels and temperatures are low, and no plants can survive.

The "deep ocean" starts in this zone. It's home to some bizarre creatures such as deep-sea anglerfish and vampire squid.

4km (2.5 miles)

ABYSSOPELAGIC ZONE
The Abyss

Lots of creatures in the Abyss feed on dead animals drifting down from the zones above.

The Abyss makes up **83%** of the total area of Earth's oceans. In most places, this zone touches the sea floor. The only parts of the sea that are deeper than this are trenches.

6km (3.7 miles)

HADAL ZONE
The Trenches

Almost 11km (6.8 miles) deep, the Mariana Trench in the Pacific Ocean is the deepest part of the ocean.

Animals that live down here have to survive enormous pressure and temperatures close to freezing.

Legendary
HEROES

Storytellers have always told tales of mighty and daring individuals – some real people, some fantastical beings. Here are just a few of them, shown alongside symbols associated with their heroic deeds.

GILGAMESH

- 4,000 YEARS AGO
- SUMER (NOW IRAQ)
- GREAT STRENGTH

Defeated a wicked ogre and Taurus the bull. Later led a revolt against an evil king.

PERSEUS

- 2,800 YEARS AGO
- ARGOS, GREECE
- SWORD FIGHTING

Slayed Medusa – a snake-haired monster – and rescued Princess Andromeda.

SITA

- 2,500 YEARS AGO
- AYODHYA, INDIA
- LOYALTY

Survived a year in captivity, and a trial by fire – sitting within the flames, unharmed.

HUA MULAN

- 1,700 YEARS AGO
- NORTHERN CHINA
- DETERMINATION

Disguised herself as a male soldier and fought against China's enemies for a decade.

KING ARTHUR

- 1,200 YEARS AGO
- BRITAIN
- HONOR

Gathered and led a team of knights to defend Britain from enemy forces.

CÚ CHULAINN

- 1,300 YEARS AGO
- IRELAND
- FIGHTING

Defended his home town single-handed against the army of Queen Medb.

KEY

Time of oldest surviving stories | Main location | Notable power/skill

YENNENGA

600 YEARS AGO

GHANA / BURKINA FASO

RIDING & FIGHTING

Fought on horseback to help defeat the enemies of the Kingdom of Dagbon.

SUN WUKONG THE MONKEY KING

400 YEARS AGO

CHINA

CUNNING

Journeyed to the edge of the universe and peed on God's fingers.

HUNAHPU & XBALANQUE THE HERO TWINS

2,200 YEARS AGO

MAYA EMPIRE

SPORTING PROWESS

Slayed an evil bird-god, and avenged their father by winning a ball game in hell.

MĀUI

1,000 YEARS AGO

SOUTH PACIFIC

GREAT STRENGTH

Lifted the Hawaiian islands from the sea using his magic fish hook.

ST OLGA OF KYIV

1,100 YEARS AGO

UKRAINE

HOLINESS

Avenged the murder of her husband the king, ruled in his stead and promoted Christianity.

MARIE LAVEAU

150 YEARS AGO

NEW ORLEANS

VOODOO MAGIC

Healed the sick, and it is said her spirit still grants wishes made at her tomb.

Mythical MONSTERS

Mixed-up monsters

MANTICORE

PERSIA (IRAN)

DEADLY STING

A lion with the head of a human and a scorpion's sting – deadly to all but elephants.

GRIFFIN

MIDDLE EAST

HEALING FEATHERS

A lion with the head and wings of an eagle, who hoards gold.

COCKATRICE

ENGLAND & FRANCE

DEATH STARE

Hatching from a chicken's egg warmed by a toad, this is a cross between a rooster and a dragon.

Shape-changers

HULI JING & KITSUNE

CHINA & JAPAN

FAR-SIGHT & HEARING

Many-tailed foxes who can change into humans to cause mischief and woe.

WEREWOLVES

EUROPE

CURSE-SHARING

Humans cursed to turn into wolves during a full Moon. Their bite passes the curse to others.

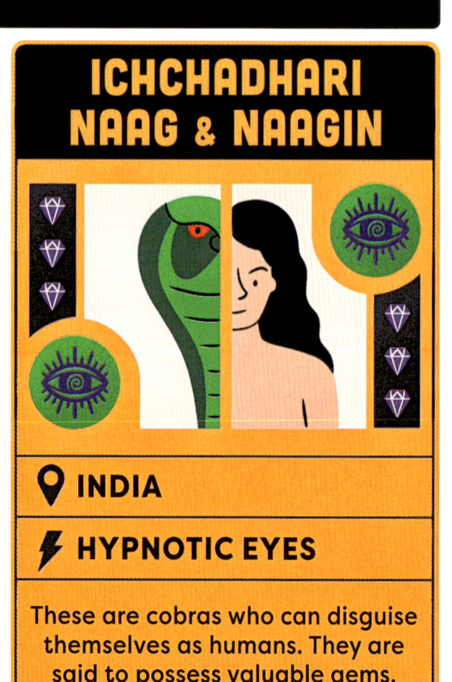

ICHCHADHARI NAAG & NAAGIN

INDIA

HYPNOTIC EYES

These are cobras who can disguise themselves as humans. They are said to possess valuable gems.

From shape-shifting beasts to creatures risen from the dead, monsters take many terrifying forms. Here are some examples described in myths from around the world. Read on if you dare...

KEY
- Location
- Power/skill

Gigantic monsters

THUNDERBIRD

AMERICA

LIGHTNING EYES

A bird that can create thunder by flapping its wings, and shoot lightning from its eyes.

TIDDALIK

AUSTRALIA

APPETITE

A small frog who grew bigger and bigger as he drank all the fresh water in Australia.

JÖRMUNGANDR

SCANDINAVIA

BIGGEST OF ALL

A sea serpent that can wrap its body around the Earth, bringing on the end of the world.

Monsters who have risen from the grave

VAMPIRES

WORLDWIDE

CHARM

Living corpses who spread evil, and must feed on human blood to survive.

GASHADOKURO

JAPAN

INVISIBILITY

Spirit formed from the bones of dead warriors, who attacks and eats unwary travelers.

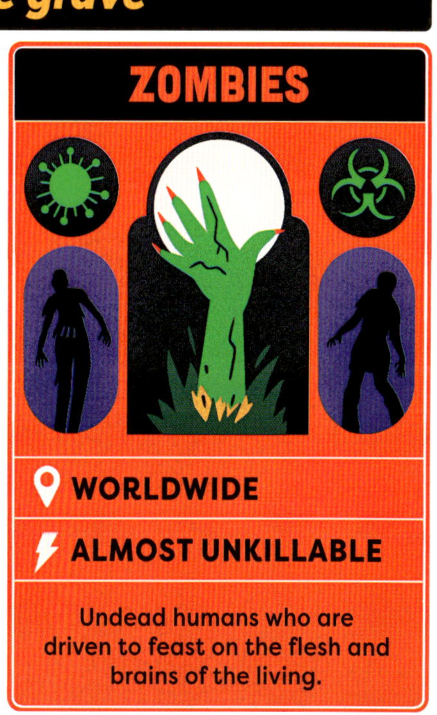

ZOMBIES

WORLDWIDE

ALMOST UNKILLABLE

Undead humans who are driven to feast on the flesh and brains of the living.

The branches of SCIENCE

SCIENCE is the study of the world and the universe around us by observing and by doing experiments.

There are lots of different specialist areas or branches. Here are just some of them.

CHEMISTRY

The study of elements (the basic "building blocks" of substances), their natures and reactions

INORGANIC CHEMISTRY

The chemical properties of metals and minerals

ORGANIC CHEMISTRY

The chemical properties of compounds containing carbon

PHYSICAL CHEMISTRY

The physical nature of substances, and how this affects their structures and reactions

CRYSTALLOGRAPHY

The make-up of chemical compounds in crystal forms, present in many substances from minerals to human DNA

PHYSICS

The study of matter (non-living things), forces and energy

GEOPHYSICS

The physical processes of the Earth

OCEANOGRAPHY

Ocean environments, including their chemistry and biology

METEOROLOGY

Weather

VOLCANOLOGY

Volcanoes

SEISMOLOGY

Earthquakes

ASTROPHYSICS

The physics and chemistry of objects in space

ASTRONOMY

Stars and planets

There are three main branches of science: **chemistry, physics and biology**. Each includes many more specialized areas.

Sometimes, an area combines more than one of the main branches. For example, biochemistry involves both chemistry and biology, especially human biology.

BIOCHEMISTR
Chemical processes in living things

PARTICLE PHYSICS
How the particles that make up atoms behave, including radioactivity

BIOLOGY

The study of all living things on Earth – how they behave, adapt and survive as species

BOTANY
Plants, including classifying and naming as well as studying their habits

ZOOLOGY
Animals, including birds, reptiles, amphibians and insect life

ECOLOGY
The relationships between living things, including humans, and their environment

HUMAN BIOLOGY
Our bodies and how they work

MICROBIOLOGY
Microbes and microorganisms (the very smallest living things), including viruses and bacteria

PLANT PATHOLOGY
Plant diseases

PALEONTOLOGY
Fossils and dinosaurs

ENTOMOLOGY
Insects

MARINE BIOLOGY
Life in the oceans

CONSERVATION
Protecting and caring for the natural environment

GENETICS
How characteristics are passed down through generations

MEDICINE
Human health (see page 22)

NEUROSCIENCE
How brains work

MYCOLOGY
Fungi

All the colors of a... ...RAINBOW

From purple and red to all the colors in between, every colour has a story to tell.

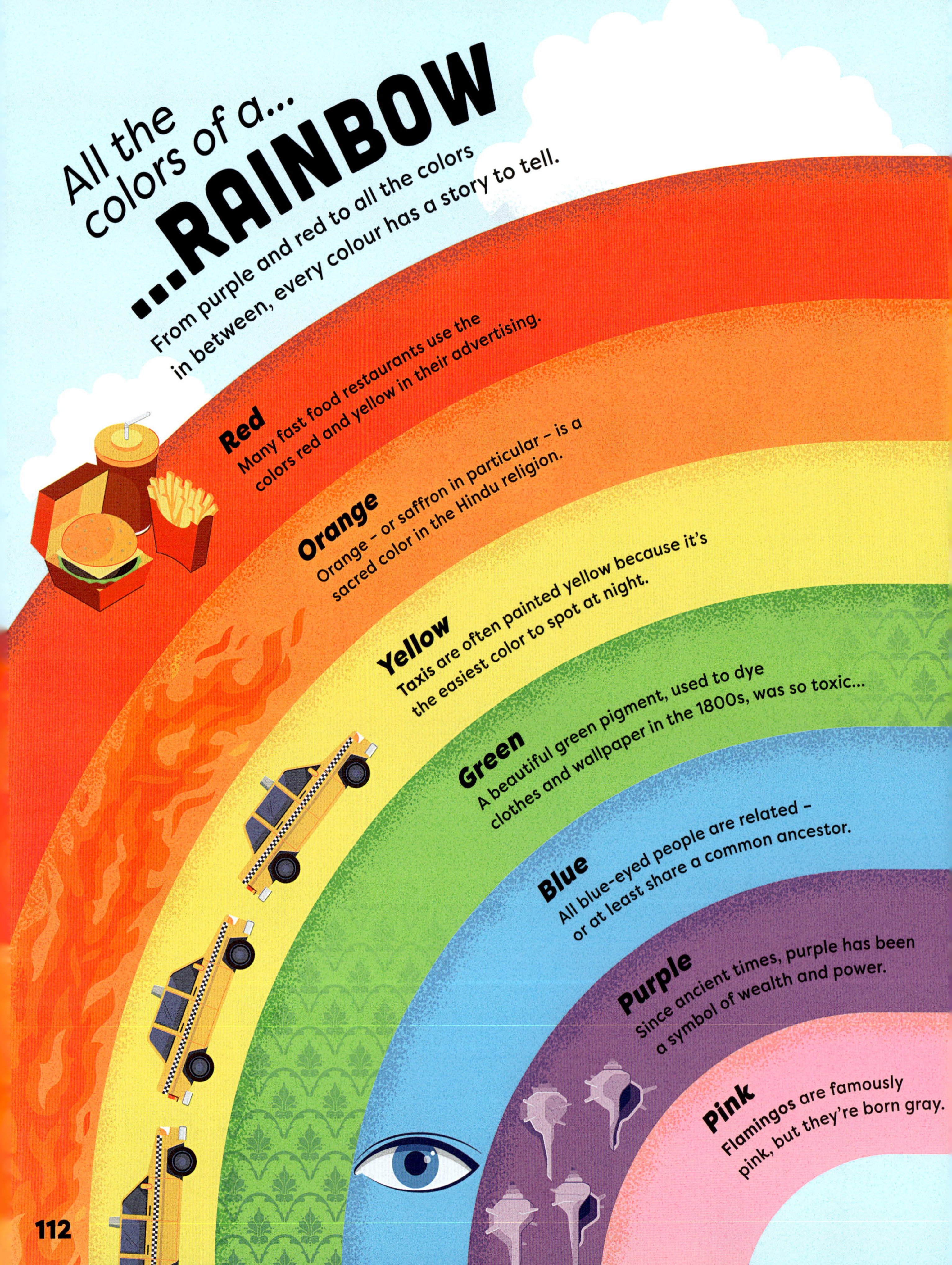

Research suggests that this combination of colors can make us feel hungry - yellow is associated with **warmth** and **comfort**, while red is thought to make us feel **impulsive**. This is known as the **ketchup and mustard theory**.

According to Hindu mythology, it's the color of **sunset, sunrise and fire**. Hindu saints wear saffron robes as a symbol of **purity and sacrifice**.

The idea was born in America in the early 1900s, when businessman John Hertz painted his fleet of taxis bright yellow to stand out against the streets of **Chicago**. Since then, many taxi companies around the world have adopted the same color.

...it caused people to faint and become seriously ill. Known as **Scheele's Green**, it contained **arsenic** which is poisonous when breathed in.

Scientists think that one person, who lived **more than 6,000 years ago**, carried a gene mutation (change) that caused blue eyes. Over thousands of years, this gene mutation spread across the world. Before this, all people were thought to have brown eyes.

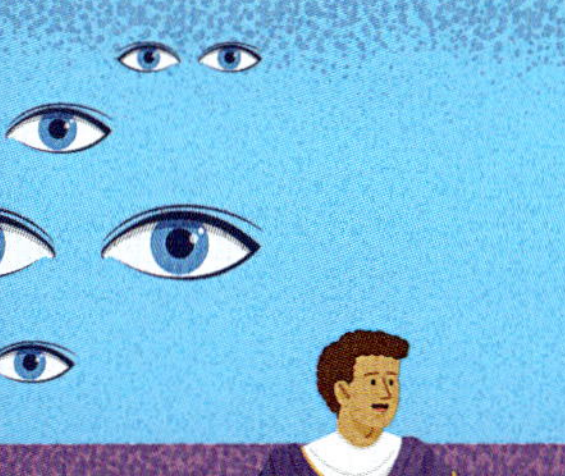

Tyrian purple was a pigment made from sea snails gathered from the coastal city of Tyre, in what is now Lebanon. The dye was so prized that only the Roman Emperor was allowed to dress entirely in purple.

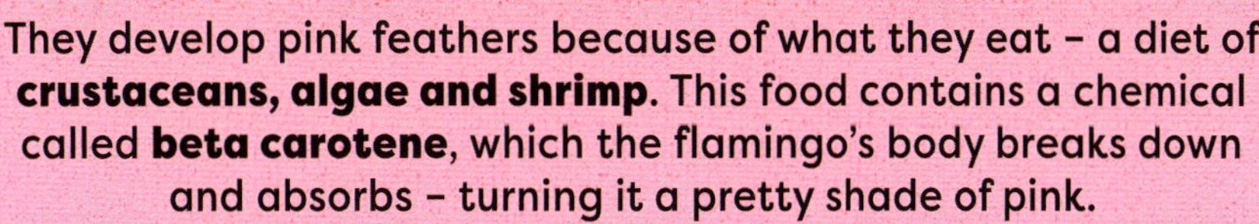

They develop pink feathers because of what they eat - a diet of **crustaceans, algae and shrimp**. This food contains a chemical called **beta carotene**, which the flamingo's body breaks down and absorbs - turning it a pretty shade of pink.

Discovering DINOSAURS

For over **165 million years**, reptiles called dinosaurs dominated the land. They ranged from cat-sized creatures to beasts bigger than buses.

KEY

■ **When it lived** (MYA = millions of years ago)

● **Length** (measured from head to tail)

🍴 **Diet**

Velociraptor

■ 75-71 MYA

● 2m (6.6ft)

🍴 Meat

Velociraptors are often shown as scaly, but they were probably covered in feathers.

Ankylosaurus

■ 68-65 MYA

● 8m (26ft)

🍴 Plants

Bony plates and a strong, club-like tail helped Anklyosaurus defend itself against predators.

Tyrannosaurus

■ 68-65 MYA

● 12m (39ft)

🍴 Meat

Human for scale – they weren't around at the same time!

Facts from feathers

Everything we know about dinosaurs comes from fossils – rocky remains left by dinosaurs that died and sank into soft ground.

Their skin usually rotted away before it could fossilize, but some dinosaurs had feathers which fossilized well.

Birds are closely related to dinosaurs. Comparing the shapes of cells in bird feathers to those in fossilized feathers gives clues to the colors of feathered dinosaurs.

Microraptor

- ■ 125-113 MYA
- ● 0.8m (2.6ft)
- 🍴 Meat

Microraptors had four wings. They could glide, and maybe even fly.

Spinosaurus

- ■ 112-94 MYA
- ● 14m (46ft)
- 🍴 Fish and possibly other dinosaurs

Diplodocus

- ■ 154-152 MYA
- ● Up to 30m (98ft)
- 🍴 Plants

Triceratops

- ■ 68-65 MYA
- ● 9m (30ft)
- 🍴 Plants

Stegosaurus

- ■ 155-150 MYA
- ● 9m (30ft)
- 🍴 Plants

ANCHIORNIS
Sausage-shaped cells mean very dark feathers.

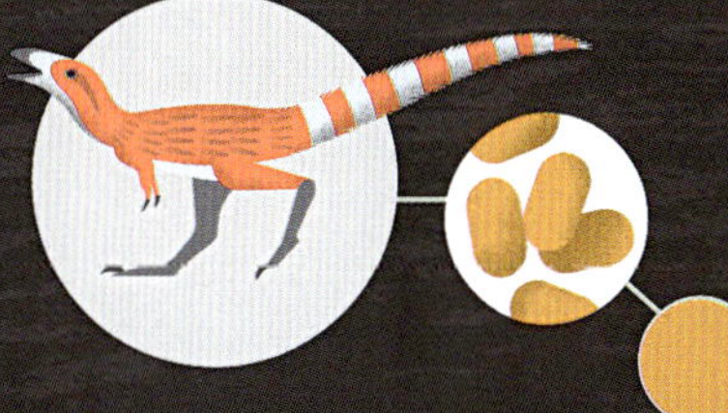

SINOSAUROPTERYX
Circular cells suggest orange feathers.

CAIHONG
Flattened cells are linked to shimmering feathers.

DID YOU KNOW...

OVER 50,000

tennis balls are used every year over the two weeks of the Wimbledon Championships in London.

EXTREME WORLD

The world's hottest places...

56.7°C *(134°F)* **Furnace Creek, Death Valley, USA**

55°C *(131°F)* **Kebili, Tunisia**

54°C *(129°F)* **Mitribah, Kuwait**
Turbat, Pakistan
Tirat Zvi, Israel

Even HOTTER than the HOTTEST place on Earth is the air that surrounds a lightning bolt. It's **30,000°C (54,032°F)** – that's around five times hotter than the surface of the sun.

...and the world's coldest

-63°C *(-81.4°F)* **Snag, Yukon Territory, Canada**

-67.8°C *(-90°F)* **Oymyakom, Russia**

-69.6°C *(-93.3°F)* **Verkhoyansk, Russia**

-89.2°C *(-128.6°F)* **Klinck AWS, Greenland**

Vostok Station, Antarctica

You can find all these extreme places on this map.

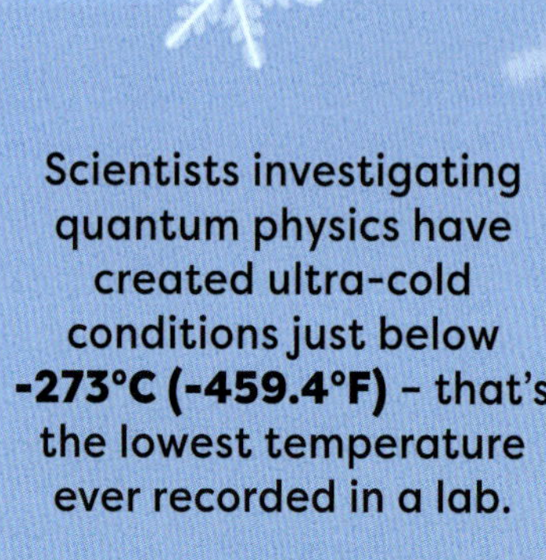

Scientists investigating quantum physics have created ultra-cold conditions just below **-273°C (-459.4°F)** – that's the lowest temperature ever recorded in a lab.

Most lightning

At the mouth of the **Catatumbo River** in **Venezuela**, lightning displays can last up to nine hours for up to 300 nights each year.

The world's wettest place...

The town of **Mawsynram**, in northeastern India, has an average rainfall of **11,971mm (471in)** every year. It's so wet, people wear big rain shields made from bamboo.

...and the world's driest

Surprisingly, the world's driest place is not a hot, sandy desert, as you might imagine – it's the **McMurdo Dry Valleys**, in Antarctica. The region has an average of **100mm (4in)** of snowfall a year, but no rain.

Deadliest hailstones

In 1986, the **Gopalganj area of Bangladesh** was pelted with hailstones that weighed up to **1.02kg (2.25lb)** and were the size of grapefruits.

Largest acidic lake

A lake in the middle of **Kawah Ijen** – a volcano in **Java, Indonesia** – measures **1,000m (3,280ft) long** and **600m (1,970ft) wide**. It contains enough sulfuric and hydrochloric acid to eat through metal.

BUILDING *to* LAST

The very first buildings were simple shelters made of mud, wood, leaves and reeds. Over time, people found new materials and methods and built much larger and longer-lasting structures. Here are some of the earliest or best-known of each type.

Stone

The earliest stone walls were fitted together carefully, piece by piece, to hold everything in place.

GÖBEKLI TEPE, TURKEY (around 9,500BCE)

Some of the oldest stone buildings ever found were uncovered here in 1994.

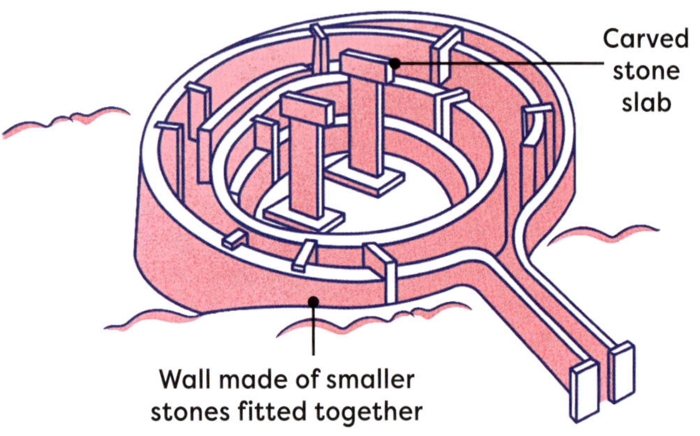

Bricks and mortar

The first bricks were made from sun-dried mud. Later, bricks were baked in kilns, making them stronger. Mortar, the "glue" that sticks bricks together, made the building process faster, easier and stronger still.

MEHRGARH, PAKISTAN (around 6,500BCE)

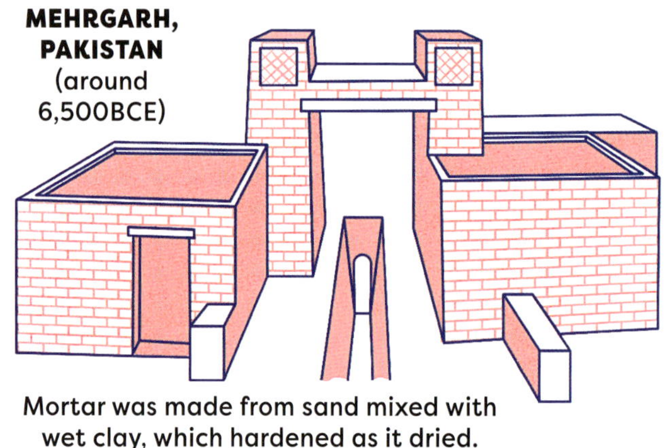

Mortar was made from sand mixed with wet clay, which hardened as it dried.

Columns and lintels

The Ancient Greeks placed wide roofs on strong lintels – horizontal beams – supported by even stronger stone columns.

PARTHENON, GREECE (447-432BCE)

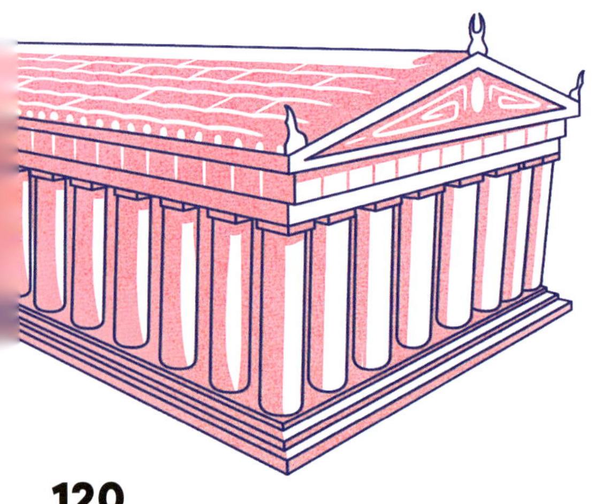

Round arches

The Romans discovered that round arches spread downward pressure more evenly than lintels on columns, making arches much stronger.

PONT DU GARD, FRANCE (40-60CE)

This aqueduct, or water bridge, brought fresh water to the Roman Colonia Nemausus (now the city of Nîmes).

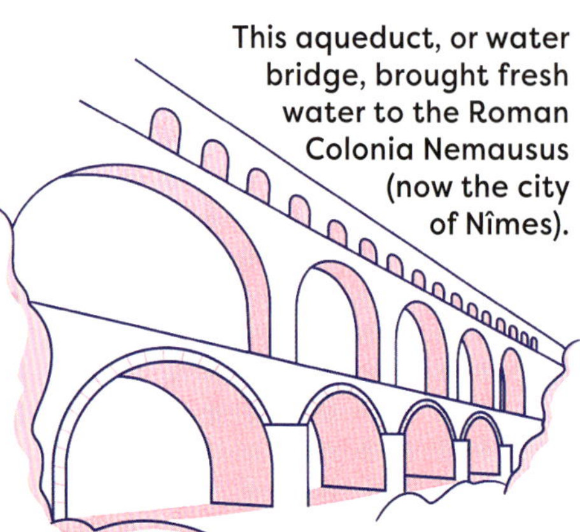

Domes

A dome is a strong three-dimensional arch shape. It distributes pressure evenly to the walls below it. This allowed architects to create spectacular high open spaces beneath the domes.

HAGIA SOPHIA, TURKEY (532-37)

Gothic arches and buttresses

Stonemasons in the Middle Ages discovered that pointed arches distributed weight even better than round ones.

These arches and supporting shapes, called buttresses, made it possible to build soaring, awe-inspiring places of worship.

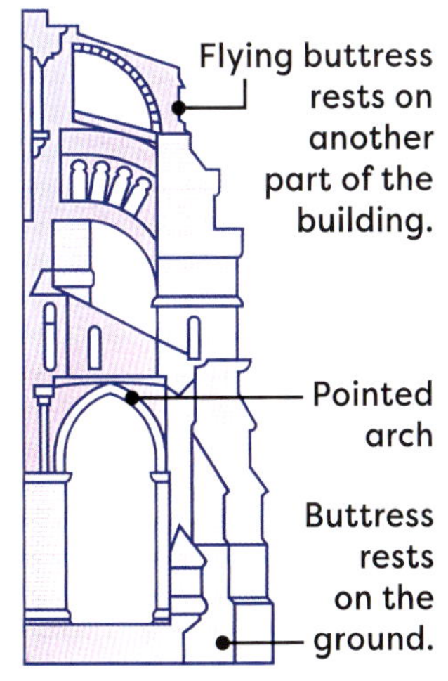

CHARTRES CATHEDRAL, FRANCE (1194-1221)

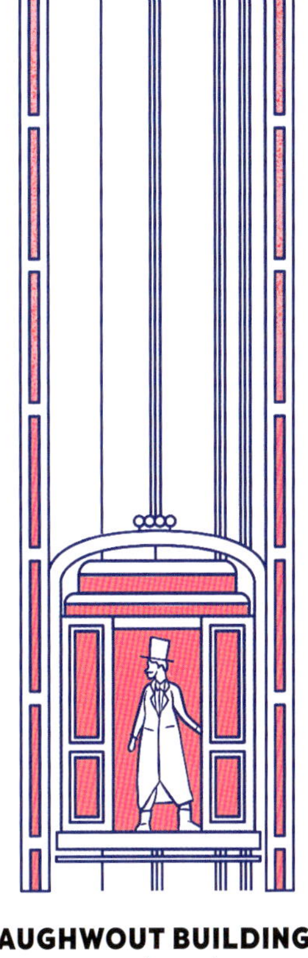

HAUGHWOUT BUILDING, USA (1857)

Iron framework

From the 18th century, blast furnaces could melt industrial quantities of iron and then form it into complex shapes. These were lighter than stone but incredibly strong. Bridges, then train stations, factories and town halls were built using iron frameworks and later steel ones.

IRONBRIDGE, UK (1777-79)

Plate glass

Plate glass could be produced in large sheets, then held in a wood or iron frame. This created vast, airy spaces filled with natural light.

CRYSTAL PALACE, UK (1850-51)

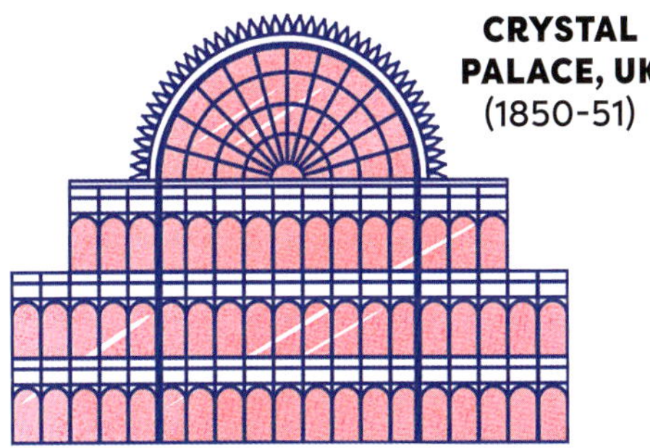

This magnificent building housed London's Great Exhibition of 1851.

Elevator

Even when people *could* build tall buildings, there was no way to reach the higher levels quickly and safely. Then in 1857, the first passenger elevator was installed in a New York department store. Elevators became essential to the city's skyscrapers, whether they were ten floors high... or over 100.

Reinforced concrete

Designers in the 20th century adopted clean, straight lines and shapes using concrete reinforced with steel rods. Soon, builders were using the techniques for factories and apartment blocks.

VILLA SAVOYE, FRANCE (1928-31)

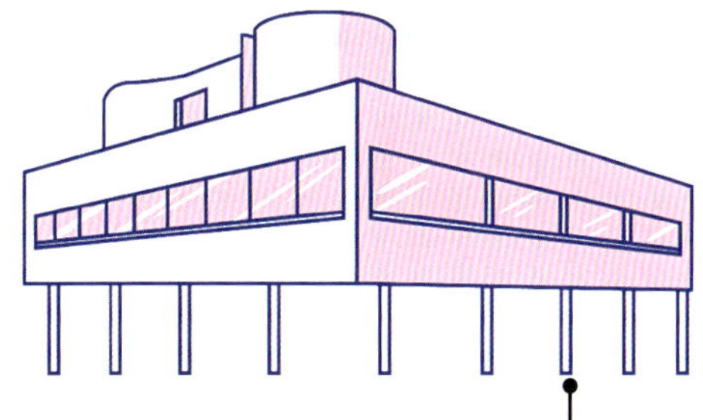

Narrow concrete columns are surprisingly strong.

Computer-aided design

Computers allow architects to create complex flowing shapes, and to test that these will be safe and stable when built. Architect Zaha Hadid was inspired by smooth river pebbles.

GUANGZHOU OPERA HOUSE, CHINA (2005-10)

Green design

Many architects are looking to nature to make buildings more energy-efficient, as well as pleasant places to live. Trees and plants can filter the air, provide shade and attract birds, bees and butterflies, increasing biodiversity.

VERTICAL FOREST, MILAN, ITALY (2008-14)

Plants are watered with filtered wastewater.

COUNTING *on and on to* INFINITY

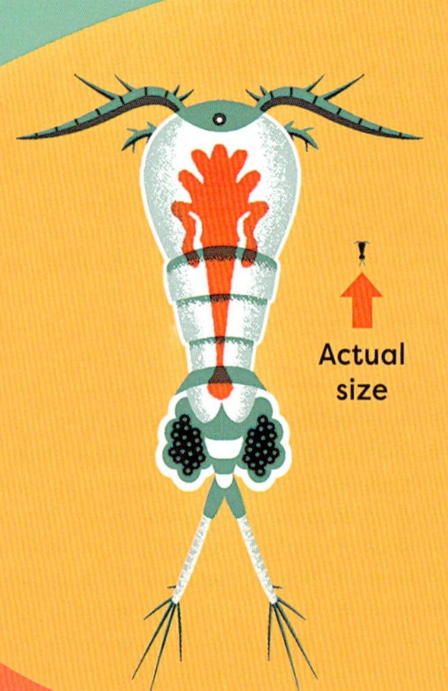

1

eye of a cyclops

At 3mm (0.1in) long, this tiny freshwater animal has just one eye. It is named after the one-eyed monsters of Greek mythology.

2

moons of Mars

Planet Mars has **two moons**, named Phobos and Deimos. Phobos orbits the planet three times a day, whereas Deimos orbits once every 30 hours.

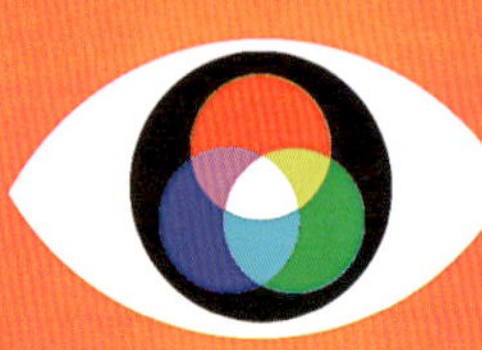

The primary colors of LIGHT – the colors we see on a television or computer screen – are red, green and blue.

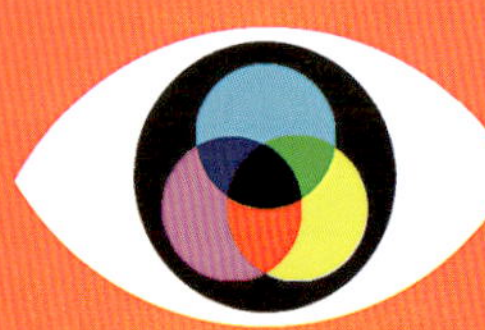

The primary colors of PIGMENT – used when mixing paint or in a color printer – are cyan, magenta and yellow.

3

primary colors

Most of the colors that people can see are a mixture of three colors, known as primary colors. Light and pigment have different primary colors.

is unlucky

In many East Asian countries, including Japan, China, Korea and Vietnam, the number **4** is said to bring bad luck. This is because the word "four" sounds like the word "death" in their languages.

People who fear the number 4 suffer from **tetraphobia**.

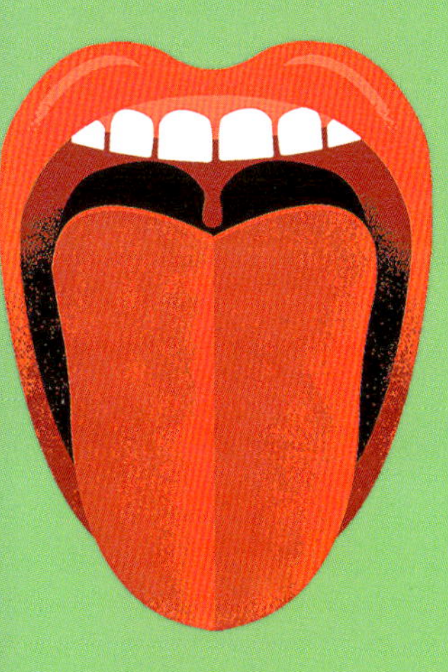

5

tastes

Humans recognize five basic tastes: **saltiness**, **sweetness**, **bitterness**, **sourness** and **umami** – savoriness. Umami means "deliciousness" in Japanese.

6

sides of a snowflake

Nearly all snowflakes have six sides. They're made of ice crystals that usually form around a speck of dust.

7

metals of antiquity

In ancient Africa, Europe and Asia, humans only knew about – and used – **gold, silver, copper, mercury, tin, iron** and **lead.** Historians call these the seven metals of antiquity.

8

ball pool

Eight-ball, also known as pool, is a game played on a billiard table. To win, a player must sink the black eight-ball into the right pocket after all their other balls have been sunk.

9

Norse worlds

In Norse mythology, originating in Scandinavia more than 1,000 years ago, there are nine worlds joined together by a great tree called Yggdrasil.

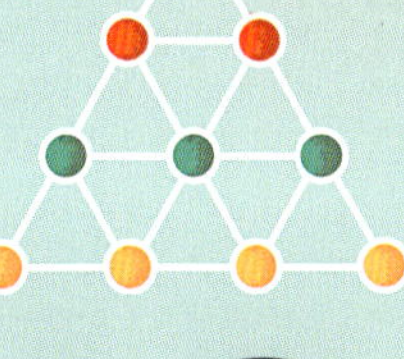

10

is a divine number

Ancient Greek philosopher Pythagoras and his followers believed 10 was a divine number. They worshipped a symbol with ten points called the **tetractys**.

Infinity

This symbol represents infinity. Infinity is the idea that numbers or quantities can get bigger and bigger as you count on...

...and on with no imaginable end.

LIQUID *or* SOLID?

Most of the stuff you can see is either solid or liquid. Sometimes, it changes from one to the other – or into gases and sometimes even electrified plasma. Scientists call these **states of matter**. It's all to do with how much their atoms are vibrating...

Solid

In solid state, atoms are held together in a set shape. They're always vibrating a little, but not enough to move apart from each other.

Liquid

In liquid state, atoms vibrate more, and they can move apart a little – enough to form a pool at the bottom of any container they are in.

Gas

In gas state, atoms vibrate even more, so they can literally bounce off each other. This means they spread out to fill the whole of any container.

Plasma

In plasma state, atoms vibrate so much they shake off tiny parts of themselves, called electrons. This creates an electrical charge.

LESS ENERGY

MORE ENERGY

HOW TO CHANGE STATES

It's possible to change the state of a substance by giving it more or less energy. **Adding energy** to a solid – for example, by heating it up – may turn it into a liquid. **Taking energy away** from a liquid – for example, by cooling it – may turn it into a solid.

This diagram shows the name given for each change of state.

SUBLIMATION
MELTING
VAPORIZATION
IONIZATION
Solid
Liquid
Gas
Plasma
FREEZING
CONDENSATION
RECOMBINATION
DEPOSITION

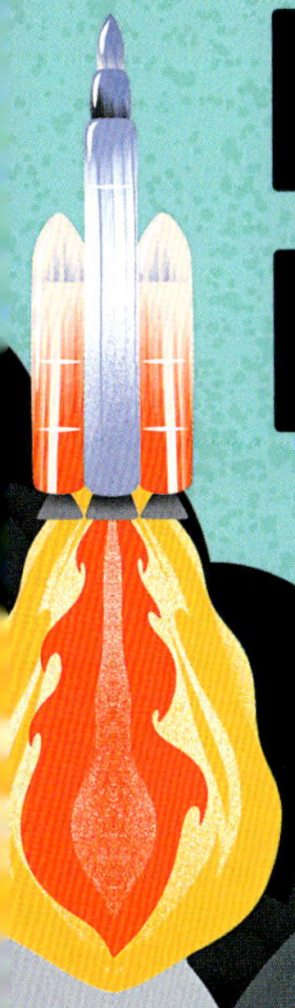

LAWS *of* NATURE

There are some things about the world that scientists have observed are ALWAYS true. These are called **laws** or **principles**. Here are just a few, named after the scientist who first explained them.

NEWTON'S LAW OF GRAVITATION

Gravity is a force that pulls objects together. The size of that force depends on how far apart they are, and how much matter – atoms, molecules and so on – each object holds.

Isaac Newton
English physicist and mathematician, 17th century

HOOKE'S LAW OF ELASTICITY

How far an object stretches is proportional to the amount of force being used to stretch it.

Robert Hooke
English scientist, 17th century

ARCHIMEDES'S BUOYANCY PRINCIPLE

If an object is in a liquid or gas, the amount of force pushing up on the object from below is the same as the weight of fluid that is being pushed out of the way by the object.

Archimedes
Greek philosopher, over 2,200 years ago

NEWTON'S LAWS OF MOTION

FIRST: If an object is not being acted on by a force, it will either stay still, or continue moving at a constant speed, in a straight line.

SECOND: Any force acting on an object will change its motion, depending on the size and direction of the force, and the mass of the object.

THIRD: When one object exerts a force on another, an equal and opposite force is applied back.

HEISENBERG'S UNCERTAINTY PRINCIPLE

At the level of particles smaller than atoms, it's impossible to measure every detail. For example, if you can measure the precise location of a particle, you cannot also determine its exact movement.

Werner Heisenberg
German physicist, 20th century

BERNOULLI'S PRINCIPLE OF AIR FLOW

Air is considered a fluid. When the flow of a fluid gets faster, the pressure of that fluid on any other object is reduced.

Daniel Bernoulli
Swiss mathematician and physicist, 18th century

AVOGADRO'S LAW OF PRESSURE

All gases of the same volume and temperature must contain the same number of atoms or molecules.

Amedeo Avogadro
Italian scientist, 19th century

BOYLE'S LAW OF PRESSURE

At a steady temperature, if the volume of a gas goes up, its pressure will go down.

Robert Boyle
Irish chemist, 17th century

The changing MOON

On some nights the Moon is the brightest thing in the sky, but from one night to the next, it seems to change shape or to vanish altogether. But why?

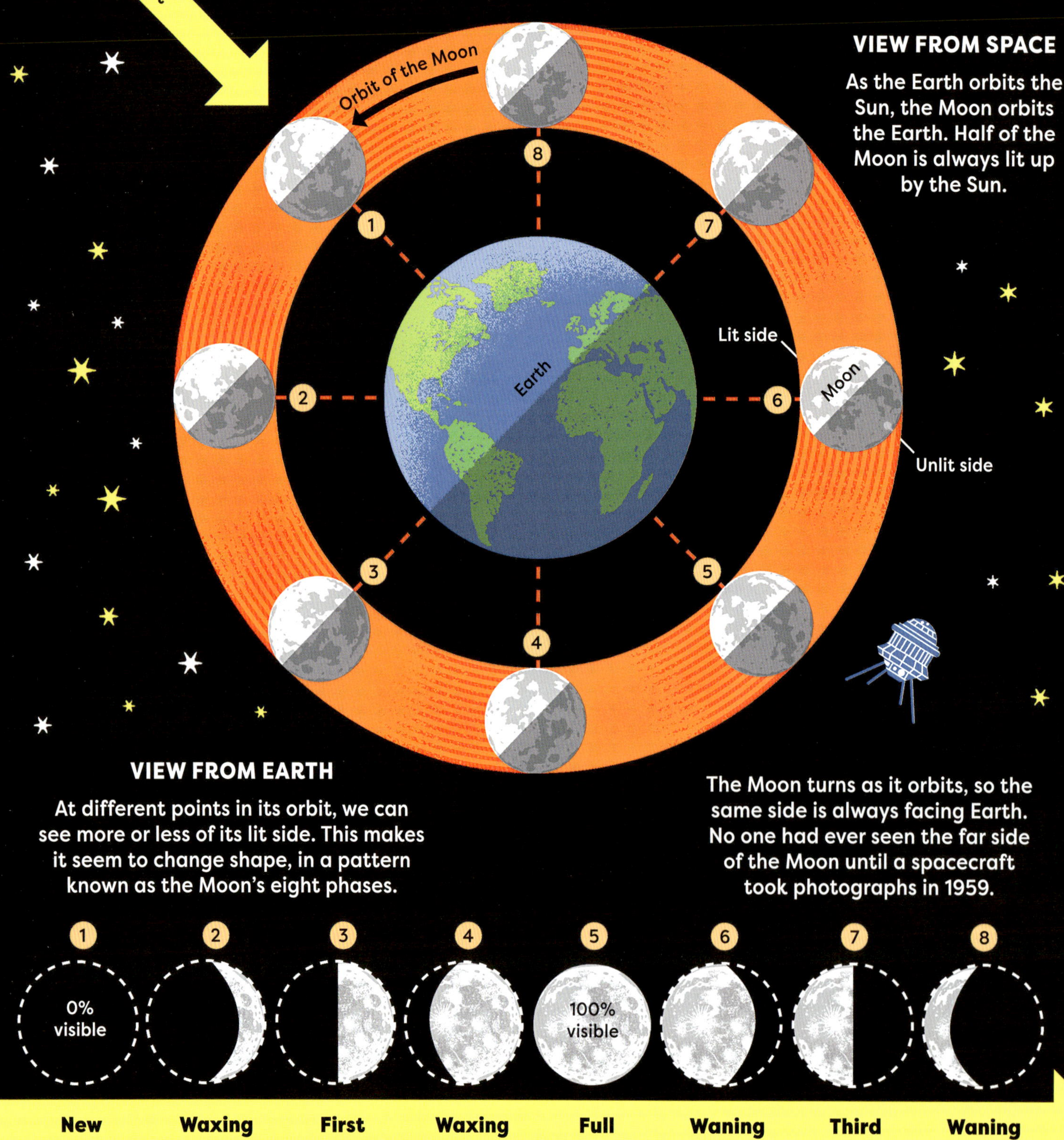

VIEW FROM SPACE

As the Earth orbits the Sun, the Moon orbits the Earth. Half of the Moon is always lit up by the Sun.

VIEW FROM EARTH

At different points in its orbit, we can see more or less of its lit side. This makes it seem to change shape, in a pattern known as the Moon's eight phases.

The Moon turns as it orbits, so the same side is always facing Earth. No one had ever seen the far side of the Moon until a spacecraft took photographs in 1959.

1	2	3	4	5	6	7	8
0% visible				100% visible			
New Moon	**Waxing crescent**	**First quarter**	**Waxing gibbous**	**Full Moon**	**Waning gibbous**	**Third quarter**	**Waning crescent**

A full cycle of this pattern takes one "lunar month" – around **29.5 days**.

It takes **27.3 days** for the Moon to **orbit** (go around) the Earth.

The average distance between Earth and the Moon is **384,400km (238,855 miles)**.

The Moon is moving away from Earth at a rate of about **3.8cm (1.5in)** every year.

Moon markings

The dark patches on the Moon were created billions of years ago by huge volcanic eruptions. In different parts of the world, people have spotted different images in these patches.

MOON RABBIT
East Asia and the Americas

In East Asia, moongazers see a rabbit making rice cakes or mixing a potion. Moon rabbits exist in indigenous American folklore, too.

TREE IN THE MOON
Hawaii

In Hawaiian folklore, a woman named Hina makes cloth for the gods from a banyan tree in the Moon.

WOMAN IN THE MOON
New Zealand

According to Māori legends, this woman is Rona. She insulted the Moon, who snatched her up in anger.

Eclipse

A **solar eclipse** happens when the Moon moves directly between the Sun and the Earth. In a **partial eclipse**, the Moon blocks out some of the Sun. In a **total eclipse**, it blocks out ALL of the Sun and turns the sky dark.

Total eclipses happen about once every 18 months, but they can only be seen from the same place roughly once every 375 years.

Watching an eclipse

Even when it's partly blocked by the Moon, looking at the Sun damages your eyes.

You need special eclipse glasses to watch one safely. Normal sunglasses will NOT give your eyes enough protection.

What makes a CAKE?

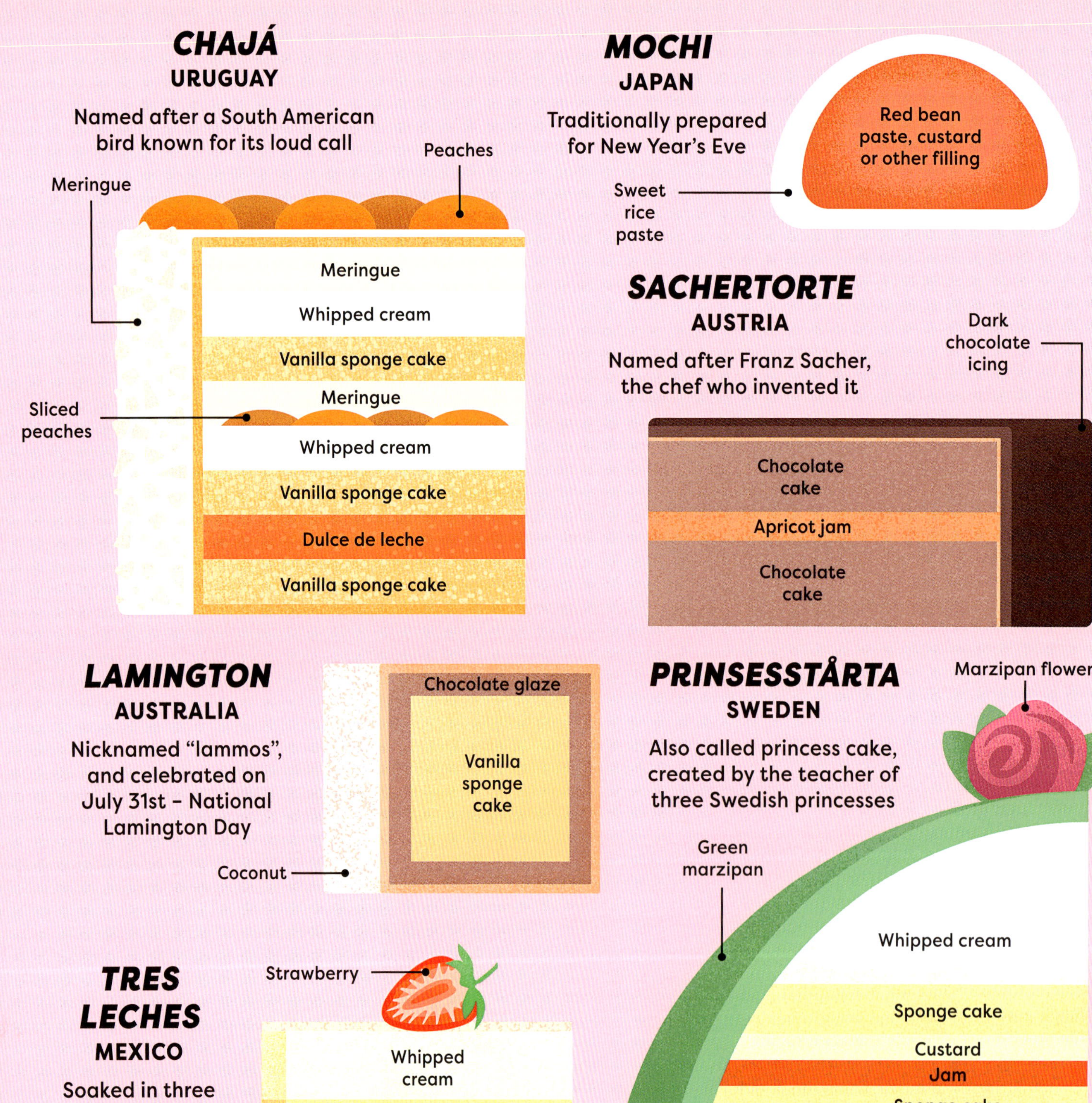

A cake is a sweet, soft treat that's usually baked. Different countries have invented their own versions, creating a huge variety of cakes with different shapes, layers and tastes. **YUM!**

UBE CAKE
PHILIPPINES

Bright purple from the ube – a type of purple yam with a nutty, vanilla-like taste

Ube sponge cake
Cream cheese frosting
Ube sponge cake
Cream cheese frosting
Ube sponge cake

Many cakes are made with eggs. Whisking eggs traps millions of tiny air bubbles in the mixture, helping the cake rise in the oven.

Before modern whisks were invented, cooks often used bundles of twigs tied together at one end.

BÛCHE DE NOËL
FRANCE

Also known as Yule log, and traditionally served at Christmas

HUMMINGBIRD CAKE
JAMAICA

Also called doctor bird cake, after Jamaica's national bird – the scissors-tail hummingbird, or doctor bird

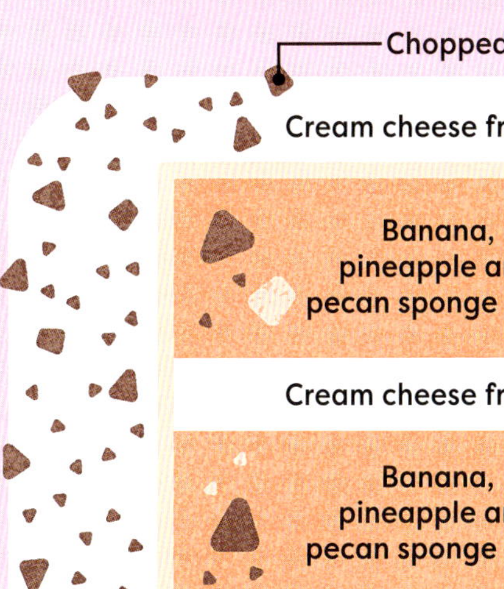

BATTENBERG
ENGLAND

Named to celebrate the wedding of Queen Victoria's granddaughter to Prince Louis of Battenberg

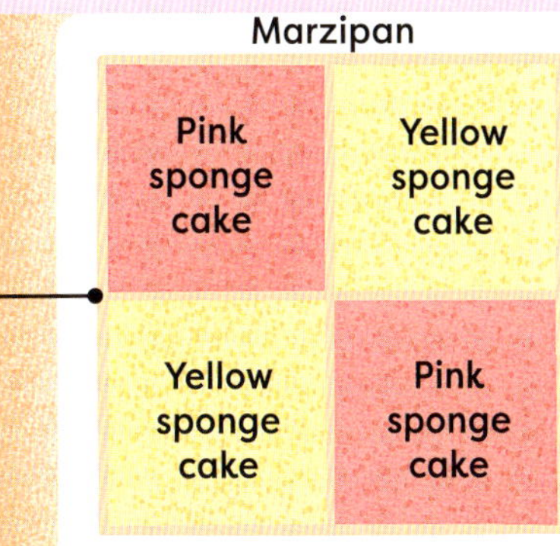

BOLO DE GINGUBA
ANGOLA

Named after its key ingredient – peanuts, known as ginguba in Angola

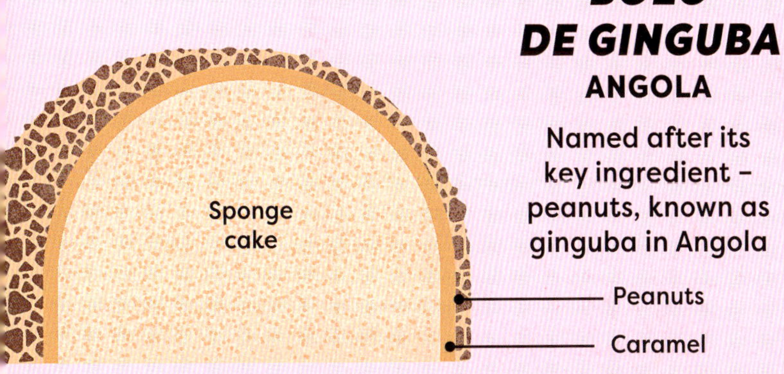

Martial ARTS

Martial arts were originally developed for warriors to perfect their skills of attack and defense. They have become popular as forms of self-defense, fitness and mental training. Some of the best-known are carried out without weapons.

WRESTLING

From: place and period uncertain

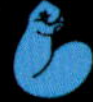

Tackle your opponent and try to throw them to the ground.

ORIGIN: modern rules used in Olympic wrestling were first devised in Ancient Greece, 7th century BCE

MUAY THAI *"Thai boxing"*

From: Thailand, 17th century

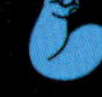

Attack and block opponents using your hands, feet, elbows and knees.

OTHER NAMES: Art of the eight limbs, Thai kickboxing

JUDO *"the gentle way"*

From: Japan, 1880s

Tackle your opponent and wrestle them to the ground until they surrender.

SAFETY: students also learn how to break a fall safely when they're thrown – this is called *ukemi*, the art of receiving attacks

TAE KWON DO

From: Korea, 1950s

Strike and kick your opponent.

EQUIPMENT: padded protectors for the head and chest, called *hogu*

BOXING

From: place and period uncertain

Punch your opponent's upper body while dodging or feinting (misleading them).

ORIGIN: existed for thousands of years, with rules first devised in Ancient Greece, 7th century BCE

CAPOEIRA

From: Brazil, 16th century

Time your moves to music and compete using acrobatics, dance and self-defense.

ORIGIN: developed by enslaved Africans and Brazilians to train in martial arts, disguising it as dance

KEY:

 Focus on punching and/or striking

 Focus on grappling and/or throwing

 Uniform includes a colored belt to show skill level

 Focus on kicking

 Focus on other moves

(Black belts are given to martial artists of the highest skill level.)

AIKIDO *"the way of harmonious spirit"*

From: Japan, 1940s

Disable your opponent with defensive strikes, tackles and throws.

ORIGIN: a combination of traditional Japanese religious beliefs with martial arts

JUJUTSU *"gentle art"*

From: Japan, 1530s

Disable your opponent by using their own strength against them. One of the deadliest martial arts.

ORIGIN: developed by samurai (Japanese warriors) to fight against armed opponents

TAI CHI

From: China, 17th century

Focuses on deep breathing, a meditative state of mind and slow movements.

OTHER NAMES: Shadow boxing, Taiji boxing

SUMO

From: Japan, 8th century

Push or throw your opponent out of a ring.

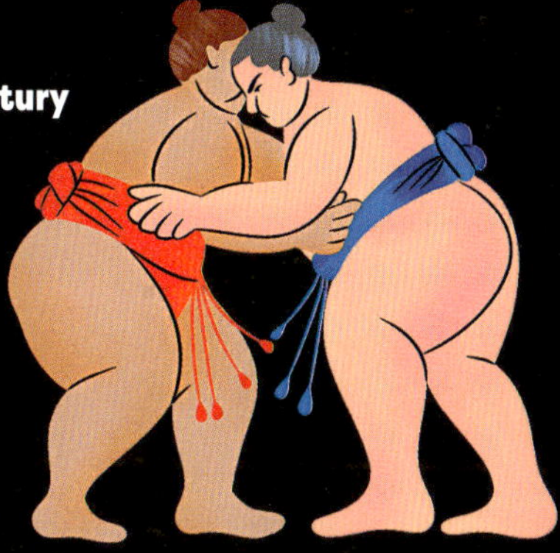

PRO TRAINING: sumo wrestlers follow a strict lifestyle and eat a special diet to keep their strong, heavy physique

KARATE *"empty hand"*

From: Japan, 17th century

Kick, strike and block your opponent. One of the most popular forms of self-defense.

STYLES: there are many styles of karate, each teaching slightly different techniques

SHAOLIN KUNG FU

From: China, 6th century

   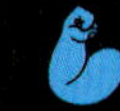

Some styles are based on animals, such as the dragon, tiger and snake, from Chinese folklore.

ORIGIN: developed by monks at Shaolin Temple to strengthen their bodies

CELEBRATE!

All around the world, people gather together at festivals to celebrate their beliefs, cultures and ways of life. Here are some of the most famous festivals in the world.

Splish, splash, splosh!

WESAK

Buddhists worldwide

Water is poured over the shoulders of statues of the Buddha – the founder of Buddhism.

HOLI

India

Hindus smear each other with water and powdered paint and welcome the arrival of spring.

SONGKRAN

Thailand

People spray each other with water in the streets to wash away the old year.

Fabulous feasts

HANAMI

Japan and Japanese communities

Picnics are held under the blossoming cherry trees to celebrate the coming of spring.

EID AL-FITR

Muslim communities worldwide

To celebrate the end of Ramadan, the Muslim month of fasting, Muslims feast on sweet foods.

Eid Mubarak! This means "blessed celebration" in Arabic.

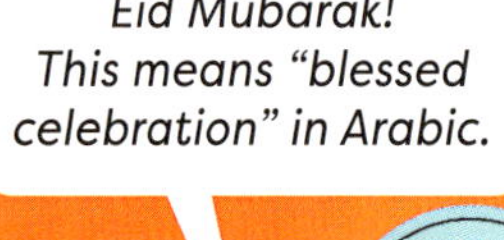

CHRISTMAS

Christians and many people worldwide

People eat a traditional meal, decorate Christmas trees with lights and give each other gifts.

Sparkle and glow
DIWALI
India and Indian communities
Known as the festival of lights, people light lamps called "diyas" to celebrate the triumph of good over evil.
LUNAR NEW YEAR
East Asian communities
Feasts, fireworks and parades are held to celebrate New Year in the lunar calendar.
HANUKKAH
Jewish communities worldwide
In the early evening, people light candles on a "hanukkiah" to remember a miracle that happened 2,000 years ago, and to celebrate religious freedom.
Dressing up
HALLOWEEN
The US and many places worldwide
Children in spooky costumes go from door to door asking for treats. People used to believe giving spirits gifts would ward off trouble.
BOO!
VENICE CARNIVAL
Venice, Italy
The city holds grand costume balls, and people wear decorative masks to celebrate a military victory in 1162.
DAY OF THE DEAD
Mexico and Mexican communities
Families dress up as skeletons and join parades to remember their dead relatives and ancestors.

DID YOU KNOW...?

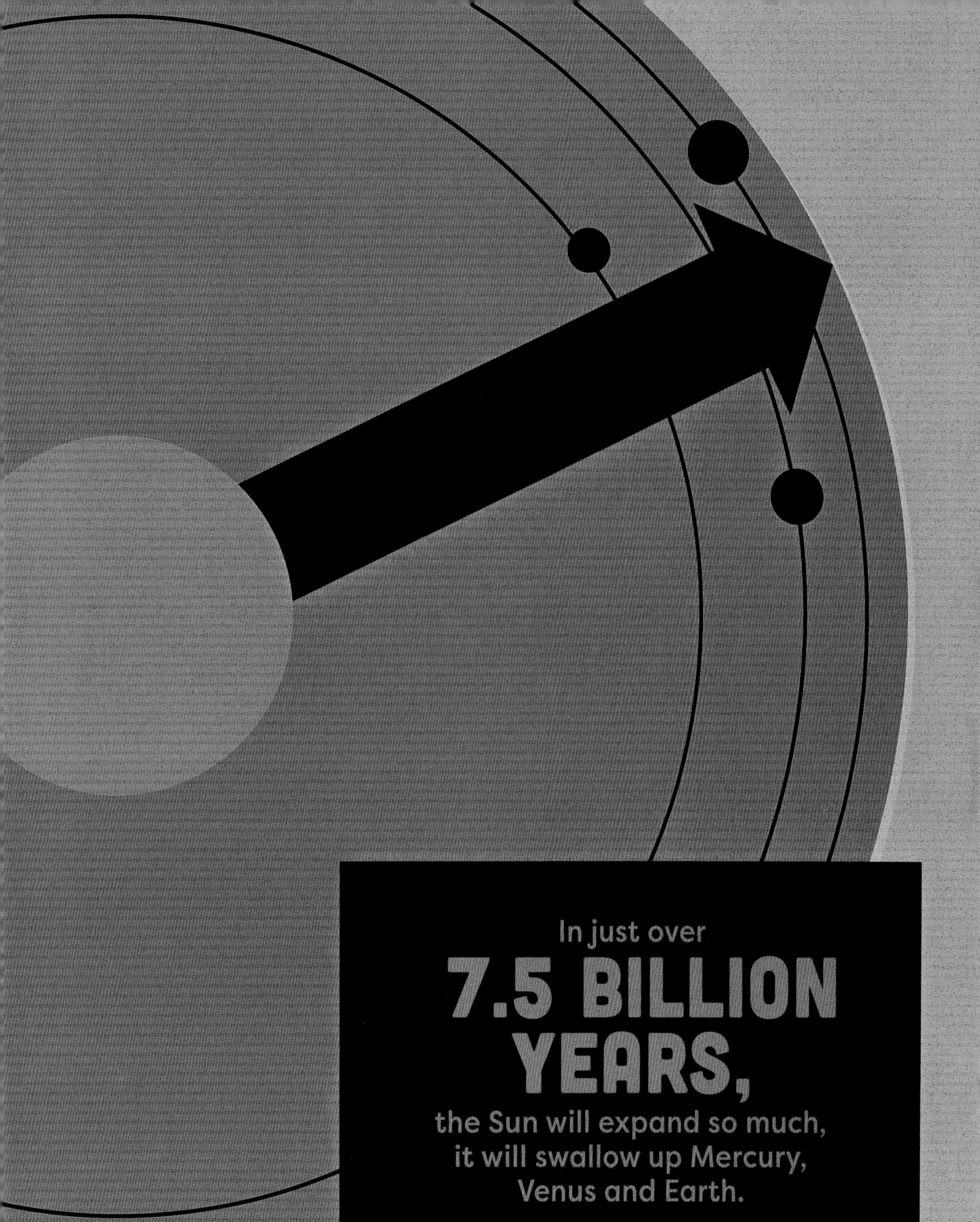

In just over

7.5 BILLION YEARS,

the Sun will expand so much, it will swallow up Mercury, Venus and Earth.

DISGUSTING!

Some would say these are the ickiest foods in history...

KEY
- ✱ Smells like
- ◆ Tastes like

Natto

Japanese dish made from fermented soybeans. Often eaten for breakfast with rice.

- ✱ Rotten cheese
- ◆ Strong cheese with a stringy, slimy texture

Durian

Large Southeast Asian fruit with spiky green rind and soft yellow flesh, banned in some hotels and on public transport.

- ✱ Rotten onions or raw sewage
- ◆ A rich almond custard (it's said)

Casu Marzu

Traditional cheese from Sardinia, Italy, now banned. Casu Marzu was left in the open until maggots started to hatch. This apparently softened the cheese and gave it more taste.

Live maggots can jump up to 15cm (6in) from the cheese surface. Ewww!

- ✱ Super-ripe cheese
- ◆ Blue cheese and black pepper, only wrigglier

Garum or liquamen

Highly prized Ancient Roman sauce made with fish guts fermented in salt for up to three months.

You wouldn't want to live next to a garum factory...

...or kiss someone who'd overindulged.

- ✱ Rotten fish, of course
- ◆ Better than it smells, a bit like Asian fish sauce mixed with soy sauce

Surströmming

Swedish speciality made from salted and fermented herring. The fish carries on fermenting after it is canned, producing gases that make the cans swell and sometimes explode under pressure.

Best opened outdoors!

- ✱ Rotten eggs, rotting fish and vinegar. May cause vomiting.
- ◆ Overripe blue cheese and extremely dead fish

DANGEROUS!

...while these are definitely some of the ***riskiest.***

KEY | **!** Risks

Deathcap mushroom

Edible mushrooms often have an "evil twin" that looks similar but has unpleasant or even fatal effects. Partly-grown deathcaps look similar to field mushrooms, but they don't usually grow in the same places.

! Eating just half a mushroom cap can kill within hours.

Mushrooms for dinner, darling?

When the Roman Emperor Claudius died suddenly, many believed he'd been poisoned with deathcap mushrooms... by his wife.

Peanuts

A delicious treat in peanut butter or cookies... unless you have a peanut allergy. This is rare but can be very serious.

! An allergic reaction known as anaphylactic shock. This causes swelling of the throat, difficulty breathing, dizziness and fainting.

If you have an allergic reaction to peanuts, you need an adrenaline injection as quickly as possible.

Blood clams

A type of shellfish once popular in China, now banned by law.

! The clams were often harvested from polluted water containing viruses that caused dysentery, hepatitis A and typhoid fever.

In 1988, over 300,000 people in Shanghai developed hepatitis A after eating blood clams.

Fugu

Japanese pufferfish. By law, chefs must train for three years before they can prepare and serve it without the dangerous bits.

! Fugu liver contains a deadly poison, tetrodotoxin. Even a tiny amount can cause paralysis and death.

Ackee

A soft fruit originally from West Africa, imported to the Caribbean. It's often eaten with saltfish.

! The fruit pulp is poisonous when unripe. Fruit must be left to "yawn" or split open, and the black seeds thrown away.

Animal

SUPERPOWERS

For humans, ultra-high speed or super strength, thousand-year lifespans or the ability to regrow body parts are the stuff of science fiction. But there are animals that can do all these things.

Leaps and bounds

Flea

Cat fleas can jump vertically up to **20cm (7.9in)**, that's to say 80 times their body length.

And they can jump up to **48cm (19in)** horizontally – around **200 times** their body length.

This line shows the actual height of a flea jump

Incredible strength

Some species of rhinoceros beetles, also called Hercules beetles, can move up to **850 times** their own body weight.

That's the equivalent of one person shifting nine fully-grown male elephants.

Mighty bites

Saltwater crocodiles have a bite almost **four times** as powerful as a tiger's or a lion's... and over **20 times** more powerful than the average human bite.

Fastest animals in the...

...air — Peregrine falcon — **389km/h (242mph)**

...land — Cheetah — **112km/h (70mph)**

...water — Sailfish — **54km/h (33mph)**

Cheetahs can run at more than twice the speed of the very fastest humans – but only for short distances.

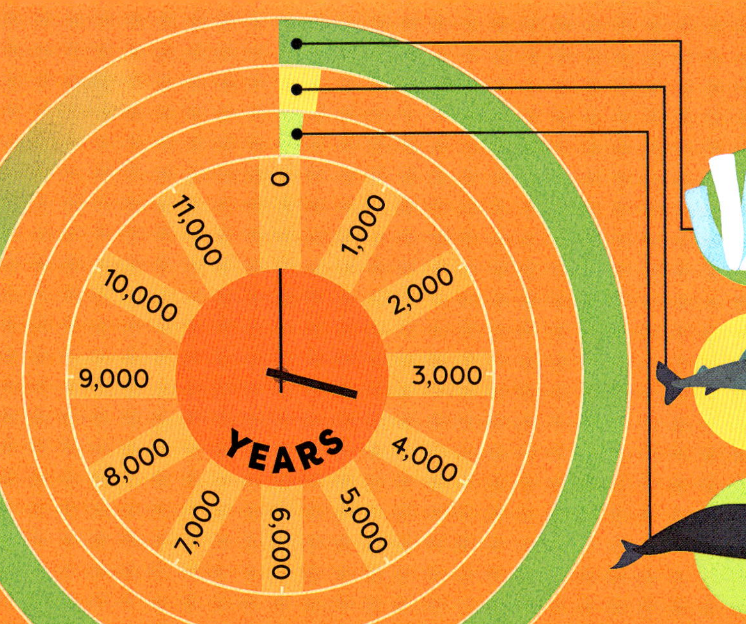

Living for centuries

Longest-living creature in the ocean:
Glass sponges, thought to be **10,000 years old** or even more

Longest-living fish:
Greenland shark, **250 years** (some scientists believe up to **500 years**)

Longest-living mammal:
Bowhead whales, up to **200 years**

Regenerating body parts

Salamanders, the amphibian family that includes newts, have an amazing ability to repair damage to their internal organs, eyes and brains. Some can even regrow entire missing limbs and tails.

Hypnotic powers

Cuttlefish can change the color cells of their skin. They sometimes use rapid color-changing effects to hypnotize prey such as crabs.

Natural antivenom

North American opossums can survive the bites of venomous snakes. They do this by producing a type of protein that neutralizes the poison.

Scientists are studying how this works, hoping to find an effective, low-cost antivenom that can be used by humans.

Almost indestructible

Tardigrades, or water bears, are microscopic eight-legged creatures. They can put themselves into a state of suspended animation (slowing all their body processes right down) to survive...

...temperatures far below zero...

...extreme dryness...

...years without food or water...

...exposure to radiation.

I've been alive for several decades... although for much of that time I was just a dried-out dormant dot, waiting for my living conditions to improve.

The natural lifespan of a tardigrade is just a few weeks... but those few weeks can be spread through many years.

Bright STARS

Viewed from Earth, stars beyond the Sun appear as points of light. Sometimes, it's just possible to make out hints of red or blue. In fact, stars exist in several colors.

Astronomers classify stars in various ways. One involves seven types of stars, each with a different letter, based on their surface temperatures. Their temperature – measured in units called Kelvin (K) – affects their color.

B-TYPE

10,000-28,000K
Example: **Rigel**

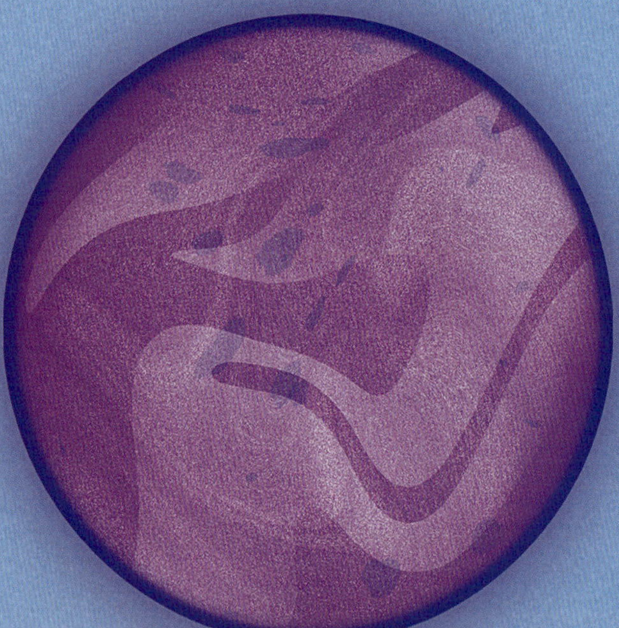

O-TYPE

Hotter than **28,000K**
Example: **μ Columbae**

BLACK *holes*

Black holes are the remnants of MASSIVE stars that have exploded. Astronomers have suspected their existence for over a century – but the first definite observation of a black hole wasn't made until 2016.

BLACK HOLES ARE...

...BLACK.

They have such a strong gravitational pull, that they suck in light itself. They are, literally, invisible.

...NOT HOLES.

They were named in the 1960s by astronomers who predicted that they would *appear* as holes, showing a gap where light cannot escape.

A-TYPE

7,500-10,000K
Example: **Vega**

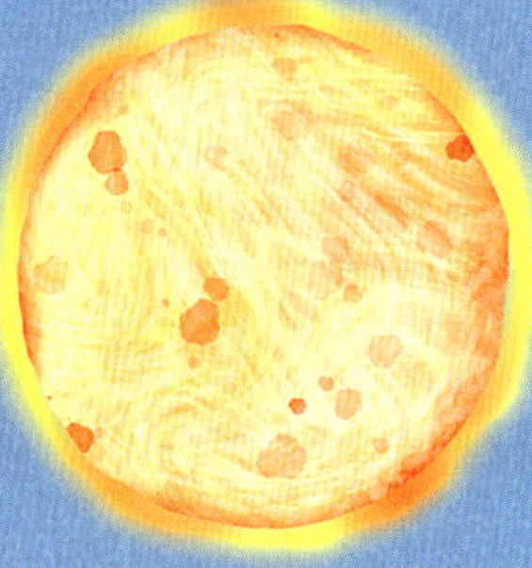

F-TYPE

6,000-7,500K
Example: **Procyon A**

G-TYPE

5,000-6,000K
Example: **Tau Ceti**

K-TYPE

3,500-5,000K
Example: **Aldebaran**

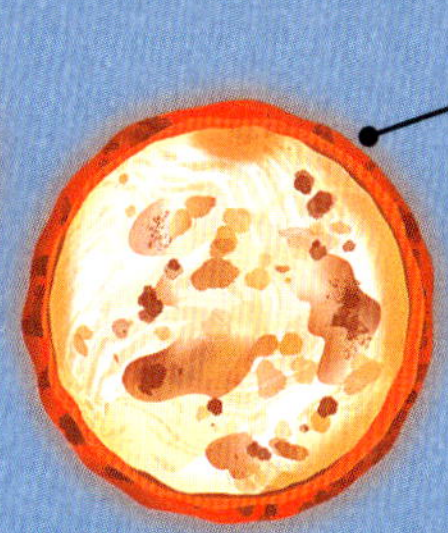

M-TYPE

2,000-3,000K
Example: **Antares**

Parts of a hole

Although the central body of a black hole is invisible, it is typically encircled by heat and light – remnants of the explosion of the original star.

Relativisitic jet
A stream of energy, observable by X-ray telescopes

Accretion disc
A disc of stuff pulled into orbit around the black hole

Event horizon
The outer limit of the extreme gravitational pull of the black hole

Photon sphere
A plume of light beyond the edge of the event horizon

Singularity
In the very middle of the invisible part is the actual remnant of the exploded star, an incredibly tiny ball.

Don't get too close

If anything were to go beyond a black hole's event horizon, something extraordinary would happen to it...

...the front end would get sucked in faster than the back end, stretching it out into a shape very like spaghetti.

So far, only TWO black holes have been observed by telescope:
MESSIER 87
SAGITTARIUS A*

Epic JOURNEYS

From the risky to the record-breaking, here are some of the most amazing journeys around the world made by people and animals.

The symbols shown next to these incredible journeys are color-coded to match the lines on the route map below.

THE *VICTORIA*

85,700km (53,250 miles)

The *Victoria* was the first ship to sail around the world. It left Spain in 1519 and completed the voyage in 1522.

ARCTIC TERN MIGRATION

70,900km (44,050 miles) round trip

Arctic terns migrate further than any other animal on the planet. Every year, they fly from the Arctic to the Antarctic and back to avoid the harsh winters.

PAN-AMERICAN HIGHWAY

Around 30,000km (19,000 miles)

The world's longest road runs from Alaska to Argentina, passing through 14 countries, with a short break between Panama and Colombia.

PROJECT AFRICA

Over 16,000km (9,940 miles)

In 2024, an athlete named Russell Cook became the first person to run from the southern tip of Africa to the most northern point, in Tunisia. The journey took 352 days.

HIGHWAY 1

14,500km (9,010 miles)

This network of highways runs all the way around the coast of Australia. Locals call it the Big Lap. It's the longest highway in a single country.

TRANS-SIBERIAN RAILWAY

9,289km (5,772 miles)

The world's longest continuous rail journey connects east and west Russia, the world's widest country. It crosses almost 4,000 bridges and takes over six days.

SILK ROAD

7,000km (4,300 miles) in total

For more than 1,500 years, from around 130BCE, the Silk Road was one of the world's most important trade networks. It linked China to the Middle East and Europe, enabling people to trade silk, tea and other goods, and exchange ideas and knowledge.

TRANSOCEÁNICA BUS ROUTE

6,200km (3,850 miles)

This bus route connects Rio de Janeiro in Brazil to Lima in Peru. It has a journey time of over 100 hours.

GREAT MIGRATION

Up to 3,000km (1,860 miles)

Every year, in East Africa's dry season, millions of wildebeest and thousands of zebra and gazelle set off to find water and grass. The walk crosses two countries, past hungry crocodiles, big cats, hyena and wild dogs.

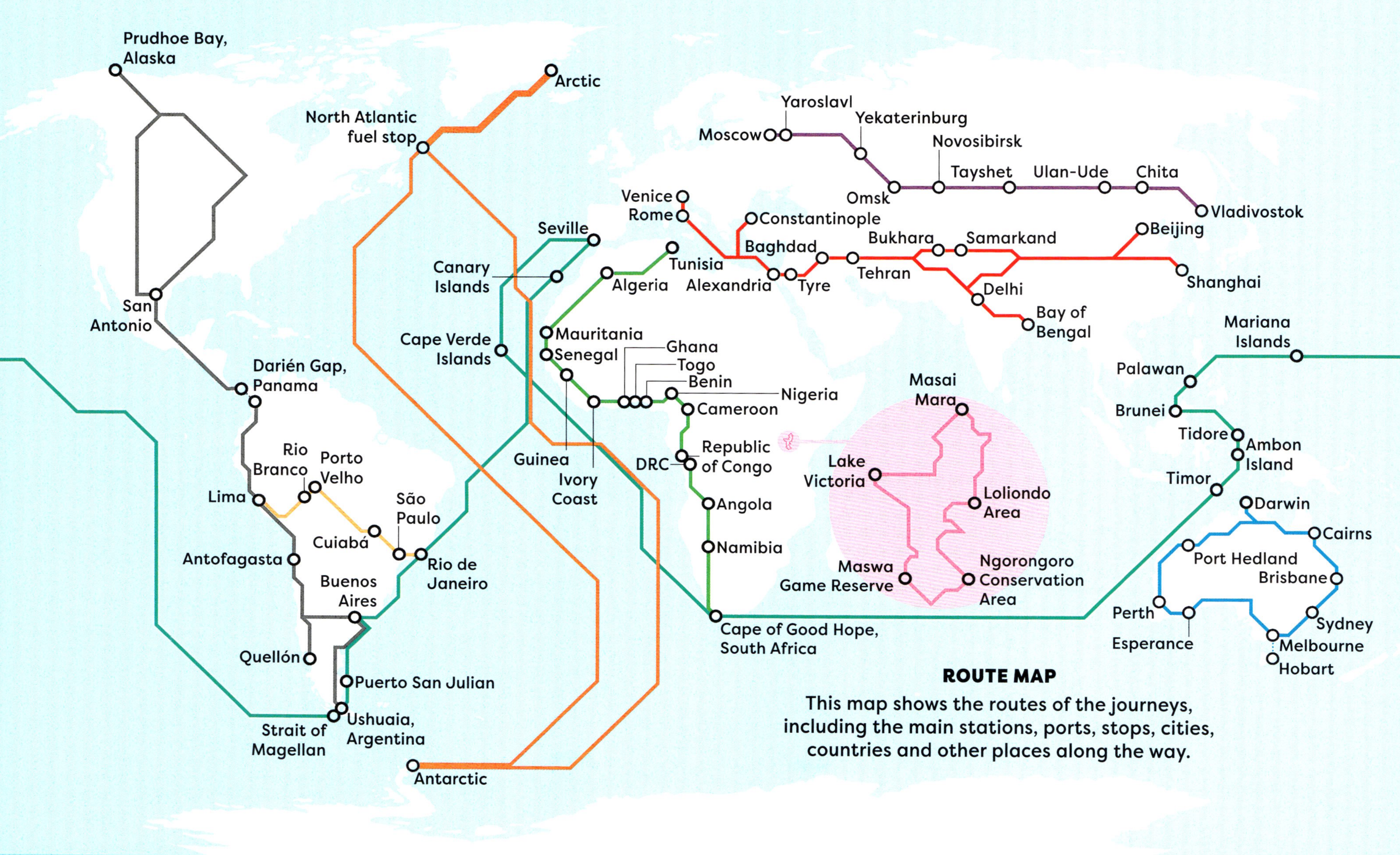

ROUTE MAP

This map shows the routes of the journeys, including the main stations, ports, stops, cities, countries and other places along the way.

Making ART

You can make art from **anything**. Here are just a few of the many ways artists work with different materials.

INK WASH PAINTINGS

Ink wash painters illustrate using mainly black ink. They dilute the ink with water to lighten its shade.

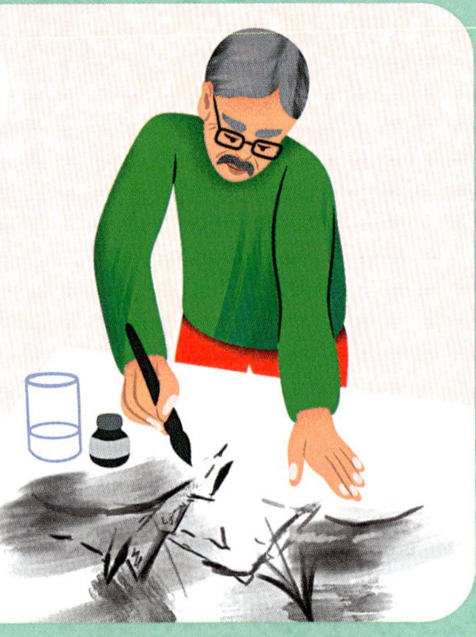

PAINTING

Painters apply pigments to a surface. Almost any surface can be painted – from canvas and wood panels to old cans and bottles.

CALLIGRAPHY

Calligraphers arrange letters, symbols and decorations to create art from words. They often use pens or brushes.

WEAVING

Weavers turn threads of yarn and other materials into sheets of fabric or even sculptures. They use many weaving methods to create patterns or pictures.

PHOTOGRAPHY

Some photographers work with cameras that capture images onto film. They use a variety of techniques to transfer their images onto paper and create special effects.

DIGITAL ART

Digital artists use computer programs. These can simulate any art technique, but still require a lot of skill and work from the artist.

PAPERCUTTING

Artists craft intricate paper designs by cutting out shapes, often using nothing but a single knife blade.

COLLAGE

Collages are artworks made by cutting up or ripping and sticking together all kinds of things, including magazines, book pages, photographs and leaves.

SCREEN PRINTING

On a mesh screen, the artist blocks out areas that aren't part of their design. Then, they use a tool to push ink through gaps in the screen and print the design onto paper or fabric.

BLOCK PRINTING

Printmakers engrave images into blocks of wood, metal or lino rubber. Then, they roll ink onto the surface and print the image on paper.

The print is the mirror image of the image on the printing block.

POTTERY

Potters or ceramicists shape soft clay into objects such as jars and dishes. These are then hardened by heating them in a special oven called a kiln.

SCULPTURE

Sculptors chisel, model and shape materials into three-dimensional works. Materials include marble, bronze, wood and plastic.

OLYMPIC *sports*

For many athletes, the Olympic Games, usually held every four years, are the ultimate test of sporting achievement. When the first modern Olympic Games were held in 1896, there were just **9 sports** and **43 events**. Now athletes tackle over **30 sports** and **300 events**.

Winter sports

The main Olympic Games are followed by the **Winter Olympics**. These usually involve around 14 disciplines, including...

Alpine skiing
Bobsleigh
Curling
Figure skating
Ice hockey
Luge
Skeleton
Ski jumping
Snowboarding

PARA sports

At the **Paralympics**, athletes with a wide range of impairments show off their incredible abilities in sports such as...

Para cycling
Para equestrian
Goalball
Para judo
Shooting Para sport
Sitting volleyball
Para swimming
Para triathlon
Wheelchair basketball

Surprising sports

Some events, disciplines and even sports are added and others taken away from each Games. Examples that have made rare appearances are...

Cricket
Croquet
Lacrosse
Motor boating
Polo
Skateboarding
Solo synchronized swimming
Tug-of-war
Roller hockey

ATHLONS
GO GO GO!

Some Olympians are not satisfied with single events. They compete in skills from several disciplines, sometimes from more than one sport. These are the "-athlons" – officially known as **combined events.**

The Olympic Games originated more than 2,800 years ago in Greece. In the Ancient Olympics, star athletes competed in a **pentathlon** – a contest across five different events.

Here are the four combined events included in the modern Olympics.

Triathlon
3
events

Modern pentathlon
5
events

Heptathlon (women)
7
events

Decathlon (men)
10
events

These diagrams show you which events feature in the five different -athlons.

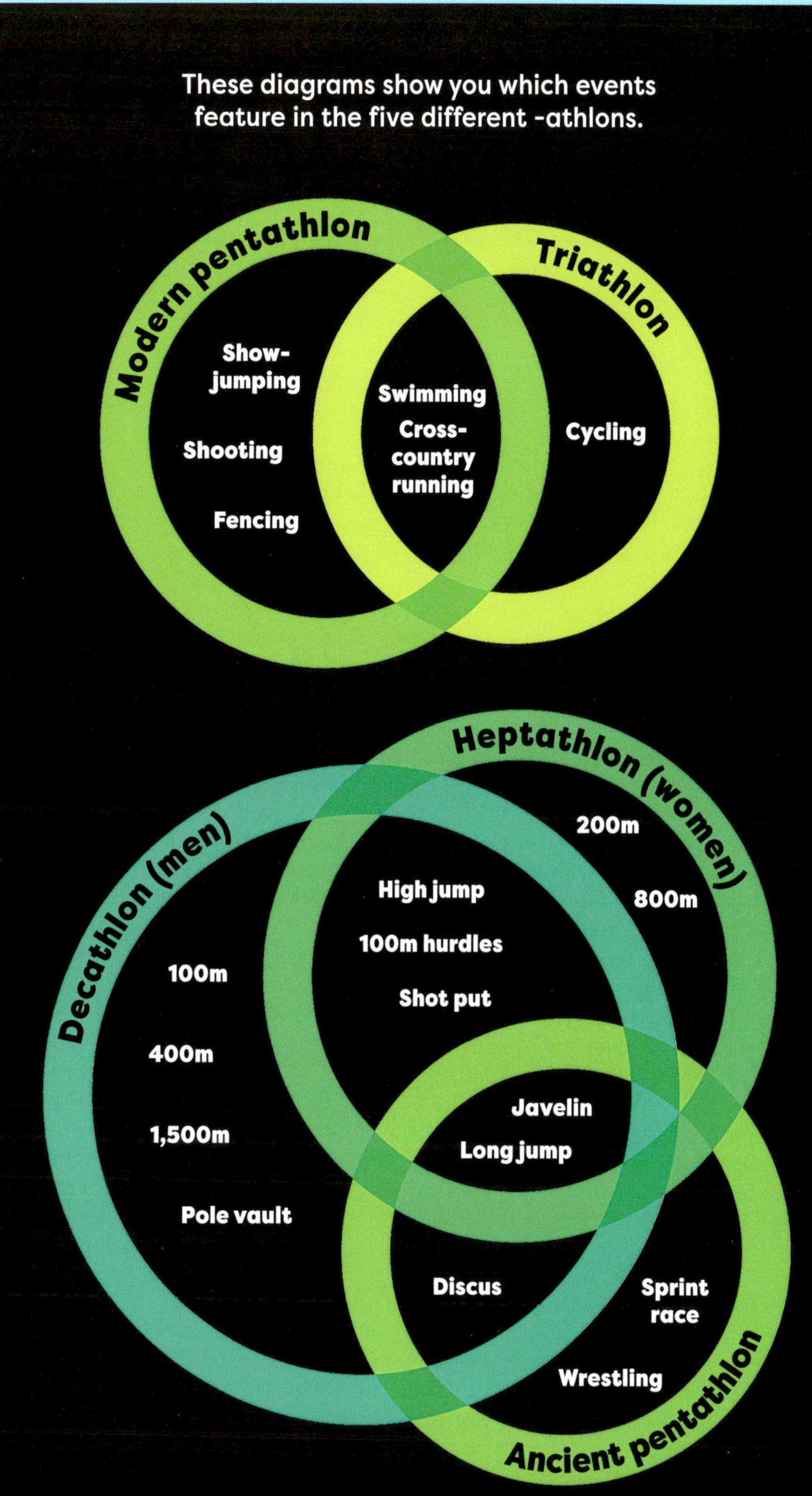

WHEN IS A BEAR ...NOT a bear?

There are **eight** different kinds of bears around the world. The scientific name for the bear family is *Ursidae*.

On its hind legs, a **brown bear** stands up to **2.4m (7.8ft) tall**.

Name
Scientific name
- Continent
- Habitat
- Max height on four legs
- Max weight
- Diet
- Also known as...

Many languages developed their own alternative names for bears, especially the fearsome **brown** or **grizzly bear**.

Maybe people were superstitious, thinking it would be dangerous to call a bear *a bear*.

American black bear
Ursus americanus
- North America
- Mountains and forests
- 0.9m (3ft)
- 240kg (530lb)
- Mainly plants
- Maskwa, nanu, shash

Giant panda
Ailuropoda melanoleuca
- China
- Mountains with bamboo forest
- 0.9m (3ft)
- 160kg (350lb)
- Bamboo
- Bamboo eater, bamboo bear, silverdog, China bear

Brown or Grizzly bear
Ursus arctos
- North America, Europe and Asia
- Mountains, forests and grassland, often near rivers
- 1.5m (5ft)
- 760kg (1600lb)
- Berries, nuts, seeds, grains, insects, fish, smaller mammals, carrion (dead animals)
- Brown one, shaggy one, honey eater

Spectacled bear
Tremarctos ornatus
- South America
- High-altitude forests and grassland
- 0.9m (3ft)
- 200kg (440lb)
- Mainly plants and fruit
- Andean bear, mountain bear, jukumari, ukumari, ukuku

Sun bear

Helarctos malayanus

- Southeast Asia
- Tropical forests
- 0.7m (2ft)
- 65kg (145lb)
- Insects, honey, fruit
- Dog-face bear, Malay bear, honey bear

Polar bear

Ursus maritimus

- The Arctic
- Ice sheets
- 1.6m (5ft)
- 760kg (1600lb)
- Seals, walrus, beluga whales, fish, bird eggs, carrion
- Ice bear, white bear, Nanuk, rider of icebergs, sea deer, old man in the fur cloak

Sloth bear

Melursus ursinus

- South Asia
- Forests and grassland
- 0.9m (3ft)
- 145kg (320lb)
- Ants, termites, fruit
- Kaathe bhaalu, honey bear

Asiatic black bear

Ursus thibetanus

- South and East Asia
- Mountains and mixed forest
- 1m (3ft)
- 200kg (440lb)
- Fruits, nuts, leaves, insects, deer, wild boar, cattle, carrion
- Moon bear, white-chested bear

Definitely NOT bears

These animals are sometimes confused with bears, although they're not members of the bear family.

Red panda

Ailurus fulgens

- Asia (Himalayas)
- High mountain forests
- 34cm (13.5in)
- 7.7kg (17lb)
- Bamboo.
- The name panda probably comes from a Nepalese word meaning bamboo-eater.

Koala

Phascolarctos cinereus

- Australia
- Eucalyptus groves
- 58cm (23in)
- 13kg (29lb)
- Eucalyptus leaves (must be fresh)
- Koala bear (they looked like small bears to early European visitors, but are in fact more closely related to kangaroos).

Where in the WORLD?

Earth has a surface area of over **500 million** km² (**190 million** square miles). That's MASSIVE. So how do we pinpoint where anything is?

Coordinate positions

The surface of the Earth is divided up by horizontal lines of **LATITUDE** and vertical lines of **LONGITUDE**.

North Pole

South Pole

LATITUDE lines describe how far **NORTH** or **SOUTH** a location is.

The Earth's widest part, the **EQUATOR**, is at **0°** latitude.

LONGITUDE LINES describe how far **EAST** or **WEST** a location is.

These start at **0°** at the **PRIME MERIDIAN**, which runs through Greenwich, in London.

They go up to **180°E** and **180°W**.

The **NORTH POLE** is at **90°N**, and the **SOUTH POLE** is at **90°S**.

You can describe any location on Earth using these coordinates. For example, the Usborne London office is at **51.5218°N, 0.1080°W**.

GPS – the global positioning system

The **GPS** helps us find our location and navigate the world, thanks to a network of **30 satellites** that orbit the Earth.

Navigation satellites send out radio waves in every direction.

HERE'S HOW IT WORKS

Devices pick up waves from the nearest satellite. Combining information from four satellites is enough to find your exact location.

Searching the INTERNET

The internet is a **huge** network of computers linked by cables and **Wi-Fi**. Connecting to it lets you access the **World Wide Web** – a colossal collection of information. Here's what actually happens whenever you use it:

1 Say you want to watch a cat video on your laptop.

Your laptop connects to the internet via Wi-Fi, thanks to a tiny chip inside it.

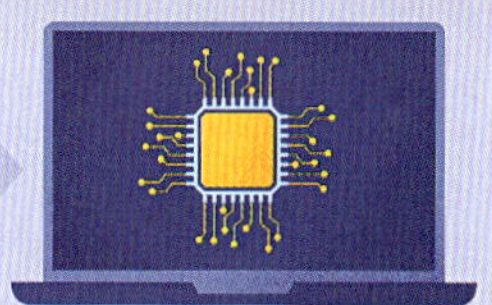

2 You open up a **WEB BROWSER**.

Browsers are applications that let you see what's available on the World Wide Web. They are like the doors to a library.

3 Then, you type "funny cat video" into a **SEARCH ENGINE**.

There are **BILLIONS** of web pages on the World Wide Web. A search engine finds the ones that are relevant.

funny cat video

4 It sends a list of sites back to you.

This data makes its way to YOUR laptop, which like every device connected to the internet has a unique identifier – an **IP ADDRESS**.

5 You choose a site and watch your video.

The website splits audio and visual data into chunks called **PACKETS** to send to your laptop. They're put back together as the video plays.

How do search engines actually work?

INDEXING

Search engines scan web pages to find out their content. This information is stored in a giant database, called an **INDEX**.

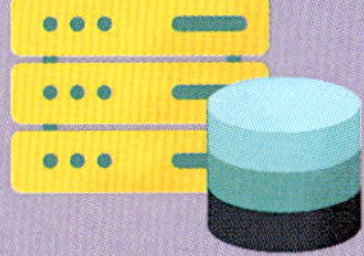

RANKING

When you look something up, the search engine runs through its index at great speed. It returns a list of websites that are related to your query, ranked by most relevant first.

CRAWLING

Search engines use programs called **CRAWLERS** or **SPIDERS** to check web pages for new information. This keeps their indexes up to date.

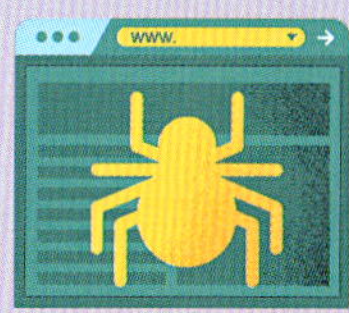

DID YOU KNOW...

Alpine bumblebees can fly as high as

9,000M

(29,500ft) – that's higher than the peak of Mount Everest.

Every VOTE counts

Most countries around the world hold **elections** to help choose a government. The basic idea is whoever gets the most votes wins. But there are lots of voting systems, and lots of ways to count votes. Here are the most common.

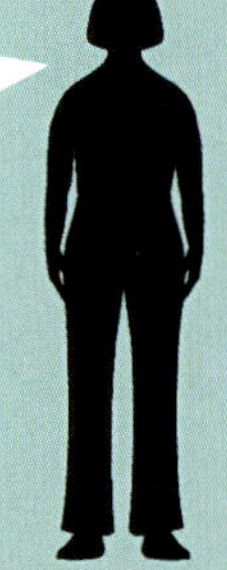

Vote for individuals

Sometimes, an election is a choice between individuals – for example, to become a country's President.

Vote for a representative

In some elections, people choose a representative who then has the power to cast a vote on their behalf.

Who gets your vote?

Votes are commonly cast by marking an X on a **ballot paper** or **voting card**.

Vote for political parties

Most often, people who want to run a country belong to groups called **political parties**. In some elections, voters have to choose which party they prefer. The party itself chooses leaders to take charge.

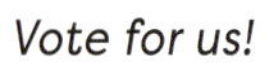

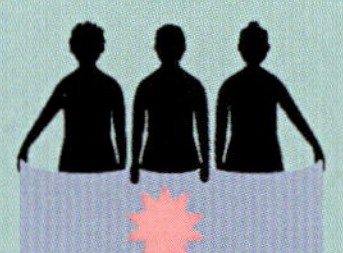

Spoiled ballot papers

Some people mess up their voting cards, or write complaints on them. This is sometimes called **spoiling a ballot paper**.

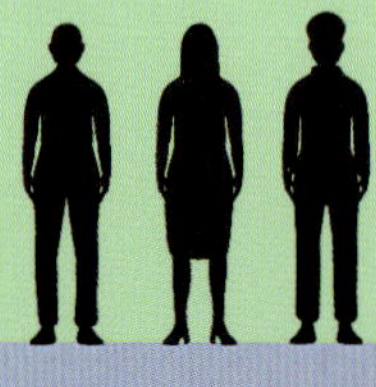

How are votes counted?

Here are three common systems.

Two-round system

In this system, voting and counting usually happen over two rounds.

Round 1: Voters choose one candidate from a list.

If any candidate gets more than 50% of all votes, they win. If not, voting goes to a second round.

Round 2: This time, voters usually choose between the top two or three candidates from the previous round.

The winner is whoever gets the most votes after Round 2.

Alternative vote, or ranked choice vote

Instead of picking just one candidate, voters are asked to mark candidates in order of preference. Then, the votes are counted over several rounds.

Round 1: The number of first preference votes is counted. If anyone gets more than 50% of these, then they win. If not, the count goes to a second round.

The candidate with the least votes is removed. All ballot papers with that candidate as first preference are counted again, looking at the second preference.

This process is repeated until one candidate has more than 50% of votes.

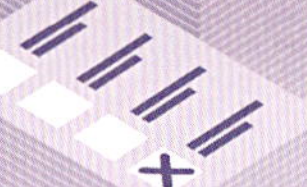

First past the post

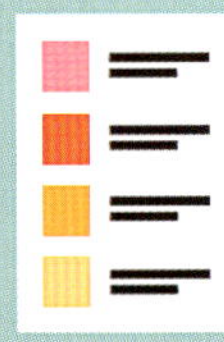

Every voter picks just ONE candidate from a list. Whichever candidate gets the most votes, even down to a single vote, wins the election.

More PRECIOUS than GOLD

For many, gold is the ultimate status symbol. It's rare and difficult to mine, but lasts for thousands of years. At times in history, though, other things have been valued even more highly.

Purple dye

Up to 3 times the value of gold

From around 3,500 years ago, spiny sea snails were used to make Tyrian purple dye. It took over **250,000 snails** to produce just enough dye for one cloak.

The dye was disgustingly smelly, but produced a rich, intense hue which actually grew stronger over time.

Agarwood

1 to 2 times the value of gold

Agarwood comes from the heart of aquilaria trees. When insects eat the wood, the trees sometimes produce a resin known as **oud**. It has a smoky, woody scent, used in perfumes.

Around **50kg (110lb)** of agarwood is needed for just 5g (less than a quarter ounce) of oud oil.

Truffles

Prize specimens: up to twice the value of gold

Truffles are a fungus with an intense smell and taste. Skilled truffle hunters and their dogs go out to find them in locations which they keep strictly secret.

In 2022, a rare white truffle weighing 700g (1.5lb) was bought at auction for almost **$200,000**.

Stigma

Saffron

2 to 4 times the value of gold

Saffron is a spice that adds a rich yellow and a distinctive taste to food. It is harvested by hand from the pollen-covered stigma of autumn crocus flowers. These are then slowly dried over charcoal fires.

It takes around **5,000 flowers** to produce 25g (1oz) of saffron.

Platinum

For most of the 20th century, platinum was worth more than gold, but gold is now more valuable.

When Spanish explorers in South America first found platinum, they called it "little silver" and thought it had almost no value.

How wrong they were. From around 1900, designers began combining platinum with diamonds. Aristocrats and millionaires around the world went wild for their dazzling creations.

Californium

Around 675,000 times the value of gold

Californium is a radioactive element, first made in a lab at the University of California at Berkeley in 1950.

It's extremely difficult to produce, but even in tiny quantities it has a wide range of uses, including in nuclear reactors and in some cancer treatments.

Pineapples

By 1760, worth a quarter of the value of gold (but much rarer)

On his second return from the Americas in 1496, explorer Christopher Columbus presented a single pineapple to the King and Queen of Spain. For centuries, pineapples were extremely difficult to grow in Europe, so they became **rare status symbols.**

Then, in the 19th century, the invention of canning food made them easy and affordable for anyone to buy.

Tulip bulbs

At height of craze, 100 times the value of gold

Tulips were introduced to Europe in 1554. The most prized blooms had white streaks on pink, red or purple petals, the result of a rare virus.

By 1637, in what became known as **tulip mania**, people in the Netherlands were prepared to buy a single bulb for the price of a house. However, within weeks, the price had crashed to less than 1% of its peak.

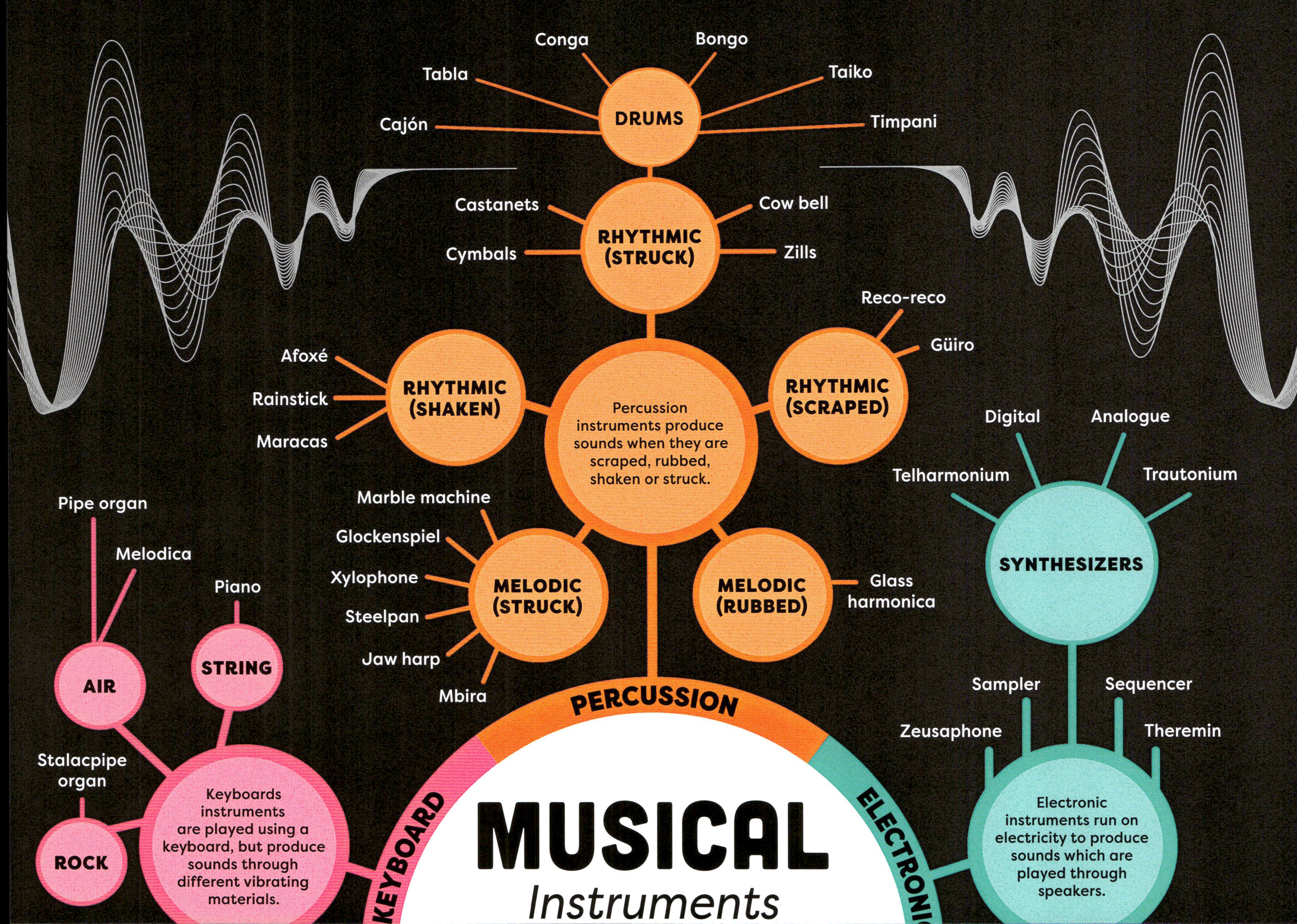
MUSICAL
Instruments
PERCUSSION
Percussion instruments produce sounds when they are scraped, rubbed, shaken or struck.
DRUMS
Conga
Bongo
Tabla
Taiko
Cajón
Timpani
RHYTHMIC (STRUCK)
Castanets
Cow bell
Cymbals
Zills
RHYTHMIC (SHAKEN)
Afoxé
Rainstick
Maracas
RHYTHMIC (SCRAPED)
Reco-reco
Güiro
MELODIC (STRUCK)
Marble machine
Glockenspiel
Xylophone
Steelpan
Jaw harp
Mbira
MELODIC (RUBBED)
Glass harmonica
KEYBOARD
Keyboards instruments are played using a keyboard, but produce sounds through different vibrating materials.
AIR
Pipe organ
Melodica
STRING
Piano
ROCK
Stalacpipe organ
ELECTRONIC
Electronic instruments run on electricity to produce sounds which are played through speakers.
SYNTHESIZERS
Digital
Analogue
Telharmonium
Trautonium
Sampler
Sequencer
Zeusaphone
Theremin

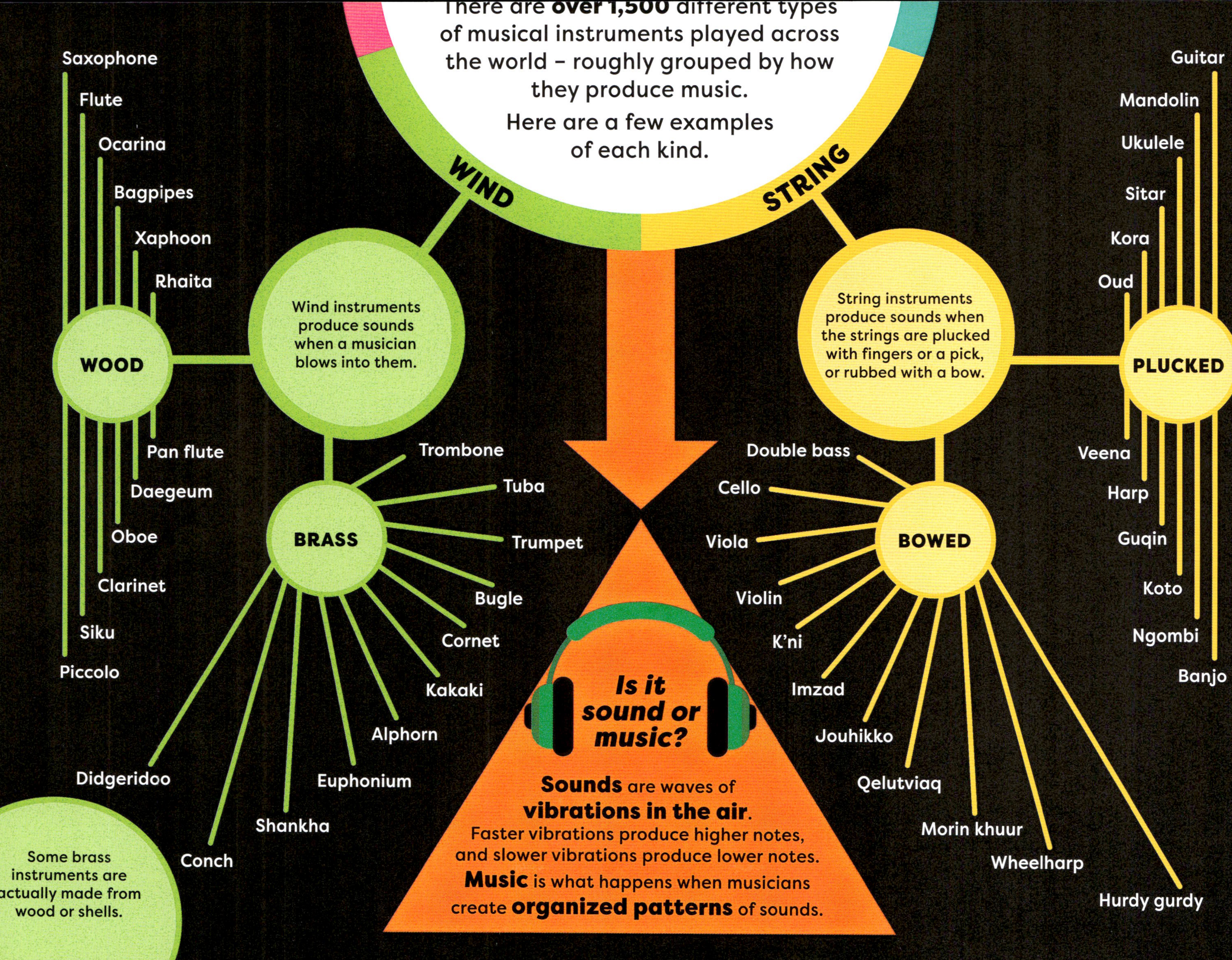

There are **over 1,500** different types of musical instruments played across the world – roughly grouped by how they produce music.
Here are a few examples of each kind.
WIND
STRING
Wind instruments produce sounds when a musician blows into them.
WOOD
Saxophone
Flute
Ocarina
Bagpipes
Xaphoon
Rhaita
Pan flute
Daegeum
Oboe
Clarinet
Siku
Piccolo
BRASS
Trombone
Tuba
Trumpet
Bugle
Cornet
Kakaki
Alphorn
Euphonium
Shankha
Conch
Didgeridoo
Some brass instruments are actually made from wood or shells.
String instruments produce sounds when the strings are plucked with fingers or a pick, or rubbed with a bow.
PLUCKED
Guitar
Mandolin
Ukulele
Sitar
Kora
Oud
Veena
Harp
Guqin
Koto
Ngombi
Banjo
BOWED
Double bass
Cello
Viola
Violin
K'ni
Imzad
Jouhikko
Qelutviaq
Morin khuur
Wheelharp
Hurdy gurdy
Is it sound or music?
Sounds are waves of **vibrations in the air**.
Faster vibrations produce higher notes, and slower vibrations produce lower notes.
Music is what happens when musicians create **organized patterns** of sounds.

RAINFOREST *life*

Rainforests are warm, wet places, found in regions near the equator known as the tropics. They have four distinct layer, each of which is home to an astonishing variety of life.

Emergent layer

This bright, sunny layer is the very top of the rainforest. Some of the trees here grow up to **60m (200ft)** tall.

Canopy layer

This leafy layer can be around **6m (20ft)** thick. It's home to most of the plants and animals of the rainforest.

Understory

It's warm, dark and damp in the understory. Short bushes and shrubs grow here.

Forest floor

It's so dark down here, plants find it difficult to grow. All kinds of animals live among the rotting leaves and twisted tree roots.

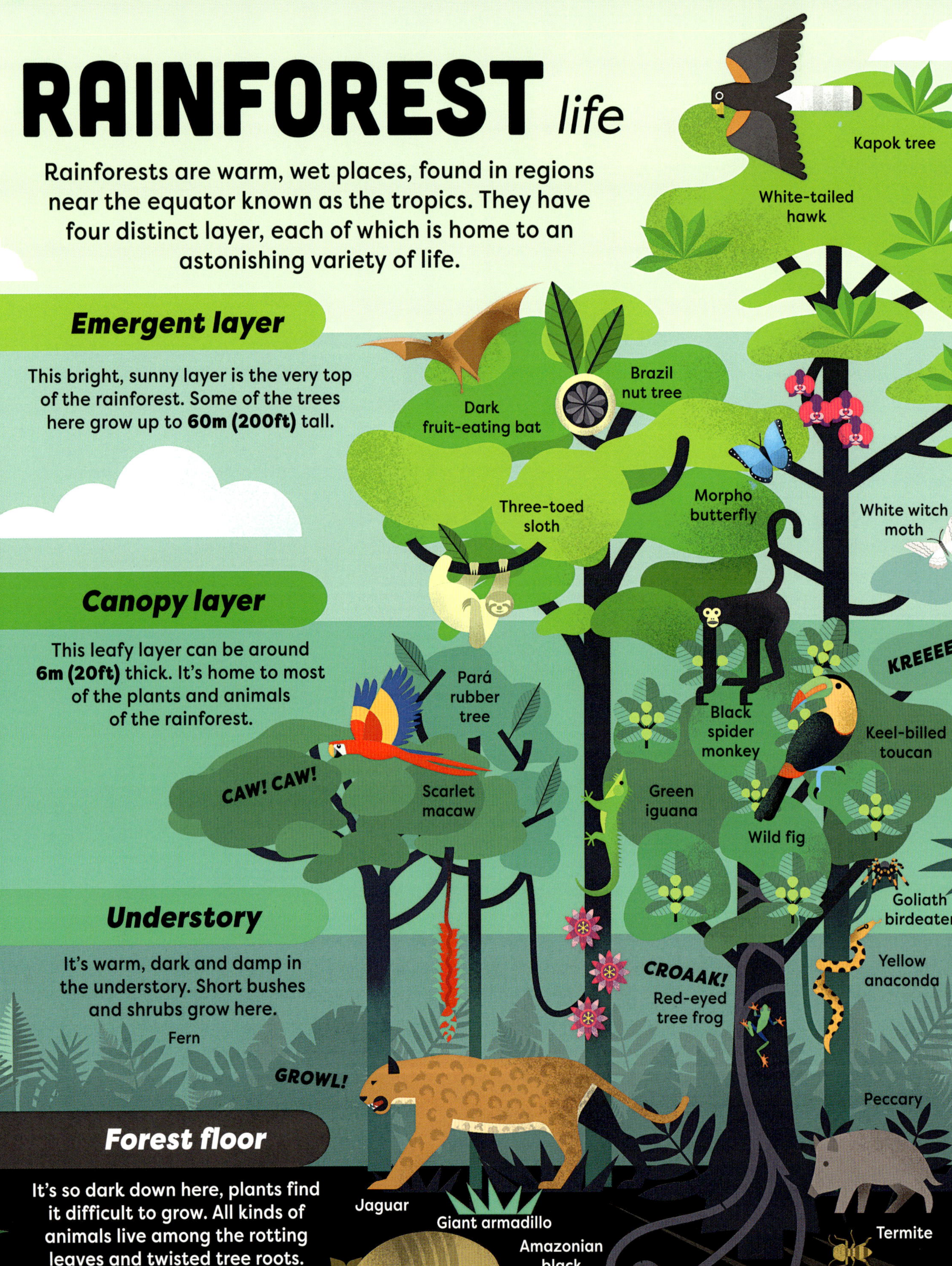

Lush leaves

Every leaf in a rainforest tells a story. From the big, glossy leaf of a rubber tree to the small, waxy leaf of a kapok tree, each leaf is adapted to suit its environment.

KAPOK TREE LEAVES

These leaves in the emergent layer are small and waxy so they won't get dried out by the hot sun.

12cm (5in) wide

RUBBER TREE LEAVES

Glossy rubber tree leaves have pointed tips, called DRIP TIPS. Rainwater slides off the leaf quickly so the tree doesn't rot.

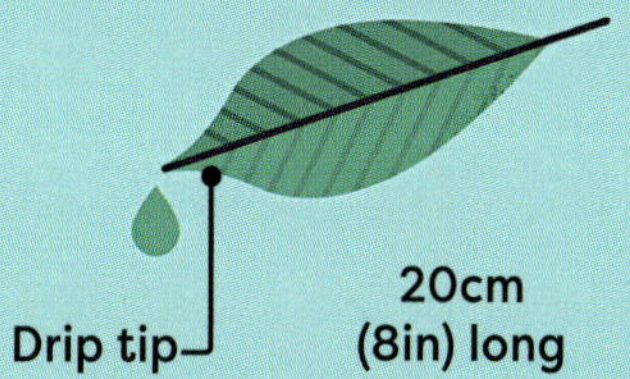

PHILODENDRON LEAVES

Dominating the understory, philodendron leaves are wide and flat to catch any flecks of sunlight that filter through to the ground.

1m (39in) long

GIANT WATER LILY

These huge leaves grow up to **3m (10ft)** wide. The undersides are coated with spikes, which help stop fish from eating them.

3m (118in) wide

Spikes

Deadly plants

Some of the most dangerous plants in the world lurk in the shadows of a rainforest. Read on if you dare...

CASTOR OIL PLANT

1 Known as the most poisonous plant in the world, its seeds contain ricin – a highly toxic substance. Chewing the seeds can be fatal. When they are pressed to make oil, however, the oil contains no ricin so can be used in medicine and also in cosmetics.

PITCHER PLANT

2 This plant traps insects – and sometimes other small animals – in big, cup-shaped leaves so it can feed on the bodies.

GYMPIE-GYMPIE

3 Very fine hairs on this plant's leaves give an agonizing sting, which can leave its victims suffering with a burning pain for weeks, months... or even years.

STAR *gazing*

Since ancient times, people have gazed up at the night sky and seen patterns that look like animals, objects or mythical characters. We call these **CONSTELLATIONS.**

There are **88** constellations recognized today by the International Astronomical Union.

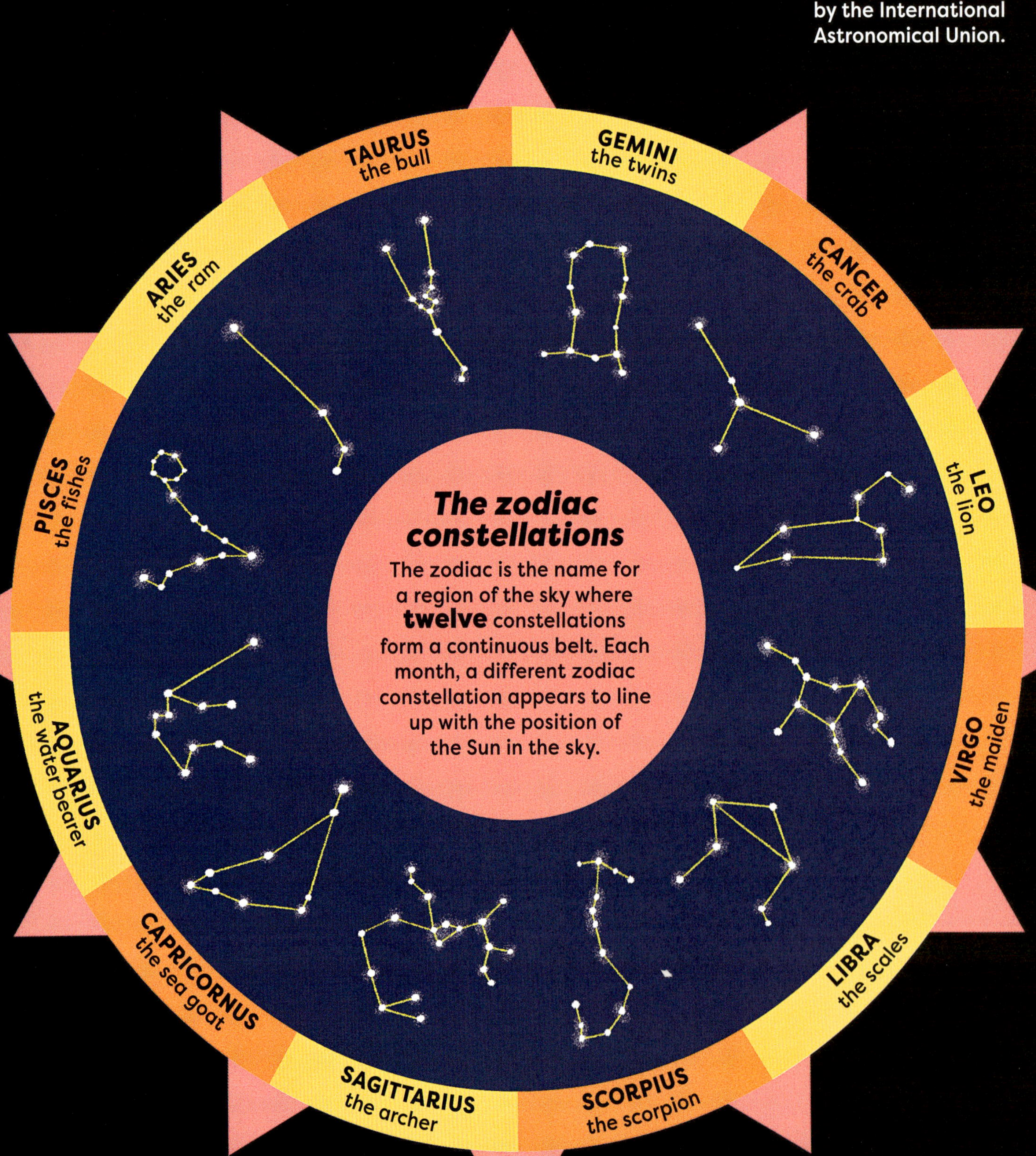

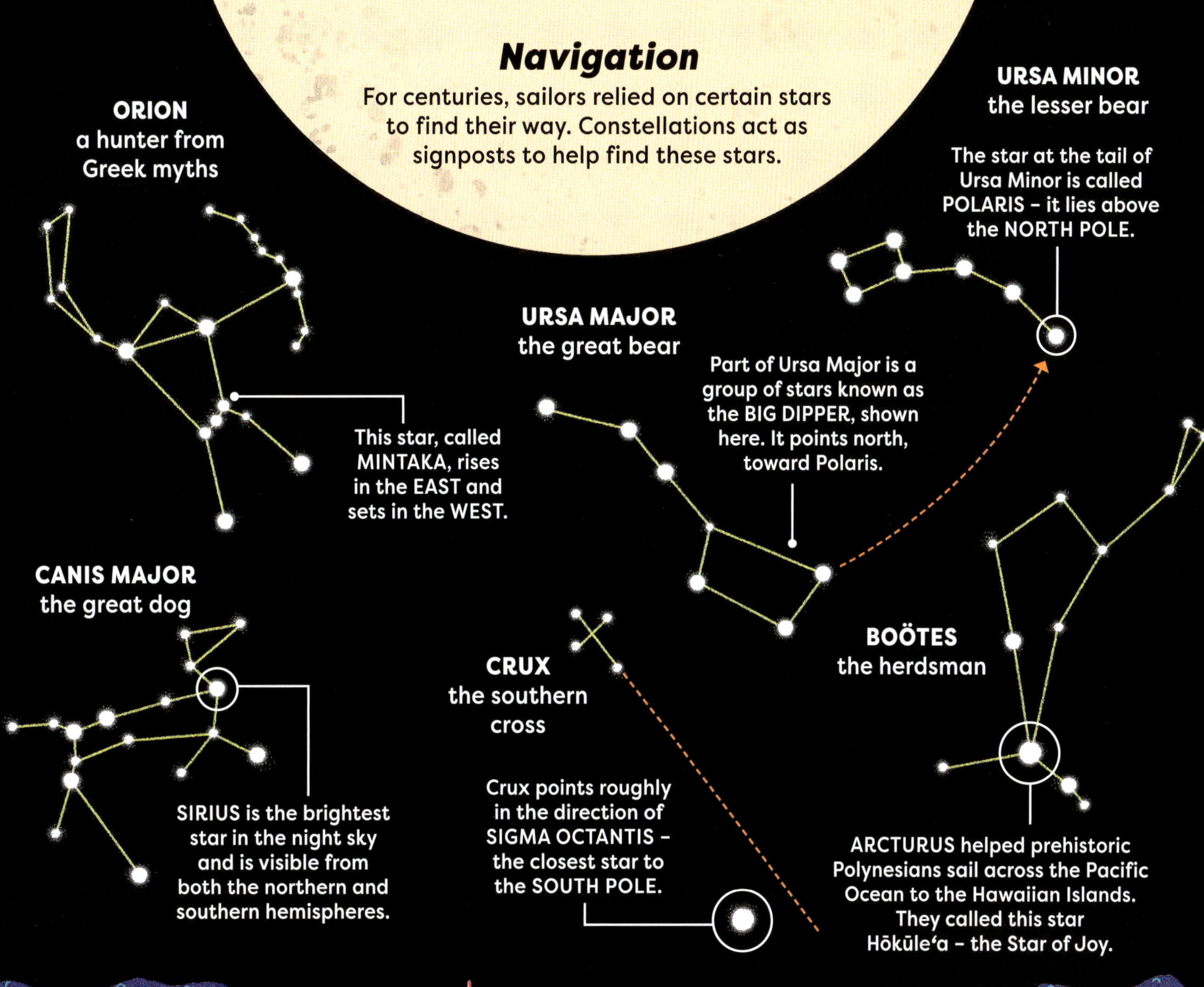

The rest of the 88 constellations

Andromeda
Antlia
Apus
Aquila
Ara
Auriga
Caelum
Camelopardalis
Canes Venatici
Canis Minor
Carina
Cassiopeia
Centaurus
Cepheus
Cetus
Chamaeleon
Circinus
Columba
Coma Berenices
Corona Australis
Corona Borealis
Corvus
Crater
Cygnus
Delphinus
Dorado
Draco
Equuleus
Eridanus
Fornax
Grus
Hercules
Horologium
Hydra
Hydrus
Indus
Lacerta
Leo Minor
Lepus
Lupus
Lynx
Lyra
Mensa
Microscopium
Monoceros
Musca
Norma
Octans
Ophiuchus
Pavo
Pegasus
Perseus
Phoenix
Pictor
Piscis Austrinus
Puppis
Pyxis
Reticulum
Sagitta
Sculptor
Scutum
Serpens
Sextans
Telescopium
Triangulum
Triangulum Australe
Tucana
Vela
Volans
Vulpecula

WHAT IS AI?

AI is short for **Artificial Intelligence**. It's all about getting computers to think like humans. The dream is to create machines that can absorb ALL the information in the world, and use it to answer tricky questions. So far, AI computers focus on three challenges: making *predictions*, *recommendations*, and *decisions*.

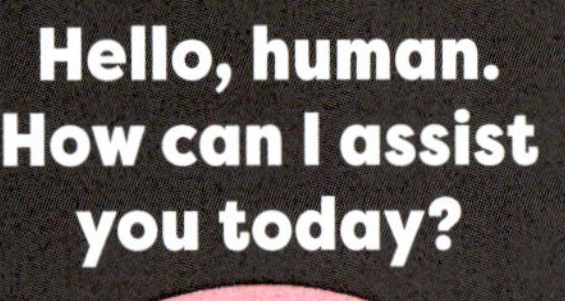

Recommend something for me!

Search engines

Search engines use AI to show websites most useful to YOU.

They work by scanning LONG lists of websites that match your search terms, and have been most visited by people similar to you.

Also used for:

Music players

Video players

Meal planners

Predict what's going to happen!

Chatbots

Chatbots answer questions by predicting the best words to put in a sentence, in order.

The system is based on pattern analysis of millions of books, websites and chat threads.

Also used for:

Weather forecasting

Stock market analysis

Data entry

Take over, so I can relax!

Self-driving cars

Self-driving cars can decide by themselves how fast to move, when to stop, and where to steer.

Each decision is based on information from sensors on the car, combined with lots of pre-set data.

Also used for:

Route planning

Drone cameras

Cookers

What humans do better than computers

Understand the meaning of words and phrases

Learn how to play lots of different games

Understand when a request makes no sense

Create art

Pick up and move objects

Come up with new ideas

Learn multiple very different skills, such as knitting or cycling

Recognize other people's feelings

Recognize objects and sounds in the real world, even in noisy, crowded places

What computers do better than humans

Do the same task again and again, without getting bored or tired

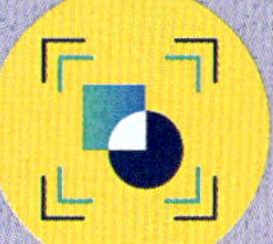
Identify objects, images and sounds – as long as they are digital

Read and write at high speed

Control machines

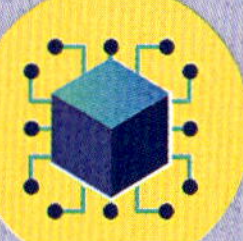
Learn new problem-solving skills

Remember lists of facts

Play games of skill or speed – as long as they're computer games

Parts of a BIRD

Did you know there are over 10,000 types of birds? They have evolved to live in all kinds of habitats around the world, and are astonishingly varied.

Birds hatch from hard-shelled eggs.

From the tiniest hummingbirds to the heaviest ostriches, birds come in a spectacular array of shapes and sizes. But they all have these things in common.

WINGS

Flapping wings enough to fly takes powerful muscles. These are supported by a strong, V-shaped bone called the **furcula**, or **wishbone**.

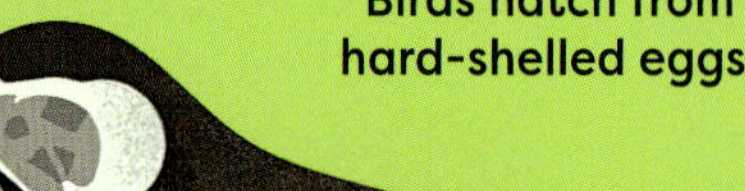

Furcula

FEATHERS

Feathers keep birds warm and dry. They are coated in a type of oil, which makes water slide off.

TOOTHLESS BEAK

Some birds have jagged edges on their beaks, but they're not teeth.

BIRD BONES

Bird bones are filled with air pockets. They help birds take in more oxygen, which provides plenty of energy for flying. They are also strong but very light.

Flightless birds

Although they all have wings, not all birds can fly. Here are some examples.

Penguin

Oily, waterproof feathers are perfect for diving and swimming.

Kakapo

Weka

Ostrich

Incredibly powerful leg muscles make this the fastest running bird.

Cassowary

Kiwi

This bird has very tiny wings, hidden under its feathers.

Types of BEAKS

Birds have beaks of different shapes, depending on what they eat and whether they forage or catch prey.

MULTITASKING

Crow

For catching small animals, pecking at grains and opening seeds

CARCASS SCAVENGING

Vulture

Good at ripping off meat from dead animals

FRUIT EATING

Toucan

For cracking open large fruits

AERIAL FISHING

Kingfisher

Perfect for diving and spearing fish

DIP NETTING

Pelican

Excellent for scooping fish out of the water

Types of WINGS

The shapes of birds' wings are specially adapted to suit the way they fly.

ACTIVE SOARING WINGS

Albatross

Long, narrow wings are excellent for gliding on air currents above oceans for over 16,100km (10,000 miles).

PASSIVE SOARING WINGS

Eagle

Long, broad wings catch rising columns of hot air, so birds soar through the sky with minimal flapping.

HIGH-SPEED WINGS

Falcon

These powerful wings flap to zoom through the air for long periods of time.

HOVERING WINGS

Hummingbird

These short wings flap rapidly, letting birds hover in one position to drink nectar from flowers.

Types of FEET

For birds that stand, swim or hunt, the shape of their feet is also important.

CLIMBING TREES

Woodpecker

SWIMMING AND PADDLING

Duck

Webs between toes

SCRATCHING THROUGH SOIL FOR FOOD

Chicken

RUNNING QUICKLY

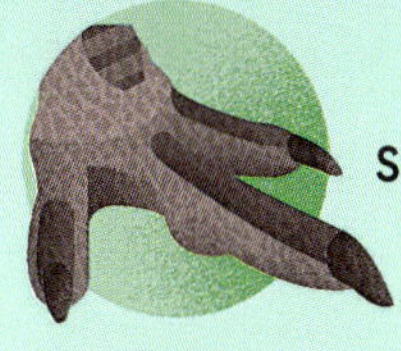

Emu

Strong toes

PERCHING

Robin

GRASPING PREY

Owl

Sharp talons

About the BRAIN

The brain is an organ inside your head. Your brain is unique. It makes sense of everything you see and hear, stores and processes memories, information and thoughts, and sends signals that control your movements and body functions.

Parts of the brain

Different parts of the brain, known as **LOBES**, are involved in different tasks.

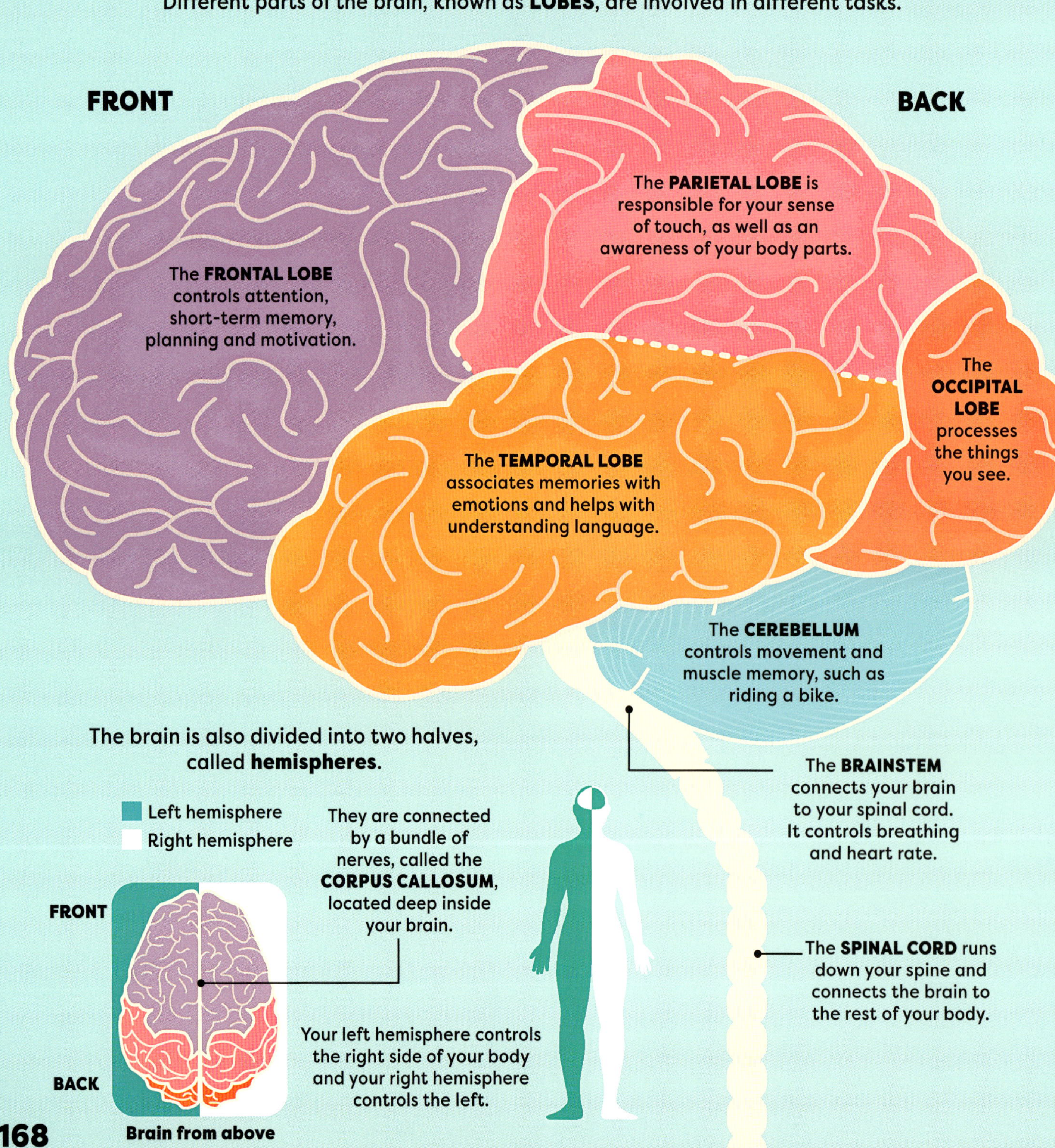

Nervous connections

A human brain is made up of **86 billion** cells called **NEURONS**. Neurons carry messages between your brain and your body through pathways called **NERVES**. These make up your **NERVOUS SYSTEM**.

Neurons carry information and messages as **electric signals**.

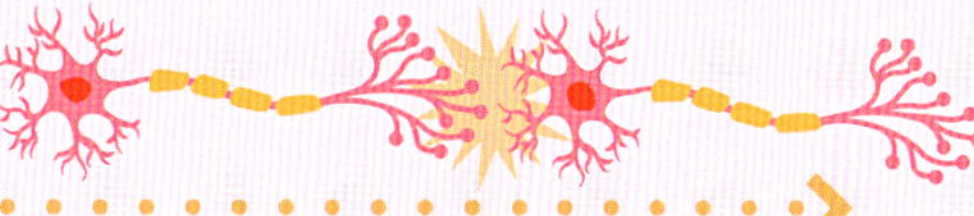

There are three main types of neurons. Here's how they work together whenever you touch something.

1 Say you touch a fluffy feather. **Sense cells** in your **fingertips** gather information and send sense signals.

2 **SENSORY NEURONS** pick up these sense signals and carry them to your **brain**.

3 **INTERNEURONS** in your brain piece together these signals. They decide how you **react** to this sensory information...

That tickles!

...and send **response** instructions back down to your body.

4 **MOTOR NEURONS** carry these instructions to your **muscles** so you can move in response to what you've touched.

Hahaha!

Neurons in your brain send more electric signals when you're **thinking** – enough to power a lightbulb.

While you're asleep, your brain goes over the things you've learned. This helps **store knowledge and memories** for the long term.

Ouch!

Have you ever touched something that's a bit too hot? Usually, you pull your hand away very quickly. When sense cells encounter something that could hurt you, sense signals don't go to the brain.

Instead, signals go to your spine, then **straight to your muscles**, so you can react fast enough to avoid getting hurt.

If you could unravel all the neurons in a human brain, they'd wrap around the Earth **20 times**.

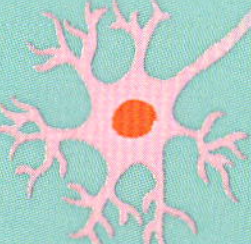

DID YOU KNOW...

A million seconds =
11.5 DAYS.
A billion seconds =
31.5 YEARS.

A trillion seconds =
31,710 YEARS.

Feeding the **WORLD**

Did you know that, whatever your diet, most of your food energy comes from plants? The ones we rely on most are known as **staple crops.**

Staple crops can be stored and eaten all year round, making them an **essential part of people's everyday diets**. Here are the world's top six staple crops and some other ingredients from around the world.

MAIZE

Over **1.2 billion tons** are grown every year.

Ground into flour and eaten as flatbread, tortillas and breakfast cereals; also as sweetcorn.

Just **three** staples – maize, wheat and rice – give us **over half** the energy value of all the food we eat.

WHEAT

0.8 billion tons grown every year

Ground into flour and eaten in bread, noodles, pasta, pizza, cakes and cookies.

RICE

0.8 billion tons grown every year

Boiled or steamed, ground into flour and made into noodles.

POTATOES

0.4 billion tons

Boiled, baked or fried, and also made into snacks.

CASSAVA

0.3 billion tons

Boiled and then mashed or fried; also made into flour or tapioca.

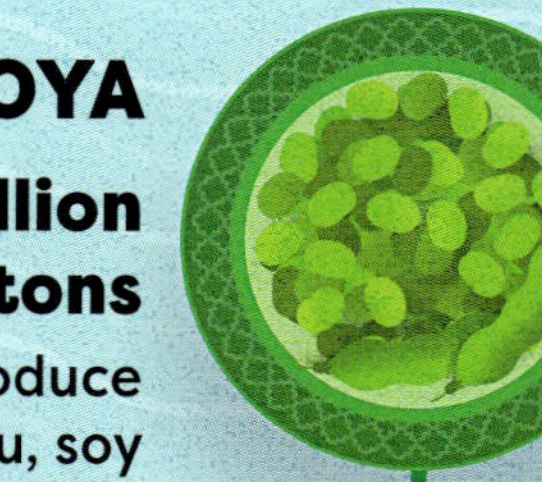

SOYA

0.4 billion tons

Used to produce soy milk, tofu, soy sauce and miso paste, or cooked and eaten as edamame beans.

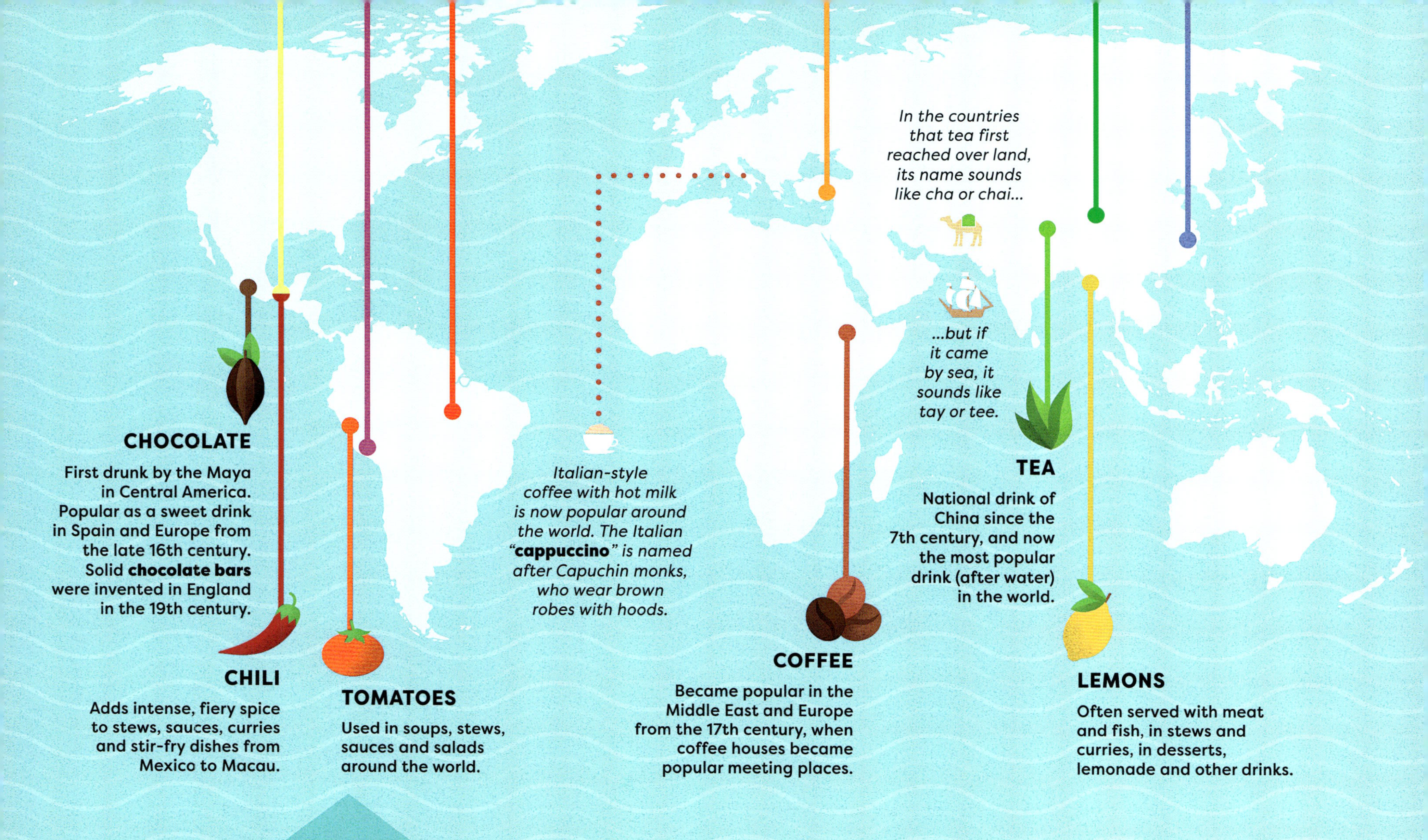

CHOCOLATE

First drunk by the Maya in Central America. Popular as a sweet drink in Spain and Europe from the late 16th century. Solid **chocolate bars** were invented in England in the 19th century.

CHILI

Adds intense, fiery spice to stews, sauces, curries and stir-fry dishes from Mexico to Macau.

TOMATOES

Used in soups, stews, sauces and salads around the world.

*Italian-style coffee with hot milk is now popular around the world. The Italian "**cappuccino**" is named after Capuchin monks, who wear brown robes with hoods.*

COFFEE

Became popular in the Middle East and Europe from the 17th century, when coffee houses became popular meeting places.

In the countries that tea first reached over land, its name sounds like cha or chai...

...but if it came by sea, it sounds like tay or tee.

TEA

National drink of China since the 7th century, and now the most popular drink (after water) in the world.

LEMONS

Often served with meat and fish, in stews and curries, in desserts, lemonade and other drinks.

This map shows where the staple crops, and other popular ingredients, originally came from.

Can you imagine **curries** without chili, or **pizza** and **pasta sauce** without tomatoes? These ingredients first grew in South America but the dishes developed in India, Thailand and Italy. Now they're popular worldwide.

Amazing INVENTIONS

Some inventions came about by accident...

MICROWAVE OVEN
1945

Invented after a physicist working on a device that emitted microwaves (a type of electromagnetic wave) noticed that the waves had melted a chocolate bar in his pocket.

SUPER GLUE
1942

A team of scientists trying to create a clear plastic accidentally made a substance that stuck to everything it touched.

STICKY NOTES
1968–77

A chemist tried to make a super-strong glue, but instead created a very weak one. Years later, another scientist had the idea to use it for removable notes.

Others were inspired by nature...

SHINKANSEN BULLET TRAINS
1990s

The long pointed shape of a kingfisher's beak lets it dive into water with barely a splash. Giving these high-speed trains the same shape lets them whizz quietly through the air, along a track.

Air

HOOK-AND-LOOP FASTENER
1940s

An engineer came home from a walk to find burdock seeds stuck to his clothes. The tiny hooks on the seeds gave him an idea for a new type of fastener.

SELF-COOLING BUILDINGS
1990s

A Zimbabwean architect created a building that catches cool breezes and removes rising hot air. It was inspired by the shape, holes and vents of termite mounds.

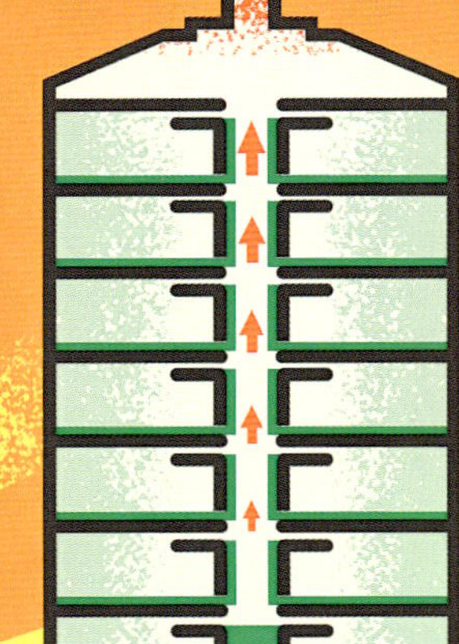

From the revolutionary to the ridiculous, people have been thinking up ideas for new inventions since prehistoric times.

But not all inventions come about in the same way.

Inventions that changed history...

WHEEL
Around 5,500 years ago

Invented in Sumer – an ancient civilization in what is now Iraq. The wheel enabled people to travel further and faster, and to carry heavy loads on animal-drawn carts.

COMPASS
At least 2,000 years ago

The first compasses were created in China. Spinning compasses helped people find their way, letting them travel far from home to explore and trade.

PRINTING PRESS WITH MOVEABLE TYPE
600 years ago

German goldsmith Johannes Gutenberg was not the first to invent printing. But his press was the first with metal letters that could be moved and rearranged. This meant books were much faster and cheaper to print.

Older than you might think...

TOILET PAPER
Around 1,500 years ago

The Chinese were the first to use toilet paper, several centuries after they had started making paper. Perforated rolls were invented in the late 1800s.

WHOOPEE CUSHION
Over 1,800 years ago

No one knows who invented this prank, but the Roman emperor Elagabalus is thought to have used an early version to surprise dinner guests.

DRINKING STRAW
Over 5,000 years ago

The first known straw, found in a Sumerian tomb, was made of gold. Modern paper straws have been used since the 1880s.

What's in a NAME?

Most last names have a particular meaning if you know how to crack the code. Can you do that for your name? Maybe it described a long-ago ancestor, and has been passed down through the family ever since.

What's your job?

Some names are based on what people used to do. The commonest last name in the UK, the USA, Canada, Australia and New Zealand is Smith. There are around 4.5 million Smiths in the world, and many versions of the same name in other languages.

Smith
English – from blacksmith

Ferreira
Portuguese – blacksmith

Kowalski
Polish – blacksmith

Schmidt
German – blacksmith

Lefebvre
French – blacksmith

Ferrari
Italian – blacksmith

Khan
Pakistani – ruler

Patel
Indian – village headman

Foster
English – forester

Clark
English, from clerk – secretary, record-keeper

Who's your father?

Some last names are based on a distant father's name or sometimes a mother's name, especially in Europe and Latin America.

Martínez
Spanish – family of Martín

González
Spanish – family of Gonzalo

Andersson
Swedish – son of Anders

Jensen
Danish – son of Jens

Wilson
English – son of Will

Davies
Welsh – family of David

Ivanov *or* **Ivanova**
Russian – son or daughter of Ivan – the commonest last name in Russia

Annasson *or* **Annasdóttir**
Icelandic – son or daughter of Anna

What do you look like?

Some last names seem to come from nicknames, often based on height or hair color.

Leroux
French – red-haired

Read *or* **Reid**
English – red-haired

Delgado
Spanish – slim

de Groot
Dutch – big, tall

Little
English – umm... not tall

Where do you live?

Sometimes it was easiest to describe people by saying where their homes were.

Attwood
English – by or in the wood

Carvalho
Portuguese – the oak tree

Dumont
French – from the mountain

da Costa
Portuguese – from the coast

Pereira
Portuguese – the pear tree

Lee *or* **Li**
Chinese or Korean, with different meanings in different dialects. One meaning is "plum tree."

Who do you serve?

Some names might look like the name of an ancestor, but actually show who that ancestor worked for.

Stewart *or* **Stuart**
Scottish – King's steward

Hall
English – the great hall – lord of the manor

King
English – the King's household

O'Neill
Irish – clan of Niall, "champion"

In Scotland and Ireland, clan names *look* like family names ("clann" means "children"). In fact, people could choose to serve a clan chief and take his family name. The chief would then protect *their* families.

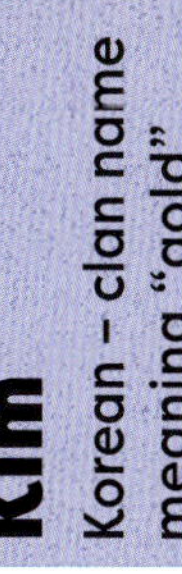

Kim
Korean – clan name meaning "gold"

Macdonald
Scottish – clan of Dómhnall, "world ruler"

Zhang
Chinese – followers of Emperor Huang Di

Are you religious?

Many names in Africa, the Middle East, India and Pakistan are based on names in Islam, either to show religious loyalty or from an ancestor named after a prophet or saint. In the Sikh religion, all men and boys take one last name, and all women and girls another.

Mohammed
Muslim – the great prophet of Islam

Ali
Muslim – son-in-law of Mohammed, and first convert to Islam

Ibrahim
Muslim – the patriarch Abraham

Singh
Sikh (men) – lion

Kaur
Sikh (women) – princess

What do you want to be?

Some popular names in India and the Middle East include personal qualities. Did these describe real people, or were they what parents most wanted for their children?

Das
Indian – of Brahmin caste (high social status)

Kumar
Indian – prince

Devi
Indian – divine

Ram
Indian – pleasing or charming, from the hero Rama

Hassan *or* **Hussain**
Arabic – handsome

STORIES *around the* WORLD

Great stories often have memorable openings and strong storylines or plots. Many stories – no matter what language they are told in – share similar elements.

Story openers

In different countries, traditional stories, such as folk tales and fairy stories, often begin with a classic opening line.

Once upon a time...
UK, USA and other English-speaking countries

Beyond seven mountains, beyond seven forests...
Poland

Once, in the old days, when tigers smoked...
Korea

Having been said and said and said...
India

Here is a story! Story it is.
Nigeria

Listen to tell it and tell it to teach it.
Chile

Types of plot

Every story has a plot filled with ups and downs and a main character or **protagonist**. Some types of plots are very common and appear in lots of stories.

RAGS TO RICHES

The protagonist starts out in poverty, but gains and loses riches along the way, winning great wealth in the end.

RICHES TO RAGS

A wealthy protagonist – often an important person with a flaw in their character – loses their fortune. This plot type is also known as a **tragedy**.

DEFEATING AN ENEMY

A protagonist must defeat someone or something – often a force of evil – that is threatening them.

Wish-granting objects

Since ancient times, people have told stories about mythical objects that grant wishes. Here are some examples from around the world:

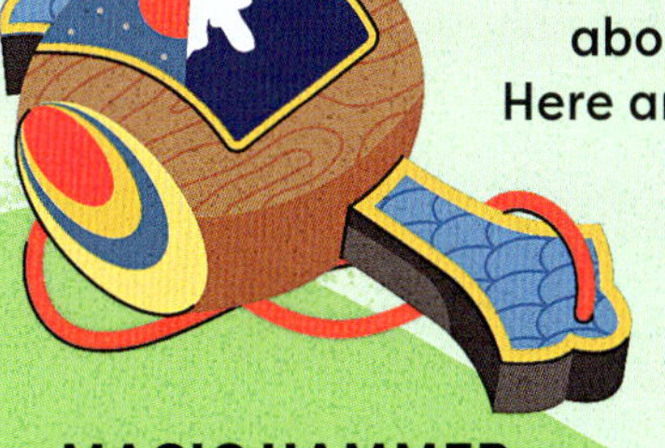

MAGIC HAMMER

This legendary Japanese hammer – called the *uchide no kozuchi* – is said to tap out anything that's wished for.

WISHING WELL

In many European folk stories, a wishing well grants wishes to anyone who drops a coin and makes a wish.

MAGIC LAMP

In many Middle Eastern folk tales, there are genies trapped in lamps or bottles. In *Aladdin*, a genie appears when an oil lamp is rubbed. The genie grants the owner wishes.

COMEDY

The protagonist experiences a series of funny or confusing events. The story always finishes on a happy ending.

QUEST

A protagonist sets out with a goal – often to find a place or look for treasure. They face obstacles and temptations as they go.

TRANSFORMATION

An event forces a protagonist to go through a transformation. The protagonist usually becomes a better person as a result.

ADVENTURE

A protagonist travels to a strange new place, but experiences difficulties along the way. They return home having learned important lessons.

WRITING
the first 5,000 years

People have been making pictures for hundreds of thousands of years. Writing came much later, and began with pictures... which became letters... which in time became emojis...

Cuneiform

(pronounced "kew-nye-form" meaning wedge-shaped)

Mesopotamia (now Iraq), from around 3,400BCE

The earliest writing that we know began as little pictures (cows, sheep, jars of grain and so on) and number symbols, pressed into clay with a sharpened reed.

In time, more stylized shapes emerged, with more abstract symbols that recorded both laws and legends.

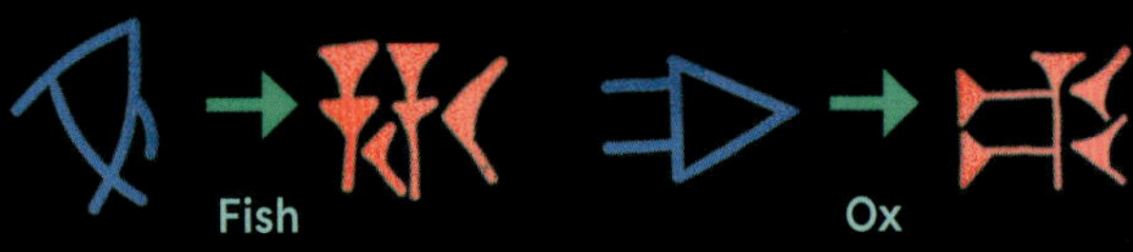

Hieroglyphics

(pronounced "hi-ro-glif-fics" meaning sacred writing)

Ancient Egypt, from around 3,200BCE

This was another form of writing based on pictures. Texts were carved into stone monuments or painted onto papyrus, an early form of paper made from reeds.

The art of reading hieroglyphics was lost for hundreds of years, and rediscovered just over 200 years ago.

The name of the boy-king Tutankhamun

The first alphabets

Ancient Egypt, from around 1850BCE

Almost 4,000 years ago, foreign workers and enslaved people in Egypt adapted a few hieroglyphic symbols to fit the sounds of their own language. This formed a set of basic letters with consonants but no vowels.

Traders from Phoenicia (modern-day Lebanon) used their own alphabet around the Mediterranean Sea. Later, the Greeks added vowels and the Romans developed the capital letters we know today.

Phoenician

ΟΔΥΣΣΕΙΑΣ Greek

AENEIDOS Roman

Alphabets move EAST

Middle East, from around 300BCE

Arabic writing developed from Eastern Mediterranean alphabets. It spread rapidly with the Islamic faith during the eighth century as the language of the Qur'an. Unlike most scripts, Arabic is read from right to left.

الصياد و الجني

Золотая рыбка

Eastern Europe, from around 860

Cyrillic – the script for several Eastern European languages, including Russian – is based on Greek. It was developed to bring Christianity to Eastern Europe, translating the Bible and prayers into local languages.

Chinese characters

China, from around 1200-1050BCE

Chinese writing also developed from pictures. It was first used to scratch on bones or turtle shells and ask questions about the future: the bones were heated in a fire, and the pattern of heat-cracks provided the answers.

Some Chinese characters in use today still look a little like those early picture forms.

Horse

Fish

खरगोश और शेर

흥부전

Other Eastern languages

South and south-east Asia, from around 300BCE (India)

Many languages in India and further east developed writing systems based on the ***syllables*** of spoken language. These include Japanese, Korean, Thai, Bengali, Tamil and other Indian languages.

Mayan glyphs

Central America, from around 300-200BCE

Like Egyptian hieroglyphs, the glyphs of the Mayan people were based on pictures. These were either carved in stone or painted onto deer skin or tree bark and made into books.

Just four Mayan books, known as codices, survive today.

Precious writing

Asia, Middle East and Europe, from around 200BCE (China)

For hundreds of years, writing was used for religious texts or for poetry, carefully copied out by hand. Writers and artists created beautiful pages by making the letters neat and even and adding decorations or pictures.

Writing is for everyone (and so is texting)

Around the world, from 1450 onwards

The invention of printing made books much easier and *much* less expensive to produce. Reading and writing were now within reach for ordinary people. Letter forms became simplified. Standard spellings were introduced.

From the 19th century, there was growing pressure for everyone to have an education… and by the 21st century, to know how to use a computer and a cell phone.

> hello

Emojis

Japan, 1990s onwards

In the 1980s, emoticons began appearing in internet chatrooms in the USA, allowing users to add smiles :) winks ;) and laughter :D to plain text.

In 1999, a Japanese company issued 176 emojis (from the Japanese words for picture and letter) to use on cell phones.

Today there are over 3,000 emojis in use, and more are added every year.

CELLS *and* DNA

Every living thing is made from tiny, microscopic parts called **CELLS**. And if you zoom in on those cells, you'll see even tinier parts called **CHROMOSOMES** that contain a chemical called **DNA**. Here's what they all do.

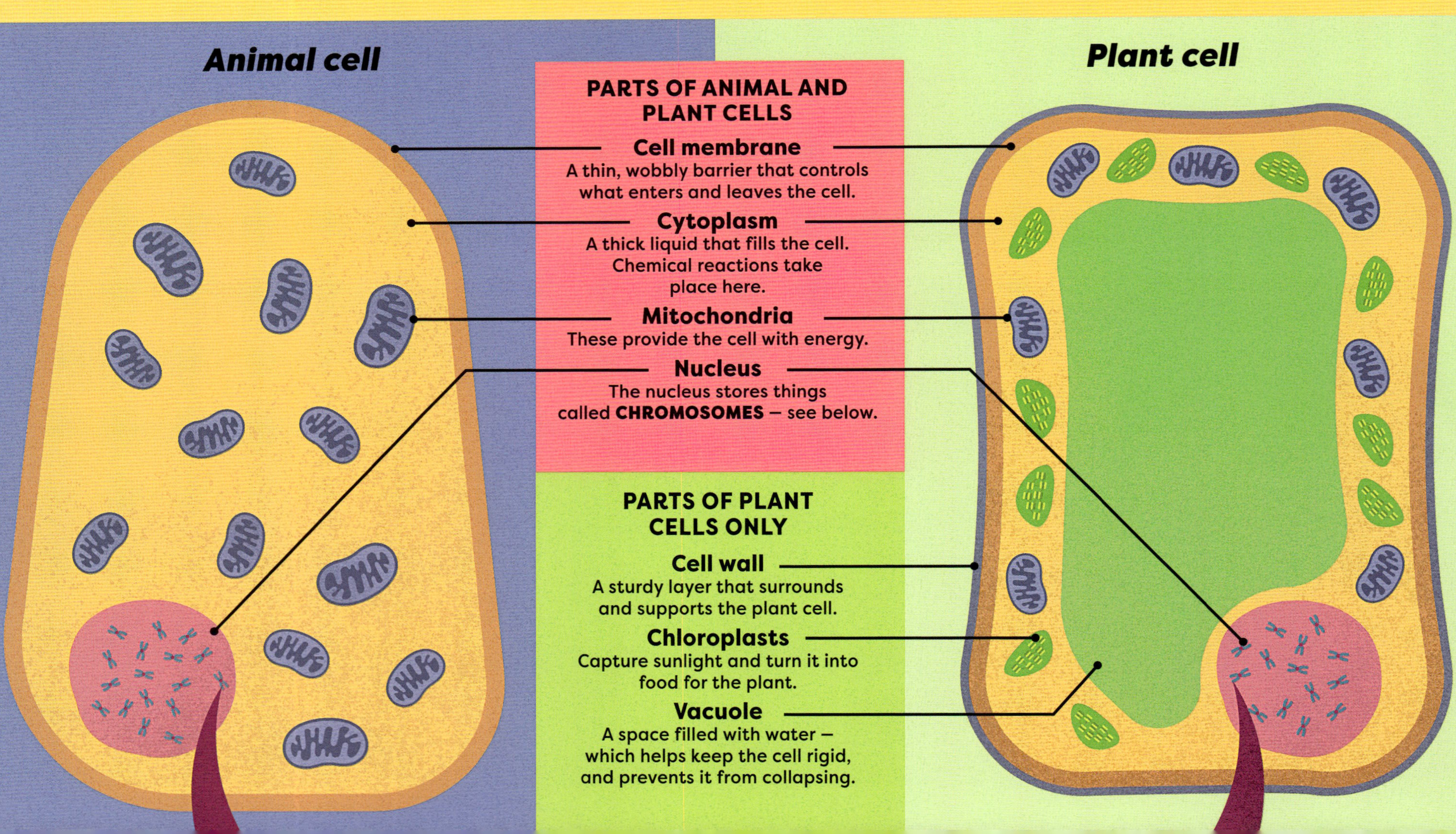

Chromosomes

Chromosomes are tiny threads containing a spiral-shaped chemical called **DNA**.

ZOOMING IN...

A typical human cell contains

46

chromosomes.

ZOOMING IN EVEN MORE...

DNA

DNA consists of two strands that wind around each other. This makes a shape called a **DOUBLE HELIX**.

The full name for DNA is **DEOXYRIBONUCLEIC ACID.**

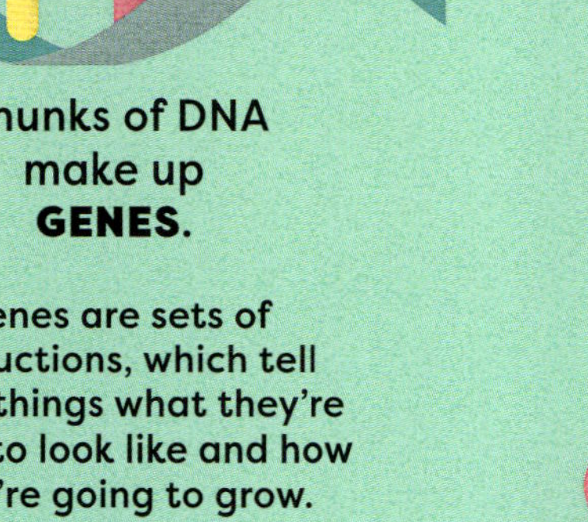

DNA is made up of blocks of chemicals called **BASES**.

There are **FOUR** of these.

Chunks of DNA make up **GENES**.

Genes are sets of instructions, which tell living things what they're going to look like and how they're going to grow.

If you stretched out the DNA from the nucleus of a single human cell, it would be around **2m (6.5ft) long**.

Genes

Your genes determine characteristics such as how tall or hairy you are, and how all the cells in your body should work together.

You share about **99%** of your genes with chimps...

...and, **amazingly**, **60%** with fruit flies.

GLOSSARY

ALGORITHM A set of step-by-step instructions – such as a computer code – explaining how to perform a particular task.

ALLERGY A condition that means a person can become sick, often very rapidly, if they come into contact with a specific trigger, such as plant pollen, peanuts or a bee sting.

AMPHIBIAN A creature, such as a frog, that lives both in and out of water.

ANCIENT GREECE The people who lived in and around Greece and their culture, especially from 3,200 to 2,300 years ago.

ARCHITECTS People with the job of designing buildings of all kinds.

ARSENIC A chemical *element* that is posionous to humans and many animals.

ASTEROID Large lumps of rock and metal found in space; sometimes they fall onto planets or moons as meteors.

ASTRONOMERS Scientists who study space and the things found in it.

ATMOSPHERE The layer of gases that surrounds Earth and other large planets.

ATOM An incredibly tiny particle; the smallest building block of an *element.*

BACTERIA A type of living thing, usually only a few *cells* in size, that often lives inside other living things.

BCE Stands for Before the Common Era, and is used to describe dates before the Year 1.

BINARY CODE A method used to represent information, especially in computer programs, using only the digits 1 and 0.

BIODIVERSITY The total range of different species in an area.

BLACK HOLE The remains of a star that has collapsed to a tiny point, which has such a powerful gravitational pull that even light cannot escape it.

BYTE An amount of digital information, roughly as much as a computer needs to remember a single letter or digit.

CE Stands for Common Era, sometimes used to describe dates beginning with the Year 1 – the traditional date given to the year Jesus Christ was born.

CELLS The basic building block of all living things, that often contains *DNA.*

CONTINENT One of the seven large land masses that cover Earth's surface, such as Asia or North America.

Here you can see some definitions of tricky words in the book. Words in *italic* type have their own entry.

COPYRIGHT LIBRARY A type of library, usually run by a country's government, that does not lend books but instead aims to store a copy of every single book published in that country.

DNA A chemical found in living things that holds the information – in groups called *genes* – needed for that living thing to build its own body and live out its life.

DOMESTICATION Breeding wild animals – over many generations – to keep as pets or use as farm animals.

ELEMENTS Any substance made up entirely of just one kind of *atom*.

EQUATOR An imaginary line running around the middle of the Earth that divides it into a *northern* and *southern hemisphere.*

EVOLUTION The gradual process by which living things change over many generations.

EXTINCTION When the last member of a *species* dies out, that species has become extinct.

FACTS Statements that give a piece of information and are true.

FOSSILS The remains of plants and animals that have, over millions of years, been turned into stone.

GALAXY A collection of billions of stars that all *orbit* around a central hub, often containing a supermassive *black hole.*

GENES Sections of *DNA* that carry a code to define one or more characteristics of a living thing, such as its size and shape.

GLIDER A vehicle that can fly through the air but does not have its own power source. It has to fall, be dropped or pulled to fly.

GOVERNMENT The group of people who are in charge of a country, usually chosen by an election every few years.

HABITAT A living thing's natural home.

HYPNOSIS A way of putting someone or something into a trance-like state.

GLOSSARY CONTINUED

KELVIN A *metric measurement* of temperature, typically used to describe extremely hot or cold things.

LARVA A young insect in the form it takes before it changes into an adult.

MAMMAL The name for any animal that has warm blood, some amount of hair or fur, and feeds its babies on milk.

MASS The scientific word to describe how much stuff an object is made of, for example its *atoms*. It is usually measured in kilograms.

MATTER The scientific word to describe everything that is made up of atoms.

METRIC MEASUREMENTS A system of measuring things, such as by length (m) or mass (kg), that is usually divisible by ten.

MIDDLE EAST The part of the world around Arabia, where Europe, Africa and Asia meet.

MIGRATION When groups of animals travel from one place to another – sometimes over great distances – for different times of year, or parts of their life cycle.

MUTATION When a living thing's *DNA* is altered in some way, causing a change in some of its *genes*.

NORTHERN HEMISPHERE The part of planet Earth to the north of the *equator*, stretching to the north pole.

OLYMPIC GAMES An international competition covering a wide range of sports, originally held in *Ancient Greece*, then revived in the 19th century, and now held once every four years in countries around the world.

ORBIT The movement of one object in space around another, such as the Moon orbiting the Earth.

ORGANS Parts of the body that carry out specific jobs, such as the brain, heart or skin.

PARASITES Living things that live in or on other, larger creatures, often eating parts of them, and causing harm rather than doing any good.

POPULATION The number of people living in a particular place, or the number of living things in a group.

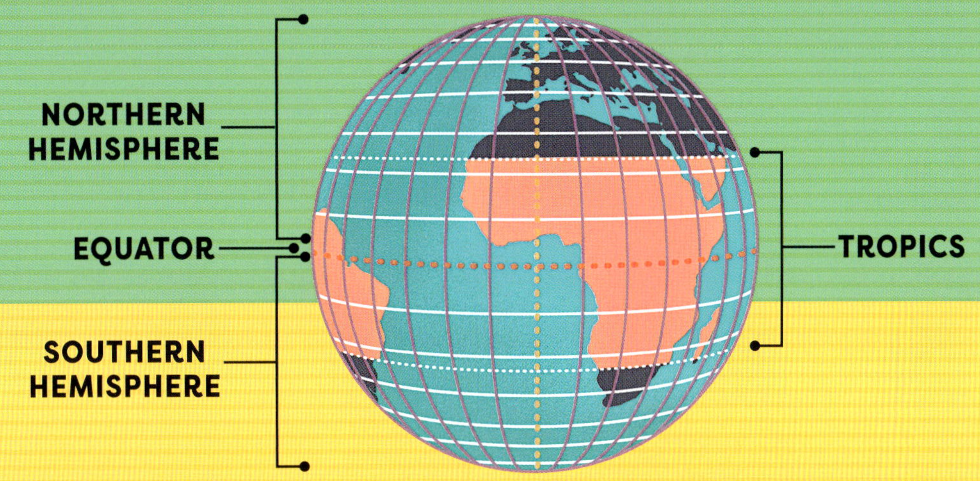

PREDATORS Animals that hunt and kill other animals to eat.

PREFIX Part of a word, at the front, that gives it a more precise meaning, such as kilo or micro in front of -gram.

PREY Animals that are hunted by *predators*.

PYRAMID A 3-D shape with a square or triangular base, whose walls meet in a point.

SCANDINAVIAN Relating to the countries and cultures of Denmark, Sweden, Norway and Iceland.

SCIENCE A way of studying the world around you, based on asking questions and doing experiments to test out answers to those questions.

SCIENCE FICTION Stories that imagine what the world would be like if something were different from how it is in the real world – for example if aliens were real – or some scientific advance, such as time travel, has been developed.

SPECIES A group of living things that can breed with each other.

SOUTHERN HEMISPHERE
The part of planet Earth to the south of the *equator*, stretching to the south pole.

TOXIN Any poisonous substance secreted by a living thing, usually passed on by touch.

TROPICS The region of Earth immediately north and south of the *equator*.

VENOM Any poisonous substance that an animal passes on deliberately, such as through a bite or sting.

VIRUS A tiny particle that attacks living things by infecting its *cells* and making copies of itself.

X-RAY TELESCOPE Telescopes that detect X-rays and help build a picture of what distant stars and *galaxies* look like.

INDEX

INDEX CONTINUED

INDEX CONTINUED

Expert consultants and fact-checkers: Sam Baer, Dr. Colin Dodd, Dr. Phoebe Griffiths, Dr. Magnus Lee, Ben Oliver, Kristina Routh, and Roger Trend.

First published in 2024 by Usborne Publishing Limited, 83-85 Saffron Hill, London EC1N 8RT, United Kingdom. usborne.com

Please follow the online safety guidelines at **usborne.com/Quicklinks**